Christianity and Depression

D1479273

Christianity and Depression

Interpretation, meaning, and the shaping of experience

Tasia Scrutton

scm press

© Tasia Scrutton 2020

Published in 2020 by SCM Press
Editorial office
3rd Floor, Invicta House,
108–114 Golden Lane,
London EC1Y 0TG, UK

www.scmpress.co.uk

SCM Press is an imprint of Hymns Ancient & Modern Ltd
(a registered charity)

H
Y
M   Ancient
N   &Modern
S

Hymns Ancient & Modern® is a registered trademark of
Hymns Ancient & Modern Ltd
13A Hellesdon Park Road, Norwich,
Norfolk NR6 5DR, UK

British Library Cataloguing in Publication data

A catalogue record for this book is available
from the British Library

978-0-334-05890-8

For Simon, with thanks for invaluable conversations, encouragement and, most of all, love.

Contents

Foreword

JOHN SWINTON

At different moments in history (and still today in different cultures and contexts), the same experiences that some now call 'mental illness' have been described quite differently: problems of living, deviant behaviour, criminality, problems with the unconscious (unconscious desires, repression, sublimation, denial and so forth), chemical imbalances, misfiring neurology, trauma, genetic predisposition, demons and angels. At different times, any one of these explanatory frameworks can become the 'standard account'; the go-to explanation that the majority hold as most accurate and significant. Those who live with unconventional mental health experiences also draw out different interpretations and descriptions of their experiences. These personal descriptions contain deep and challenging insights, perspectives and accompanying possibilities for response which are easily subsumed to more powerful cultural discourses. Those living with unconventional mental health experiences push against the idea that what they are experiencing is best explained as 'mere symptoms of underlying pathology'. Within these narratives we find deep and rich narrative descriptions of what it *means* to live with voices, to have unusual elations of mood and to deal with troublesome negative feelings that are deeper than sadness.

It is clear that the human experience of mental health challenges is contested and contestable. It's important that we recognize that our interpretations of unconventional mental health experiences matter. They matter because they deeply impact upon the ways in which we think about, interpret and respond to those who live with such experiences. Each of these explanatory frameworks leads to different forms of practice. The way that we name things determines what we think we see. What we think we see determines how we respond to what we think we see. How we respond to what we think we see determines the faithfulness of our actions.

The power of medicine

One powerful explanatory framework which guides a good deal of the current conversation around mental health comes to us from science and medicine. Within this conversation the assumption is that mental health challenges are basically the same as physical illnesses and that, eventually, we will discover a biological cause. Within this explanatory framework the root of all mental health challenges lies primarily within the purview of biomedicine. Despite the fact that we don't currently have biomarkers for the majority of mental health challenges, we are told that eventually we will discover a biological explanation that will explain the nature of mental health issues and provide us with the most appropriate medical responses. It may well be that we do in the end find biomarkers for mental health challenges, but even if we do, that won't help us fully explain the nature and cause of unconventional mental health experiences. Many people's challenges emerge from things such as deep trauma, broken relationships, loneliness, isolation, war and social injustice. These are things that cannot be altered by improvements in biomedical knowledge. It seems unlikely that medical science can offer the ultimate solution to mental health challenges that emerge from human selfishness and social and personal evil. Tempting as such simplicity might well be, biomedicine and the gifts of science are not the only ways or even necessarily the best ways in which we can understand and respond to people's unconventional mental health experiences. It is important that we pay attention to the gifts that medicine brings. However, we must be careful lest paying attention to one aspect of the issue distracts our attention away from other vital aspects that emerge from other ways of looking at the issues. The issue of paying the right kind of attention to mental health challenges is crucial, but actually quite difficult at least for Western people.

Paying the right kind of attention

In his fascinating book *The Master and his Emissary: The Divided Brain and the Making of the Western World*,[1] Scottish psychiatrist and philosopher Iain McGilchrist makes an interesting observation. After millions of years of evolution, the brain remains split into two asymmetrical hemispheres. This seems more than a little odd bearing in mind that the power of the brain is determined by its ability to make and sustain millions of connections. The number and complexity of these connections is what gives it its computational power. So why is it that the brain has come to be split into two hemispheres, connected by a bundle of tissue that passes messages between them: the corpus callosum? The corpus callosum spends much of its time *blocking* and *inhibiting* the communication between the hemispheres. Even more oddly, the corpus callosum has been getting *smaller* rather than larger over the course of evolution.

Arguing against previous views that suggest that the left hemisphere of the brain deals with reason, facts and hard logic, with the right hemisphere focusing on such things as emotions, feelings, imagination and aesthetics, McGilchrist points out that in fact both hemispheres participate in both sets of perceptions. In his view the difference between the two hemispheres is not in the way that each hemisphere processes things. The significant difference between the hemispheres is the way that each sees the world: *their different ways of paying attention to the world*. The left and right hemispheres of our brains have radically different and contradictory ways of looking at the world. In making this move, McGilchrist shifts the neurological question away from 'What does the brain do?', a question that conceptualizes the brain as machine-like, towards a different and more profound question: 'How does the brain see the world?' This revised question, *inter alia*, brings the brain into the realm of the personal.

The brain thus has two very different ways of paying attention to the world. McGilchrist offers the example of birds feeding on a pebbled surface to illustrate these two modes of attention. A feeding bird needs:

> to pay narrow-beam sharply focussed attention to what it has already prioritised as of significance – a seed against a background of grit or pebbles, or a twig to build a nest. At the same time, it must be able to bring to bear on the world a broad, open, sustained and uncommitted attention, on the look-out for whatever else may exist. Without this capacity it would soon become someone else's lunch while getting its own. Birds and animals all have divided brains, and regularly use one hemisphere for vigilant attention to the world at large, so as to make sense of it, including to bond with their mates, and the other for the narrow attention that enables them to lock onto whatever it is they need to get.[2]

What is true for feeding birds is also true for human beings:

> we use our left hemisphere to grasp and manipulate, and the right to understand the world at large and how things within it relate to one another, as well as our relationship with it as a whole. It is the left hemisphere that controls the right hand which for most of us is the one that does the grasping, and provides that aspect of language (not all of language) that enable us to say we have 'grasped' something. But it is the right hemisphere that is the basis of our nature as the 'social animal', which Aristotle saw as our defining feature.[3]

The issue between the hemispheres is therefore not thinking versus feeling, as has been previously assumed, but rather two very different kinds of thinking:

> each hemisphere has a quite consistent, but radically differ-ent, 'take' on the world. This means that, at the core of our

thinking about ourselves, the world and our relationship with it, there are two incompatible but necessary views that we need to try to combine. And things go badly wrong when we do not.[4]

McGilchrist is convinced that things have gone badly wrong, at least for Westerners. He argues that various changes within post-Enlightenment Western culture have led people, implicitly or explicitly, to give preference to the mode of attention that comes to us via the left side of our brains. We are thus culturally more attuned to giving priority to certain kinds of knowledge such as science, fact, figures, statistics than others such as stories, feelings, emotions, spirituality and art.

If we transfer this hypothesis into the realm of mental health it becomes clearer as to why we might culturally be drawn to scientific, biomedical explanations and interpretations as opposed to other ways in which we might attend to and interpret mental health experiences. Within such a context, more diffuse, personal and interrelational ways of viewing and understanding experiences may not draw the kind of attention they require.

And this is precisely the point at which Tasia Scrutton's book enters into and makes an important contribution to our knowledge and thinking about mental health challenges in general and depression in particular. She has noted certain biases and problems with the ways in which many of us interpret and respond to mental health issues. She urges us to think differently and to open our minds to fresh and new ways of interpreting mental health experiences within which theology has a fresh and transformative voice. The power of Tasia's book is that it shifts our gaze away from that which we assume to be culturally normal and helps us to pay the right kind of attention to people's unconventional mental health experiences. As such her book functions as a counter-cultural text that stands in the prophetic tradition of opening our eyes to things that we cannot see unless we have a guide and an advocate who can reframe our worlds in ways that enable us to see those things that are often culturally invisible and require theological illumination. In helping us to pay the right kind of attention to mental health challenges, she opens up the way for fresh and creative ways of responding. Readers of this book will find her work fascinating, challenging, at times dissonant, but ultimately deeply healing.

Notes

1 Iain McGilchrist (2010), *The Master and his Emissary: The Divided Brain and the Making of the Western World*, London: Yale University Press.

2 McGilchrist, *The Master and his Emissary*, p. 25.

3 McGilchrist, *The Master and his Emissary*, p. 24.

4 Jonathan Rowson and Iain McGilchrist (2013), 'Divided brain, divided world: Why the best parts of us struggle to be heard', available at www.thersa.org/globalassets/pdfs/blogs/rsa-divided-brain-divided-world.pdf (accessed 13.12.19).

Acknowledgements

Books are written by individuals, and yet I doubt this book could have been written without the support, insight and encouragement of the communities I was lucky to find myself in while writing it.

My thanks go particularly to people who read my manuscript and participated in a symposium on it in June 2019, and whose generosity and wisdom were overwhelming: David Sims, Mark Wynn, David Efird, Anthea Colledge, Zoe Longworth, Ann Catherine Swailes OP, Wendy Dossett, Stephanie MacGillivray, Al McFadyen, Simon Hewitt, and Gabrielle and Roger White. Other people also read full drafts and provided invaluable comments and suggestions: my thanks go especially to José Eduardo Porcher, David Streets, Peter Kevern and Rebekah Latour.

Since coming to the School of Philosophy, Religion and History of Science at the University of Leeds in 2012, I have been surrounded by wonderful colleagues who have encouraged and supported my work on religion and mental health. Among those who have especially contributed to discussions on the topic of this book, but who haven't been mentioned already, are Mikel Burley, Robin Le Poidevin, Scott Shalkowski, Simon Kittle, Rachel Muers, Adriaan van Klinken, Caroline Starkey, Jelena Havelka, Léa Salje, Gerald Lang, Aaron Meskin, Ed Elliott, Victor Durà-Vilà, Daniel Elstein and Thomas Brouwer.

My thanks also go to UFRGS, Porto Alegre, for hosting me during two periods of research leave in 2014 and 2015, and to the Center for Philosophy of Religion at the University of Notre Dame, Indiana, in 2011–12. Thanks especially to colleagues and friends in those places: Paulo Faria, José Porcher, Mike

Rea, Beth Seacord and Bob Roberts. And thanks to Matthew Ratcliffe for his kindness in including a 'homeless' post-doctoral hanger-on as a participant in the Durham-based Experiences of Depression project, which introduced me to a new way of thinking philosophically.

The helpful conversations I've had about the topic of this book are too numerous to capture here. A few stand out as having been particularly helpful. My thanks go to Jo Buglass, Tony Buglass, Jon Robson, Ian Kidd, Theo Hawksley, Kevin Timpe, Sam Clarke, Paul Middleton, Warren Kinghorn, John Swinton, Amber Leigh Griffioen, Rhiannan Grant, Sam Lebens, Anna Bortolan, Mike Pennington, Jon Lawson and Peter Brown.

Thanks to my parents, Margaret and Sebastian Yorke, and my (now deceased) grandmother, Henrietta Hick, for their ongoing support and love. Thanks to Lola Scrutton, Wendy Hall, and Archie and Murphy Emerson-Hall for friendship, therapeutic walks and games during the writing process.

Thanks too to universities and funding bodies who provided generous support for me to pursue research on this topic that led to the writing of this book: the Center for Philosophy of Religion at the University of Notre Dame; the Mind Association; the John Templeton Foundation and Saint Louis University, and the University of Leeds.

Thanks to journals I've published in who are letting me reuse materials, especially *Philosophy, Psychiatry and Psychology*. Thanks also go to the Alister Hardy Religious Experience Research Centre, for access to their archive.

Finally, thanks to the brilliant people at SCM Press, and especially to David Shervington for good advice, encouragement and support.

Introduction

As a child, I'd often go for walks with my grandma and our dogs in the Yorkshire countryside. One day, I saw a patch of red at the farthest end of the field we were walking in. Thinking it was a patch of wild poppies, I pointed and said, 'How lovely!' Then, realizing it was an old plastic bag, I corrected myself: 'Oh no, it's horrible!' My grandma – rather philosophically – asked me what it was that had changed my experience of the patch of red so drastically. What exactly, she asked, made me feel so differently about it?

Interpretation is central to our experience. Interpretation shapes how we see the world, what we feel about our place within it, how we will respond to the situations we encounter. Interpretation of the experience of being depressed is no exception. Someone might view depression as a biological disorder, or they might see it as a result of having led a sinful lifestyle. They might see it as an indication of being demonically possessed or, on the contrary, of being especially holy or close to God. They might regard it as a result of oppressive social structures, or as something through which a person might be transformed into a more compassionate and insightful human being. In all these cases, the person's interpretation of depression will shape how they experience and approach depression. It will affect what advice they will give to others who are depressed. If they are depressed themselves it will affect who they ask for help and what kinds of therapies they will consider in response to it.

Different Christians from various traditions believe each of the above about depression, and other things besides. This book is about the different interpretations of depression within Christianity, and how these interpretations shape people's experience of depression. It is also about the kinds of response, support and advice people get about depression in churches – and about the kind of support and advice they *should* be getting in churches.

This book is written for a number of people. It is written for Christians who suffer from depression, who want to know how to make sense of their depression in the light of their Christian faith, and to navigate the different things they might have been told in or by churches. It is written for the families and friends of people with depression, who want to know how to support them. It is written for clergy, religious and lay people within church communities, who want to know what advice to give and how best to help people. This book is also written for mental health professionals, whether themselves Christian or not. It is hoped that this book will enable psychologists, psychiatrists, mental health nurses and others to understand the different interpretations Christians may have of depression, and the way this is likely to shape their experiences and responses to depression. This is important because, in psychiatrist Harold Koenig's words:

> Knowing the impact that religious beliefs may have on the etiology, diagnosis, and outcome of psychiatric disorders will help psychiatrists better understand their patients, appreciate when religious or spiritual beliefs are used to cope with mental illness, and when they may be exacerbating that illness.[1]

This book is also written for academics who have an interest in religion and mental health, which includes people from a range of disciplines, including philosophy, theology, religious studies, sociology, anthropology and psychology. My own disciplinary background is in philosophy and theology, and especially the philosophy of religion; the book will naturally reflect this, while engaging with some work from those other disciplines.

Because this book is written for people from such a wide range of disciplines and professions, I provide a glossary at the end with definitions of some less well-known terms. This book necessarily includes a lot of complex abstract ideas; my aim in providing a glossary is to make these accessible to people who are interested and committed to thinking about these issues but who might otherwise be excluded on account of discipline-specific terminology. Also in the spirit of accessibility, in the endnotes and list of further reading I try where possible to provide references to the growing number of excellent scholarly resources that are freely available online.

Caveats, definitions, criteria and other preliminary things

Writing a book usually gives rise to a number of qualms, particularly if one is used to an academic context where ideas are often contested as soon as they are put forward. For this reason, it's customary to begin with a few 'caveats': explanations to clarify exactly what one is saying – and what one is not saying – in order to prevent misunderstanding. It's also usual to discuss terminology – here, defining and justifying use of terms such as 'depression' and 'mental illness'. Earlier I said that my book will be evaluative as well as descriptive – and so I need certain criteria by which to evaluate different Christian interpretations of depression. Below are my caveats, terminology, criteria and some other preliminary things. If it feels too dull to get bogged down in details about what I'm not saying before I've really said anything at all and you're happy to take my word for these things, you're welcome to skip to p. 18 – the following section and chapters will still make sense.

Four caveats

First, this book is about *Christian* interpretations of depression. I have already mentioned that Christian interpretations of depression will shape the experience of depression in various ways. It might sound as though I think Christians have interpretations of depression, whereas secular people or people from non-Christian religious traditions do not. That is not the case. For example, non-religious people often adopt a biological or social interpretation of depression (depression is seen to be a physical illness or else to be a result of an imperfect society), or a combination of these – which of these they adopt will have a significant impact on how they approach the experience of depression. The view held by some Christians that depression is a sin has as its corollary in some non-religious thought the idea that depression is the result of a blameworthy lifestyle – perhaps not thinking positively, being self-obsessed, not getting enough exercise or not making the effort to see friends or be sociable. And the view that depression is potentially transformative often also has secular correlates, for example in the idea that depression can give rise to greater compassion or more insight without the accompanying view that this is something to do with divine grace or God's capacity to bring good out of evil. So my decision to focus purely on Christian interpretations of depression arises not from a belief that Christians interpret experiences such as depression more than non-Christians. Rather, my focus on Christianity arises from a conviction that, if we are to engage with interpretations of phenomena such as depression, we need to do so with a degree of depth. That takes time and space – a book that tried to discuss *all* interpretations of depression and not only Christian ones would only be able to provide a superficial treatment of each interpretation. Because of my expertise I focus on Christian interpretations of depression; studies of other interpretations would be possible, valuable and helpful.

Second, talking about 'experiences' and 'interpretations' can make it sound as though interpretations (Christian or otherwise) are an 'add-on' to 'bare' experience. In fact, we do not experience something and then interpret it. Rather, our interpretation shapes our experience, such that the experience itself would be qualitatively different without the interpretation. When I was walking with my grandma and saw the patch of red, my interpretation of it as lovely or horrible didn't come after my perception of it; it was part of my perception of it. When I see a chair, provided that I live in a culture where chairs are frequently used to sit down on, I am likely to perceive not a horizontal surface propped up on four legs but, rather, something I can sit down on, or perhaps use to stand on to reach something.[2] When I see a door, I automatically see something I can pull open, walk through and close in order to keep out some noise or a draught. Depression is different from a patch of red, a chair or a door, but the way our interpretations shape our experiences also apply to it. We may see depression as something arising from our own sinfulness, or as a result of biological or neurological dysfunction requiring medication, or as something negative out of which, if we have faith, God may bring something good. In each of these cases, these perceptions of depression will shape our experience of it.

Third, my approach will be to outline and evaluate different Christian interpretations of depression. Someone might object to this approach that religious interpretations shouldn't be evaluated, since we shouldn't pass judgements on people's religious views. I reject the idea that we shouldn't judge or evaluate religious views as a kind of 'head in the sand secularism', which is founded on inaccurate perceptions that religion is 'private' and that things in the private sphere are somehow immune from evaluation and criticim.[3] 'Head in the sand secularism' is pernicious, not least because it enables oppressive beliefs and practices that happen to be religious in relation to women, gay people, people experiencing mental illness, and others to continue unchallenged. Conversely, it means that valuable and helpful aspects of religious traditions are overlooked. Because I reject 'head in the sand secularism', my own approach will be evaluative as well as descriptive: it will not only describe Christian interpretations of depression, but will also try to separate the wheat from the chaff.

Fourth, it might be objected that, by focusing on Christian *interpretations* of depression, I portray Christianity and other religious traditions as sets of beliefs held by individuals, and ignore the fact that religious traditions are also communities that involve other people, emotions, sacred places and spaces, and bodily practices as well as formal doctrines and beliefs. This is a serious criticism, since my own discipline, philosophy of religion, has recently been criticized for focusing on belief as the defining characteristic of religion, to the exclusion of other aspects of religious traditions.[4] This leads to an underestimation of the subtlety of religious traditions, or to a caricature of what these traditions involve.

By 'interpretations', I mean not only explicitly held beliefs (such as 'I believe in one God' or 'I believe that depression is caused by sin'). I also mean ways of understanding phenomena such as depression that are formed and revealed through practices such as liturgies and rituals (for example, in church services in which happiness is normative or, on the contrary, where space is made for sadness through the collective recitation of the Psalms of Lament). In addition, I mean attitudes, revealed through bodily comportment to people with depression, that are held by communities (and can come apart from attitudes professed by individuals within those communities). And I also mean frameworks for understanding experiences such as mental distress that make sense in some historical and interpersonal contexts – perhaps the tradition of the 'dark night of the soul' in Catholic communities – but may be difficult to extract meaningfully or helpfully from those contexts. (This is consistent with the way in which the term 'interpretation' is often used – for example, my interpretation that the patch of red was beautiful when I believed it to be flowers arose out of my belonging to a community in which flowers (and not plastic bags) are regarded as beautiful, which was conveyed to me from an early age by people's bodily comportment towards flowers, and so on.)

The ways in which religious traditions such as Christianity involve not only explicitly held beliefs but also practices, communities, places, emotions and so on is not the focus of this book, but I hope to include some sense of it here.[5]

Terminology: what is 'depression'?

This book focuses on unipolar depression, though much of what I say is relevant to many other kinds of mental disorder (for example, bipolar disorder and anxiety disorders), while being less relevant to some other psychiatric diagnoses (for example, autism), which require a separate discussion. By 'depression' I mean anything that might reasonably be diagnosed as a depressive disorder by a doctor, whether or not the person has been to a doctor and been diagnosed with depression. Doctors base their diagnoses on psychiatric definitions of depression, according to which depression is 'persistent sadness', or 'the presence of sad, empty or irritable mood', or 'depressed mood, or loss of interest and enjoyment', accompanied by some other symptoms. These other symptoms typically include loss of energy, change in appetite, sleeping more or less than usual, anxiety, reduced concentration or ability to think, indecisiveness, feelings of worthlessness or inappropriate guilt, and/or thoughts of self-harm.[6]

Defining depression in this way is good for demarcating the scope of this book. I have said that anything that might reasonably be diagnosed as depression by a doctor who is using a psychiatric definition of depression is within the scope of my discussion, and that other experiences are outside the scope of my discussion. However, the medical definitions are 'thin' descriptions; they tell us relatively little about the experience of depression, or what living with depression is like. For a more fine-grained understanding of depression, we need to turn to descriptions of depression by people who have experienced it. While psychiatric definitions may be helpful for diagnosing depression, it is first-hand descriptions of depression that are most useful in enabling people who have not experienced depression to understand a little about what being depressed is like.

First-hand accounts show that depression often involves a sense of isolation from others, or of being cut off from the usual, interpersonal world.[7] People report: 'I could not reach other human beings.'[8] 'Most of all I was terribly alone, lost, in a harsh and far-away place.'[9] 'Depression feels like the most isolated place on earth. No wonder they call it a disease of loneliness.'[10] 'It was like being inside a very, very thick balloon … I couldn't touch anybody, I couldn't touch anything.'[11] Reflecting on his own and others' experience of depression, sociologist David Karp writes that: 'Much of depression's pain arises out of the recognition that what might make me feel better – human connection – seems impossible in the midst of a paralysing episode of depression.'[12] Analysing first-hand descriptions of depression, philosopher Matthew Ratcliffe writes that depression is experienced as a 'prison' which is 'mine, and mine alone'.[13]

The sense of isolation in depression can be intensified by experiencing others as threatening or in other ways difficult to be around. Karp expresses this when he says: 'A paradox of depression is that sufferers yearn for connection, seem bereft because of their isolation, and yet are rendered incapable of being with others in a comfortable way.'[14] In Ratcliffe's study, people with depression report: 'The world appears to be a frightening place full of people who are bad and threatening'; 'I can feel very paranoid and unsafe, on the verge of being attacked'; 'People in general seem more hostile and uncaring when I am depressed.'[15]

Perhaps surprisingly, the body can also feel very different when one is depressed. People feel 'tired' and 'heavy': 'My body seems very heavy and it's an effort to move'; 'My entire body aches and feels like it's going to break'; 'my legs are terribly heavy; I cannot walk I feel so exhausted.'[16] People report that they have 'No energy' and feel 'Just totally run down', or that their body feels 'As heavy as lead' or 'like it's full of lead'.[17] Another person says they feel 'Exhausted, heavy limbs, aching, headaches, tired, spaced out.'[18] Some people even report sickness, nausea, a blocked nose, and a sore throat.[19]

Feeling cut off from others, and feeling tired and heavy, are by no means the only experiences characteristic of depression. In Chapter 1 we will encounter other characteristic experiences, such as a sense of diminished free will and loss of possibility, and feelings of guilt. Hopefully, though, these first-hand accounts give us some sense of some common features of depression, and go beyond the psychiatric definitions in describing what depression is like.

As the accounts above suggest, experiences of depression are diverse.[20] Not everyone who experiences depression will feel cut off from others or that their body is heavy. And if they do, there are differences between people's experiences: feeling cut off from others is not the same as feeling that the presence of others is threatening, and having a sore throat is different from feeling tired or as though one's body is made of lead. The variety of experiences involved in different cases of depression has made some people wonder if we should cease to use the word 'depression', since it's so broad and covers so many different things. If this is right, I have a problem: I have said that I am going to talk about Christianity *and depression*, and yet the experience of depression is not uniform but, rather, describes a number of diverse experiences.

I don't think this need worry us too much. When we reflect on it, it seems that quite a lot of terms we use are very broad and cover lots of different things. 'Religion' might refer to Christianity, with its belief in a creator God, or to Buddhism, which is typically non-theistic. Alternatively it might refer not primarily to beliefs at all but to a set of practices or communities or ways of living. Nor can we say that religions, even if they have various differences, are united by one core thing that they have and other things do not have. Being a football fan, for example, has many of the same characteristics as belonging to a religion in terms of commitment, and having rituals and sacred spaces, and yet is not usually classed as a religious tradition. There is no one core feature of religion that all examples of religion have in common, and that things that aren't a religion don't have. And this goes for lots of other terms we use – think about 'games', 'illnesses', 'books' and so on.

The fact that so many of the terms we use pick out diverse rather than homogenous phenomena has led some philosophers to suggest that we should see lots of concepts not as having a single core or essence, but as groups of diverse things united by family resemblances.[21] I think we should adopt this approach.

You might reasonably ask what I mean by 'family resemblances'. Within a family we might find that a mother and daughter have a similar nose, say, while the daughter's eyes are similar to her grandmother's but her mother's are not. And then the daughter's brother might have a similar nose to their grandmother but take after his father in terms of his eyes. An aunt might have a similar mouth to the mother and the son but not to the daughter or grandmother, and so on. People might say, 'We can see the family resemblance' – there are similarities that unite them as a group. But that doesn't mean that any one member of the family has precisely the same features as any other, and there is no one core feature shared by them all. I think 'depression' is like this, and so should be regarded as a 'family resemblance'-type term.

But it could be argued that it's much more natural to group families together than to group the different experiences involved in depression together. Families have a biological – a genetic – relationship, and grouping people together in terms of families occurs across history and culture. Depression isn't like that. The states we call depression have been categorized differently at other times and in other cultures. So surely it's arbitrary to group the states and experiences involved in what we call 'depression' together as depression rather than in another way. And when we look at other diagnostic categories that psychiatrists use, we see that changes in diagnostic categories in fact do occur.[22] Why should we have any faith in the category of 'depression' as valid or coherent?

In responding to this kind of objection, it might be helpful to think of the example of someone organizing a library.[23] Perhaps the person could organize the library by topic, or in alphabetical order according to the author's surname, or in alphabetical order according to the book's title. Then again, they could order it according to the year in which the book was written. If they order it by topic, they have to consider what distinctions to make – should they distinguish fact from fiction, or eastern philosophy from western philosophy? Should they put cookery books alongside gardening and pottery books, or alongside culture and travel? The experiences involved in depression could have been categorized differently, and diagnostic manuals sometimes do change the different diagnostic categories they use. The question then is not, 'Does the category of depression carve nature at the joints?' any more than we're likely to ask that question about the way a library has been organized. Rather, the question is, 'Is this a helpful way to categorize these different experiences and states in this culture at this time?'

My sense with depression is that by and large it is. We know broadly what people mean when they speak of having depression, and we know broadly what range of treatments and responses – medical, psychological, social – might help them.

This foray into the metaphysics of depression is practically important. If the family resemblances approach to depression is correct, then recognizing the heterogeneity of the experience of depression does not entail that we reject the term 'depression', or the psychiatric and psychological therapies that seek to treat depression. Defining a range of experiences as 'depression' might be practically helpful, in the same way that organizing a library in, say, alphabetical order according to author's surname might be practically helpful (by making it possible for people to find books). It is helpful, even if the library might conceivably have been arranged in another way.

Terminology: 'mental' vs 'physical' illness

If it is easier to use the word 'depression' than to define clearly what we mean by it, much the same goes for the term 'mental illness', and perhaps especially when we try to explain how mental illness is different from physical illness. Some people say that physical illness is a condition of the body, while mental illness is a condition of the mind, and so about whether people can function productively, or interact with others, or whether their ability to think and feel is diminished.[24] But, when we come to think about it, things are not as straightforward as this suggests. Mental illness also involves the body – it can be caused by biological factors such as neurological changes or drug use; it can include somatic symptoms such as feelings of heaviness, tiredness and achiness;[25] it can respond to biological therapies such as prescribed medications or exercise. Conversely, in fact we *can't* function productively, or interact with others, or think and feel as we used to, if for example we have come down with a bad flu or are paralysed by severe backache. Surely this gives us pause for thought: what basis do we have for putting one state (such as depression) in the 'mental illness' category and assuming another (perhaps flu or backache) is a 'physical illness'?[26]

This difficulty in establishing a decisive boundary between mental and physical illness has led some people, including some psychiatrists, to be suspicious of the distinction between 'mental' and 'physical' illness. One psychiatric manual, DSM-IV, puts this suspicion in the following way:

> the term mental disorder unfortunately implies a distinction between 'mental' disorders and 'physical' disorders that is a reductionistic anachronism of mind/body dualism. A compelling literature documents that there is much 'physical' in 'mental' disorders and much 'mental' in 'physical' disorders. The problem raised by the term 'mental' disorders has been much clearer than its solution, and, unfortunately, the term persists in the title of DSM-IV because we have not found an appropriate substitute.[27]

In the background of DSM-IV's suspicion of the 'mental' vs 'physical' distinction is its rejection of dualism. More particularly (although it is not specified in the passage quoted), the kind of dualism DSM-IV is referring to is 'Cartesian dualism', or the dualism put forward by the early modern philosopher René Descartes ('Cartesian' comes from 'Descartes'). Descartes believed that there are two radically different and independent substances that make up reality: matter (or the physical) and mind (or the mental). Language about the physical and the mental occurred long before Descartes, but until Descartes the physical and mental were not regarded as independent kinds of substance. For example, the term 'soul' was used by medieval theologians such as St Thomas Aquinas to refer to the 'form of the body', rather than to a spiritual reality that floats free of the body and where the real person is located.[28] It's Cartesian dualism (henceforth just 'dualism') that has largely brought a sharp distinction between terms such as 'soul' and 'mind' (on the one hand) and 'body' and 'physical' to western culture.

Dualism still has its defenders, but by and large it's been rejected, and for good reason. For example, as one friend of Descartes, the philosopher Princess Elisabeth of Bohemia, asked: if the mental and physical are independent kinds of substance, how can we account for the fact that the mental and physical interact?[29] In other words, how can we account for the fact that changes take place in my brain when I think about tax returns or polar bears, or that I temporarily relax and worry less when I drink a glass of wine? Here, the physical seems to affect the mental and vice versa, and it's not easy to explain how this is the case if dualism is true. No one has found a satisfactory answer to Princess Elisabeth's question. This and other difficulties have led most philosophers to reject dualism.

According to the passage in DSM-IV quoted above, we have two reasons to reject the distinction between mental and physical illness. First, there's much that's physical in mental illness, and much that's mental in physical illness, so that there are no clear-cut boundaries. Second, the distinction between mental and physical presupposes dualism, which is something we should reject. What are we to make of these arguments?

While it is true that there are no clear-cut boundaries between mental and physical illness and plenty of vague cases, I don't think this need worry us too much. As we have seen when discussing depression and family resemblance-type terms, there are no clear-cut boundaries when it comes to many or even most of the terms we use. What is important is that we know how to use terms and that our use of them does something helpful. This seems to be the case with terms such as 'mental illness': if my friend tells me she is worried about her mental health, I know to gently enquire about her moods and how she is feeling about the world. I know not to respond by saying, 'Oh, where does it hurt?' As one philosopher, Ludwig

Wittgenstein, puts it, the term is 'in order' because 'We know how to go on.'[30]

That the distinction between 'mental illness' and 'physical illness' is implicitly dualistic is more of a worry. Adopting dualism can mean that we can downplay the important psychological elements of physical illness, and the somatic elements of mental illness. More generally, thinking dualistically is problematic – philosophically, theologically and (as I shall argue in Chapter 3) potentially even for our mental health. The question then becomes, what is the relationship between dualism and the mental/physical illness distinction? If the mental/physical illness distinction entails dualism – if we can't have the mental/physical illness without adopting dualism – that would be a significant reason for rejecting the mental/physical distinction and seeking some alternative.

Contrary to the implication of the DSM-IV passage, I don't think the language of 'mental' and 'physical' illness does entail dualism. Language referring to the mind as distinct from the body was used long before Descartes; this was just understood in non-dualistic or less dualistic ways. It may be that, as a culture, we sometimes default to understanding the mental/physical distinction in dualistic terms because of the latent dualism in our culture – as, for example, when we 'spiritualize' mental illness (by seeing it as especially relating to sin, or demons, or holiness) but see physical illness as quite separate from anything spiritual. However, it's far from obvious that we always understand the term dualistically, and even less obvious that we necessarily do. Most people are perfectly able to discuss the effects of their antidepressants with their psychiatrist or GP, while speaking of their depression as a kind of 'mental illness'. In short, most people 'know how to go on' in other than dualistic ways. It's easier to shift meanings than replace words;[31] it therefore seems sensible to carry on using the terms 'mental illness' and 'physical illness', but try to understand and use them in other than dualistic ways.

Terminology: is depression an 'illness'?

How about the idea that depression is a mental *illness*? In Chapter 1, we will see that some people want to deny that depression is an illness at all. One well-meaning reason for this is that regarding depression as an illness is sometimes thought to lead to a denial of agency: to make depression out to be simply a misfortune that happens to someone rather than something they can do something about. Correspondingly, it's argued, telling someone they have an 'illness' renders them a passive recipient of medical help, and this can diminish their mental health further by diminishing the person's sense of self and ignoring their narrative and the things they find important. This is particularly the case if the medical help they receive ignores the views and narratives of patients and treats people purely as faulty machines to be mended.[32]

However, it seems to me that ignoring patients' voices and narratives is not an essential part of medical care but simply an unfortunate aspect of some medical culture that needs to change.[33] In addition, that depression is an 'illness' is very important in two ways. First, it tells us that we must take mental illness every bit as seriously as any other kind of illness: people who have experienced depression first-hand and those close to them know that it's every bit as debilitating and deserves compassion and understanding just as much. Second, it tells us that we should continue to provide medical care for people with depression and other forms of mental illness. Many cases of mental illness do respond well to medical treatment, and we jeopardize people's lives if we remove medical care from them. 'Illness' itself is difficult to define; there are good reasons for including depression within the category of illness alongside cancers, colds, eye infections, epilepsy and diabetes – and no good reasons not to.

Criteria

I have promised to 'evaluate' the different interpretations of depression, as well as to describe them. I think this is important: I got into philosophy as I wanted to know what to believe. Philosophy gives us helpful tools to decide what we often have: a choice of different beliefs we have to decide between. Different interpretations of depression are a case in point.

Philosophical criteria typically include things not specific to a particular religious tradition – criteria that are, as far as possible, universal or a sort of lingua franca for discerning what is true or at least might be true. Philosophical criteria include things such as coherence and consistency – in other words, whether a belief or set of beliefs 'hangs together' or whether it contradicts itself, and whether it takes account of all the facts. For example (on the topic of Chapter 4), if someone claims that a period of mental distress is a 'dark night of the soul', but the background theology on which they base that claim is out of sync with the dark night tradition, we might worry that ultimately their claim will not be coherent, because the set of beliefs they have do not hang together. Or again (on the topic of Chapter 5), if someone says that everyone's experience of depression leads to spiritual and moral growth, but ignores the fact that some people report that their depression was just a period of meaningless suffering, we might wonder if their claim is flawed because it fails to take account of all the facts.

Relatedly, a further criterion for deciding what to believe is fidelity to experience – does this view of reality correspond to people's experience of reality? If I tell you that it's raining outside, but when you look out of the window it's sunny, you have reason to doubt my assertion that it's raining outside. Likewise, as we shall see in Chapter 1, if someone – perhaps a well-meaning advisor – tells a depressed person that they are able to get out of bed, have a shower, or even get a job, but the depressed person experiences those things as impossible, we have at least some reasons for doubting that the advisor is right.

In addition to coherence, consistency and fidelity to lived experience, discerning what is helpful is also important.[34] We can't always know for sure whether something is true – so we might think instead about whether it is helpful to believe it, or say it, or act as though it is true. Perhaps you don't know whether my brusque interactions with you are the result of my shyness, or whether it's because I dislike you. You decide to believe it's a result of shyness, because it makes you relax around me and be kinder towards me. Or perhaps you don't know whether a friend's occasional smoking habit contributed to his lung cancer, but you know it would be an unhelpful response to raise it when he tells you about his diagnosis. Then again (on the topic of Chapter 2), perhaps you might decide to challenge someone about their belief that depression is caused by demons, because you have evidence that the belief is unhelpful and doing real harm.

Helpfulness is close in some ways to typical medical criteria such as clinical outcomes. But 'helpfulness' is broader than 'clinical outcomes': while 'clinical outcomes' focuses primarily on recovery and recovery time, helpfulness is a much more general category that might include recovery but could also include (for example) an illness having meaning even if recovery is not likely. We might put this by saying that helpfulness includes not only recovery but also healing.[35] Havi Carel points towards something like this sense of healing when she says, in the context of discussing her own permanent, debilitating and life-threatening illness: 'Against the objective horror of my illness I cultivated an inner sense of peacefulness and joy. I was surprised at this ... this ability to be ill and happy.'[36]

We would like all illnesses to be cured. In reality, some illnesses are permanent and some are fatal. While 'clinical outcomes' typically concerns recovery (for example, whether a particular religious belief is conducive to recovery or the reverse[37]), 'helpfulness' can refer to recovery but also to healing, meaning, hope, solidarity with those who suffer, consolation and so on.

It's hoped that this book will be read, among others, by people within the Christian tradition who want to know what to believe about depression. In addition to philosophical criteria, Christians typically use theological criteria – criteria specific to the Christian tradition – when they want to know what to believe. For example, a Christian might ask, do the Scriptures – the Bible – have anything to say about this? What wisdom can other Christians in the past whom we particularly admire – for example, theologians such as St Augustine of Hippo and St Thomas Aquinas – lend us to think about these issues? And what has the Church, for instance through the various Councils it has held when faced with dilemmas, ended up believing to be true? As we shall see, for example, the Councils of Carthage and Ephesus discerned that the fourth- and fifth-century monk Pelagius was wrong about free will, and this has implications when we come to discuss the claim that depression is a result of sin.

This book is written not only for Christians, but also for people who want to know what Christians believe about depression – for example, because they hope to understand their friends or their patients better. Theological criteria are likely to carry less weight for these readers than are philosophical criteria. Yet, religious traditions such as Christianity have been concerned, over many centuries, with the reality of human suffering. Whether the reader is a Christian or not, she may be able to engage fruitfully with Christian thought by seeing it as a kind of repository of cultural wisdom for thinking about and responding to suffering, including the suffering involved in depression.

There are internal debates within the Christian tradition about the relationship between philosophy and theology, and also about the relationship between different theological criteria (such as fidelity to Scripture and fidelity to tradition). It's not within the scope of this book to discuss these here; the kinds of criteria I am using here and the way I am using these criteria have been well defended elsewhere.[38]

Overview and structure of the book

Some people like spoilers: it helps them to focus on 'How are we getting there?' rather than 'Where are we going?' Others like the surprise of seeing how a story or an argument unfolds. For those who like spoilers, here's an overview of the book; for those who don't, feel free to skip to Chapter 1.

Chapter 1: Sin

It is sometimes claimed, for example by churches or in Christian self-help books, that depression is a sin or a result of sin. In other words, it's claimed that a particular person is depressed because they've done something wrong, or generally led a sinful lifestyle, or because they lack faith. I call this a 'sin account of depression'. In Chapter 1 I argue against this account, on the grounds that its underlying presuppositions about human free will aren't true to human experience, and are also at odds with the Christian tradition.

People who put forward sin accounts of depression not only claim that these accounts are true; they also think that sin accounts are helpful because (they claim) they provide people with hope by showing them what needs to be done in order to recover. I argue that they have this feature in common with most medical treatments and theological responses to depression, and so there is nothing especially hope-giving about sin accounts of depression. In addition to this, sin accounts of depression are overwhelmingly unhelpful in other respects. For example, sin accounts of depression encourage people who are already vulnerable to unwarranted feelings of guilt and shame to feel further guilt and shame; they alienate people from the religious communities that should be a source of strength and comfort to them; they discourage people from seeking medical and psychological help for their condition; and they deflect attention away from the social causes of depression by making depression out to be about the failings of individuals rather than of societies.

Chapter 2: Demons

The idea that demons cause depression will be totally alien to people from many Christian traditions, but very familiar to people from others. Within the latter Christian traditions, that demons cause some illness (or apparent illness) is thought to be based on the Bible, and especially the exorcism ministry of Jesus as reported in the Gospels of Matthew, Mark and Luke. But, as I show, many demonic accounts of mental illness do not faithfully reflect scriptural accounts of the demonic at all. In particular, they erroneously associate susceptibility to demonic affliction (possession or oppression) with individual sinfulness; they interpret language about 'spiritual warfare' in a politically conservative way; and they regard Jesus' activity as an exorcist as separate from his ministry of liberation, of which it was one aspect.

Demonic accounts of depression are often defended on the grounds of their apparent helpfulness. But in fact they are unhelpful for many of the same reasons as sin accounts of depression. They may also be pathogenic or illness causing in other ways – for example, by triggering or providing a focus for psychosis for those who are susceptible to it.

Chapter 3: Biology

Reacting against sin and demonic accounts of depression, some churches increasingly emphasize the fact that depression is an illness instead. Depression, it's claimed, is like a broken leg or any other kind of ailment. It needs to be treated with prescription medications, and not repentance or exorcism.

These kinds of accounts must come as a huge relief to many people in communities who have been told that their depression is the result of sin or of demonic possession. And yet, I argue, we can do better than this. These accounts risk emphasizing the biological at the expense of other important elements related to depression's causes: the psychological and the social. This chapter redresses the overemphasis on the biological by outlining and arguing for a biopsychosocial rather than a biomedical (or 'bio-bio-bio') model of depression.

While arguing for a more moderate account of the biological in depression, I also emphasize the very real importance of the biological in depression. Traditional Christianity holds that humans are a kind of animal, and so bodily through and through. It is often in forgetting that we are animals and so forgetting our vulnerability, need for stability and the companionship of others that, as a society, we make ourselves more susceptible to depression and other forms of mental illness. Sadly, Christianity has sometimes been associated with a denial of our animality and a negative attitude towards the body. In response to this, the second part of this chapter looks at parts of the Christian tradition that invite us to recognize and celebrate our bodiliness and animality: the idea of the resurrection of the body, and stories of saints' friendships with non-human animals.

Chapter 4: The dark night of the soul

Sin and demonic accounts of depression view depression as a sign of spiritual failure or distance from God. In contrast to these, language about the dark night of the soul has been used to suggest that people suffering from mental distress are in fact especially holy or close to God. This chapter looks at different ways of construing the relationship between the dark night of the soul and depression. Drawing on the writings of the sixteenth-century mystic St John of the Cross, it argues that depression should not be conflated with the dark night of the soul, but nor should the two experiences be seen as mutually exclusive. Someone may be going through a dark night of the soul, but that does not preclude them from also having depression. Relatedly, that they are or might be having a dark night of the soul is not a reason to discourage them from medical and/or psychological therapies.

The importance of these points becomes apparent when we look at the way in which Mother Teresa of Calcutta's experience of mental distress was interpreted, and when we think about whether a cure should be sought, for example through medical means, in cases of people whose distress seems to have religious or spiritual value.

Chapter 5: Can depression help us grow?

In Christian thought, God is thought to bring good out of evil: the execution and death of Jesus, for example, was the occasion for Jesus' resurrection and the hope of resurrection for the whole world. The idea of God bringing good out of evil is central to what I call a 'potentially transformative' account of depression. This is the idea that depression, like all suffering, is an evil, but that through the experience of depression some people find that they become more insightful about or happier in themselves, more compassionate or courageous, or more able to appreciate beauty and to be thankful for it.

This chapter considers a potentially transformative account of depression, focusing on the writings of the Dutch psychologist and priest Henri Nouwen. I argue in favour of a potentially transformative account of depression, on the grounds that (unlike some other accounts) it maintains that suffering is evil rather than a disguised good – and so motivates people to seek recovery – while also recognizing that experiences of suffering can have some meaning and value. I defend a potentially transformative account from several objections: that it puts pressure on people to find positive elements in their suffering, encourages glib and insensitive responses to suffering, leads to social and political apathy, and only applies to short-term and/or mild cases of depression. Responding to these objections is helpful, as it clarifies what a *good* potentially transformative account of depression looks like, and allows some core emphases for promising Christian responses to depression to come further into view.

Chapter 6: Can God suffer?

It is sometimes claimed that divine passibility, the idea that God suffers not only in the person of Jesus but in Godself, is the most fruitful emphasis for a Christian theology of mental illness. But is it plausible to think that God suffers? Christians are split on this question, and there are good arguments on either side. This chapter will help you think through this question for yourself, and takes the form of a dialogue between a passibilist and an impassibilist. In addition to enabling everyone to reach their own conclusions, the chapter encourages readers to have sympathy for both points of view, and to understand why passibilism might not be an easy solution for some Christians. In so doing, it opposes a simplistic application of passibilism as a kind of panacea or easy Christian response to questions about human suffering.

Chapter 7: Would a suffering God help?

Building on Chapter 6, this chapter begins by looking at two ways in which passibilism, the idea that God suffers in Godself, is sometimes thought to be helpful to people with depression. First, the idea of presenting God as a 'fellow sufferer who understands' provides consolation to sufferers, including sufferers of depression. Second, the idea of a suffering God destigmatizes experiences such as mental illness, and so provides a more welcoming and less alienating form of church community.

I argue that passibilism is not more helpful than impassibilism in these respects. While fellow suffering is one kind of consolation, having someone outside human suffering who points beyond suffering or offers redemption from it is also consolatory. In addition, Christ and the saints often embody both kinds of consolation, and so have the potential to destigmatize particular kinds of suffering, including mental illness. It's not clear why the being who suffers needs to be God in Godself rather than other religious figures. In relation to destigmatization what is important is that religious figures are presented not only as suffering but as suffering in ways that are usually stigmatized (for example, because they are associated with sin, shame, or sexual humiliation). Too often in both passibilist and impassibilist traditions the suffering of religiously significant figures is sanitized and so robbed of its destigmatizing power. This is true in characteristically passibilist and impassibilist traditions, whether in relation to the suffering of God in Godself, of the saints, or in relation to the person of Jesus.

Furthermore, destigmatizing mental illness is not the only work churches need to do in order to make the experience of living with depression better. Other forms of stigma, for example relating to gender, sex and sexuality, which frequently contribute to mental illness, also need to be addressed if churches are to be welcoming places. And, in addition to combatting stigma, more practical support of people with depression and for their family and care-givers is often needed.

Chapter 8: Towards a Christian response to depression

In this book I offer what might be called a deflationary account of the relationship between Christianity and depression. I argue that mental illness doesn't have a special relationship with faith or the spiritual life, and that we should regard it no differently theologically from physical illness or other kinds of suffering. I think this needs arguing for, because as a culture we have a tendency to spiritualize mental (but not physical) illnesses, and this does a great deal of harm. In the course of my argument I will talk about some of the things we shouldn't say to or about people experiencing depression: we shouldn't say it's a result of their sin, or of demonic possession, or something God has inflicted on them as a sign of their holiness, or that they must or ought to grow spiritually because of it. Along the way, more fruitful emphases for a Christian response to depression will emerge.

Chapter 8 draws out these more fruitful emphases, focusing on four themes: Christ's solidarity with those who suffer;

social sin and the political demonic; hope and resurrection; and animality and the senses. In addition to exploring these themes, I will point to some pastoral and clinical implications of this book.

Notes

1 Harold G. Koenig (2007), 'Religion, spirituality and psychiatry: A new era in mental health care', Foreword in a special issue of *Revista de Psiquiatria Clinica* 34, Supl 1, p. 5, available at www.scielo.br/pdf/rpc/v34s1/en_a02v34s1.pdf (all websites in this notes section accessed 13.12.19).

2 See Maurice Merleau-Ponty (1962), *The Phenomenology of Perception*, trans. Colin Smith, New York: Humanities Press, p. 150; Edmund Husserl (2001), *Analyses Concerning Active and Passive Synthesis: Lectures on Transcendental Logic*, trans. A. J. Steinbock, Dordrecht: Kluwer, p. 42.

3 Emma Tomalin (2015) (20 February), 'Secularism can sometimes undermine women's rights', *Open Democracy*, available at www.open democracy.net/en/openglobalrights-openpage/secularism-can-sometimes-undermine-womens-rights/.

4 See Simon Hewitt and Anastasia Philippa Scrutton (2018), 'Philosophy and living religion: An introduction to a special issue on philosophy and living religion', *International Journal for Philosophy and Theology* 79.4, pp. 349–54, and Kevin Schilbrack (2014), *Philosophy and the Study of Religions: A Manifesto*, Chichester, Sussex: Wiley-Blackwell, for a critique of belief-focused approaches in philosophy of religion.

5 For a book on philosophy of religion that does do justice to these things, see Mark Wynn (2013), *Renewing the Senses: A Study of the Philosophy and Theology of the Spiritual Life*, Oxford: Oxford University Press.

6 APA (American Psychiatric Association) (2013), *Diagnostic and Statistical Manual of Mental Disorders 5th ed.* (DSM-5), Arlington: American Psychiatric Publishing, p. 155; WHO (World Health Organization), Depression: Let's Talk, available at www.who.int/mental_health/management/depression/en/; ICD-10 Criteria for Diagnosis of Depression, available at www.brisbanenorthphn.org.au/content/Document/Pathways/LINK%20A_ICD_10.pdf.

7 This account of depression is dependent upon Matthew Ratcliffe (2015), *Experiences of Depression: A Study in Phenomenology*, Oxford: Oxford University Press. For an account of the experience of depression that is more aligned with the psychiatric description of depression (but

less detailed than Ratcliffe's analysis), see Femi Oyebode (2015), *Sims' Symptoms in the Mind: Textbook of Descriptive Psychopathology* (5th edn), China: Elsevier, pp. 270–1, available at http://zu.edu.jo/Upload File/Library/E_Books/Files/LibraryFile_151635_46.pdf.

8 Gail A. Hornstein (2009), *Agnes' Jacket: A Psychologist's Search for the Meanings of Madness*, New York: Rodale, p. 222.

9 Fiona Shaw (1997), *Out of Me: The Story of a Postnatal Breakdown*, London: Penguin, p. 40.

10 Sally Brampton (2008), *Shot the Damn Dog: A Memoir of Depression*, London: Bloomsbury, p. 1.

11 Anon, cited in Ratcliffe, *Experiences*, p. 218.

12 David Karp (1996), *Speaking of Sadness: Depression, Disconnection, and the Meanings of Illness*, Oxford: Oxford University Press, p. 16.

13 Ratcliffe, *Experiences*, p. 201.

14 Karp, *Speaking*, p. 14.

15 #66, #21, #129, cited in Ratcliffe, *Experiences*, pp. 224–5.

16 #129, #14, cited in Ratcliffe, *Experiences*, p. 76; the final quotation is from Oyebode, *Symptoms*, p. 267.

17 #357, #26, #22, cited in Ratcliffe, *Experiences*, p. 77.

18 #226, cited in Ratcliffe, *Experiences*, p. 76.

19 Ratcliffe, *Experiences*, p. 76.

20 See Ratcliffe, *Experiences*.

21 Ludwig Wittgenstein (1986/1953), *Philosophical Investigations*, trans. G. E. M. Anscombe, Oxford: Basil Blackwell, available at https://static1.squarespace.com/static/54889e73e4b0a2c1f9891289/t/564b61a4e4b04eca59c4d232/1447780772744/Ludwig.Wittgenstein.-.Philosophical.Investigations.pdf.

22 For example, there are a number of differences between DSM-5 (a psychiatric manual used especially in the USA today and published in 2013) and DSM-IV (its predecessor, published in 2000). These include Asperger's being subsumed into a new category (Autism Spectrum Disorder), changes to criteria for schizophrenia and bipolar disorder, and the removal of a bereavement exclusion clause for a major depressive episode. See APA, DSM-5, pp. 809–16.

23 I owe this analogy to K. S. Kendler, P. Zachar and C. Craver (2001), 'What kinds of things are psychiatric disorders?', *Psychological Medicine* 41, pp. 1143–50.

24 See for example Anon, n.d., 'What is the difference between physical and mental health?' *Reference.com*, available at www.reference.com/education/difference-between-physical-mental-health-e593c36dd8b1f42b, and Canadian Mental Health Association, BD Division (2015), 'What's the difference between mental health and mental illness?', *Here to Help*, available at www.heretohelp.bc.ca/ask-us/whats-the-difference-between-mental-health-and-mental-illness.

25 Thomas Fuchs (2013), 'Depression, intercorporeality, and inter-affectivity', *Journal of Consciousness Studies* 20, No. 7–8, 219–38, p. 228, available at www.klinikum.uni-heidelberg.de/fileadmin/zpm/psychatrie/fuchs/Literatur/Depression_Intercorporeality_and_Inter affectivity.pdf.

26 See Matthew Ratcliffe, Matthew Broome, Benedict Smith and Hannah Bowden (2014), 'A bad case of the flu? The comparative phenomenology of depression and somatic illness', in Matthew Ratcliffe and Achim Stephan, *Depression, Emotion and the Self: Philosophical and interdisciplinary perspectives*, Exeter, UK: Imprint Academic Ltd, pp. 163–82.

27 APA (American Psychiatric Association) (2000), *Diagnostic and Statistical Manual of Mental Disorders 4th ed.* (DSM-IV), Washington, DC: APA Publishing, p. xxx.

28 Thomas Aquinas, *Summa Theologiae*, Part 1, Question 76, available at www3.nd.edu/~afreddos/summa-translation/Part%201/st1-ques76.pdf (Alfred J. Freddosa translation). Biblical language, too, is often translated and interpreted as more dualistic than it in fact is (see Chapter 3 of this book).

29 Lisa Shapiro (2013), 'Elisabeth, Princess of Bohemia', *Stanford Encyclopedia of Philosophy*, available at https://plato.stanford.edu/entries/elisabeth-bohemia/.

30 Wittgenstein, *Philosophical Investigations*, §180.

31 Elizabeth Barnes (2016), *The Minority Body: A theory of disability*, Oxford: Oxford University Press, p. 8.

32 See e.g. C. Heriot-Maitland, M. Knight and E. Peters (2012), 'A qualitative comparison of psychotic-like phenomena in clinical and non-clinical populations', *British Journal of Clinical Psychology* 51, pp. 37–53.

33 See Havi Carel (2013), *Illness* (2nd edn), Durham: Acumen Publishing, and Havi Carel and Ian James Kidd (2014), 'Epistemic injustice in healthcare: A philosophical analysis', *Medicine, Healthcare, and Philosophy* 17.4, pp. 529–40.

34 William James (1896), *The Will to Believe and Other Essays in Popular Philosophy*, New York, NY: Longmans, Green, and Co., available at www.mnsu.edu/philosophy/THEWILLTOBELIEVEbyJames.pdf; Anastasia Philippa Scrutton (2015), 'Why not believe in an evil God? Pragmatic encroachment and some implications for philosophy of religion', *Religious Studies: An International Journal for Philosophy of Religion* 52.3, pp. 345–60.

35 Kathleen J. Greider (2007), *Much Madness is Divinest Sense: Wisdom in Memoirs of Soul-Suffering*, Ohio: Pilgrim Press.

36 Carel, *Illness*, p. 76.

37 See e.g. K. Pargament, H. Koenig and L. Perez (2000), 'The many methods of religious coping: Development and initial validation of the

RCOPE', *Journal of Clinical Psychology*, 56.4, pp. 519–43; Harold Koenig, Dana King and Verna Carson (2012), *Handbook of Religion and Health*, Oxford: Oxford University Press.

   38 See e.g. Alister McGrath (2016), *Christian Theology: An Introduction* (6th edn), New Jersey: Wiley Blackwell, especially Part 2.

I

Sin

Introduction

One of the reasons I started researching the topic of Christianity and mental health is that a friend who had contended with a serious illness and disability from birth and had particularly difficult experiences throughout her life was told by a church in the north of England that her depression was the result of her having sinned. This surprised and shocked me, and I thought this kind of message must be unusual. As I researched further, I realized that the belief that depression is the result of sin is in fact quite common, in the UK, USA and elsewhere. And while the idea is sometimes attributed only to 'lay theology',[1] in fact it is also put forward in Christian self-help books by psychologists, psychiatrists, church ministers, university professors, and other figures of authority.[2] At the same time as realizing this, I became aware that this kind of view isn't distinctively Christian or distinctively religious, despite using language about 'sin': it has correlates in some secular attitudes to depression, for example in the idea that if people with depression only tried harder, looked on the bright side, were a bit less self-obsessed, did more exercise, went out to see their friends, and so on, they would soon stop being depressed.[3]

In this chapter I'm going to examine, and argue against, a 'sin account of depression', by which I mean the idea that depression is the result of the person's own individual sins or sinfulness.[4] I will begin by characterizing a sin account of depression, drawing on the writings of published Christian self-help books and websites. After that, I'll move on to evaluating this kind of view. Much could be talked about here.[5] But as I can't talk about everything, I'm going to focus on two core claims found in sin accounts of depression as the basis of my criticism of these accounts. The first is that people with depression can choose not to be depressed. I'm going to argue against this claim on the basis that it presents an account of free will that does not take seriously the fact that human free will is not unlimited. This account of free will has in fact been rejected by the Christian Church, and so a sin account of depression is not consistent with criteria internal to the Christian tradition. Furthermore, I'll argue that free will can be more or less diminished in particular situations and, as some philosophical work on depression indicates, free will is characteristically diminished in depression. A sin view of depression is therefore not only not consistent with the Christian tradition: more universal criteria such as fidelity to lived experience should lead us to reject it.

The second core claim I'm going to argue against is that telling people with depression that they can choose not to be depressed is helpful because it provides more hope for recovery and empowerment than other accounts of depression do. I argue against this claim on the basis that other elements of 'sin' accounts, such as guilt and blame, outweigh the hopeful elements. In addition, the hopeful or empowering elements can be found in other responses to depression (ranging from medical treatments for depression to a theological emphasis on the resurrection), and these do not involve the idea that depression is the result of sin. The thrust of the chapter is that sin accounts of depression are neither plausible nor helpful, and we should reject them.

Why focus on these particular two claims in sin accounts of depression? One reason is that I think these get to the heart of sin accounts. In addition, some of the underlying presuppositions – particularly about the extent of human free will – are also found in some other, otherwise very different Christian approaches to depression, which will be discussed later. A further reason is that even people who are vehemently against sin accounts of depression can find that some aspects of them, especially relating to free will and choice, can creep back into their thought when responding to people with depression. By focusing on these core claims, I will address sin accounts of depression head on, and also cast my net somewhat wider by preparing the ground for later discussion and challenging some more general problematic assumptions.

What are sin accounts of depression?

The idea that depression is a result of sin is associated with the idea that Christian faith includes spiritual fruits such as joy. According to St Paul, 'the fruit of the Spirit is love, joy, peace, patience, kindness, goodness, faithfulness, gentleness, and self-control' (Galatians 5.22–23a).[6] Taking this single passage of the Bible out of context, the thought goes as follows: if joy is the fruit of the Spirit, and someone isn't experiencing joy, things must be awry in the person's spiritual life. One person who has been on the receiving end of sin accounts of depression characterizes them vividly:

> When dealing with people in the church ... some see mental illness as a weakness – a sign you don't have enough faith. They said: 'It's a problem of the heart. You need to straighten things out with God.' They make depression out to be a sin, because you don't have the joy in your life a Christian is supposed to have.[7]

Sin accounts tend to be extremely voluntaristic: they presuppose that people have a high degree of free will and choice with respect to attitudes, emotions, beliefs and behaviour.[8] A necessary condition of sin, on this account, is that people are able to do (and be) otherwise: the person chooses to sin, and (by extension) to be depressed. For example, in their Christian self-help book *Happiness is a Choice: The Symptoms, Causes and Cures of Depression*, psychiatrists Frank Minirth and Paul Meier write that happiness and, conversely, depression are choices, or perhaps more accurately a series of choices, and that 'by applying the contents of this book, depression is 100 percent curable ... Indeed, *happiness is a choice*'.[9] The role of free will and choice is sometimes articulated but less explicitly, as in psychology professor E. Rae Harcum's 2010 book, *God's Prescription for Mental Health and Religion: Smile if You Truly Believe Your Religion*. According to Harcum, the 'highway' to mental health is God's prescription of selfless devotion to others. The converse conclusion, that depressed people are selfish in a morally reprehensible way, becomes evident in the Preface:

> A respected social worker once said to me about a mutual friend, 'If she would just start thinking about others, instead of herself all the time, she would not have so many physical and psychological problems.' Indeed, this one brief proposition summarizes the central lesson of this book: God's prescription, the highway to mental health of individuals and of society is the highway – God's way – which includes selfless devotion and service to others.[10]

Sin accounts of depression usually focus on lifestyle changes (giving up sinful behaviour, more prayer, reading the Bible, exercise, seeing friends) as choices that will lead to recovery from depression. But sometimes proponents of sin accounts are so keen to highlight the role of choice and individual responsibility that they will even argue that the stressful or traumatic events that triggered someone's depression are also within that person's control. So, for example, Minirth and Meier say that:

> These precipitating stresses can vary from finding out your child has leukaemia to finding out your mate is having an affair. They can include any situation that you, as an individual, perceive as acutely stressful. We bring most of these stresses upon ourselves, through either direct or unconscious irresponsibility.
> ... when a battered wife comes seeking advice and consolation because her husband beats her up twice a week, we have to wonder if there is a possibility that she has a passive-aggressive personality and may have subconsciously provoking [sic] his own behavior. (Of course, this does not

diminish the husband's responsibility.) In this type of cycle, the husband usually feels very guilty following his behavior and spoils his wife for several weeks. In the meantime, she is getting from people around her the sympathy which she craves, and she is satisfying her unconscious needs to be a masochist.[11]

Here, we see victim-blaming for domestic abuse. That the victim being blamed is a woman is not insignificant; as Mathew Stanford has shown, women are more likely than men to be told that their mental distress is not an illness, but is the result of sin.[12] The alleged sin of being homosexual, too, is given a significant amount of attention in sin accounts of depression.[13]

On most sin accounts, depression never, or at least only infrequently, has a biological basis. One website advises people that 'the notion of "mental illness" is a myth. There is usually nothing wrong with your body or your brain, you are suffering the consequences of sin in your life. You do indeed feel sick, but you would get better if you repent and change your lifestyle.'[14] Characteristic of self-help books, Minirth and Meier provide a get-out clause, in this case by conceding that in some cases depression has a biological cause. However, they think that biological causes are far rarer than they are usually believed to be, and that most people use the idea that their depression has a biological base as an 'excuse' to 'avoid facing up to their own behavioural and emotional irresponsibilities as the cause of their depression'.[15] Some sin accounts recognize that neuro-logical changes take place in depression, but appeal to the fact that 'correlation does not entail causation'; for example:

Many will argue that depression is caused by a chemical imbalance in the brain. 'Specialists' in this area are still divided. When did the chemical imbalance occur, and why? Was it prior to the depression? Or was it due to the depression ... There may be a few actual cases where a physiological problem is an issue, but if the truth were known, how many of them would actually cause the depression and not vice versa?[16]

In addition to depression, closely related experiences such as anxiety and loneliness are also regarded as choices. For instance:

> Loneliness, like depression, is a choice. The only people who suffer from loneliness are those who choose not to make the effort it takes (including the occasional rejections) to build a few close friendships ... People who are lonely are in fact rejecting intimacy with others, and projecting their rejection onto those around them.[17]

> Worrying is a choice, since the apostle Paul commands us to 'be anxious for nothing'.[18]

> The Bible is quite clear on the ORIGIN of depression ... Proverbs 12:25 – Anxiety in the heart of man causes depression, But a good word makes it glad ... How quickly you recover from this state of mind and heart is all up to you, because that's a choice only you can make. That's right ... it's a choice ... Depression is a choice to listen to the lies the devil tempts you with.[19]

A further common characteristic of sin accounts of depression is that there is a hierarchy of choices according to which faith in Christ is the primary choice that provides the person with the ability to make other decisions. For example, Minirth and Meier write that only people who have a personal relationship with Christ will be able to have the power within themselves consistently to live in such a way as to avoid depression. This is based on the idea that Christians are never tempted to sin without being given a way and the power to avoid sin (implicitly, the sin *is* depression in this context). So, for example, Minirth and Meier explain that psychiatrists cringe when Christians say they can't do things, such as that he or she can't find a job: 'Any good psychiatrist knows that "I can't" and "I've tried" are merely lame excuses.'[20] Therefore, they have Christian patients substitute 'won't' for 'can't'. However:

Whenever a non-Christian patient uses the word *can't*, we let him get away with it, because we believe him ... those who choose not to accept Christ as Savior do not have the power to stay out of depression. A year or so later they get back into the same rut.[21]

Minirth and Meier also add that belief in Christ is itself a choice.[22] On this view, belief in Christ is seen as the primary choice that needs to be made in order for other choices (such as taking more exercise, seeing friends, and even getting a job) to be made at all, or to be made consistently over time, or to be successful or effective in the recovery from depression.

It's not clear from these discussions whether belief in Christ is effective by virtue of a divine intervention which takes place as a reward for or result of faith, or by a purely psychological mechanism based on (for instance) helpful practices such as prayer, or confidence that recovery is possible and/or that fullness of life is promised for Christians. Either way, for the Christian who remains depressed, it seems that the person does not really have a personal relationship with Christ, or else that they are consistently and reprehensibly making the wrong life-style choices despite their relationship with Christ, or else (and this is the least likely option in Minirth and Meier's view) that they are among the very small number of people whose depression has a biological basis. There is therefore a bias towards blaming the person with depression, whether because of a lack of faith or on account of continuing damaging or sinful behaviours.

In summary, on sin accounts of depression, there is characteristically a primary choice – having faith in or a personal relationship with Christ – which gives rise to the possibility of making good decisions about other aspects of one's life. These good decisions include giving up sinful lifestyles, becoming less selfish, reading the Bible more, doing exercise, seeing friends and so on. Becoming a Christian also seems to mean a greater degree of control over events that might precipitate depression, such as not being able to get a job or being domestically abused by one's partner.

Evaluating sin accounts: are they true?

Sin accounts of depression and their secular correlates may be popular because we want the universe to be just ('this person is suffering because they have done something wrong') and, relatedly, because we want to find ways to reassure ourselves that we won't suffer similarly ('I'm not like that, so I won't get depression'). Con Drury, a Christian, philosopher and psychiatrist in a mental hospital in Dublin, wrote of the way in which sin (including 'absence of faith') accounts are used to deceive ourselves about our vulnerability to severe mental illness:

> That we, you and I, might one day be admitted to a mental hospital in a state of despairing melancholia, or foolish mania, might become deluded or hallucinated – that is a thought not easily to be entertained. We like to think that either our intelligence, or our will power, or our piety, would save us from such a fate. I heard a sermon some time ago in which the preacher stated that the great increase in mental illness at the present time was due to the decay of faith. Anyone, he said, who had a firm belief in God would never suffer from nerves or a mental breakdown. Alas.[23]

In addition to this, sin accounts are also popular because they chime with our folk wisdom about everyday emotions and how to manage them: when we feel down, it often does help to see friends, do exercise, go outside, do something for others, and more generally shake ourselves from our Slough of Despond. And of course, well-regarded therapies such as behavioural therapies can work precisely because changing our behaviour and thoughts sometimes can change our mental states, including improving those associated with depression.

Sin accounts are extremely voluntaristic, in that they presuppose that people have a high degree of choice over a number of things, including their behaviour, emotions, beliefs, and even things that happen to them. In being extremely voluntaristic, sin accounts are similar to Pelagianism, a heresy in the early Church which taught that human free will is sufficient to live a blameless life. Pelagius himself, an austere British monk writing in the context of what he saw as Roman immorality, was concerned that Christians were using the idea of human frailty as an excuse for their failure to lead a Christian life. Although Pelagius doesn't link sin to depression, he sounds like a milder version of Minirth and Meier when he writes that:

> It affords endless comfort to transgressors of the divine law if they are able to believe that their failure to do something is due to inability rather than disinclination, since they understand from their natural wisdom that no one can be judged for failing to do the impossible and that what is justifiable on grounds of impossibility is either a small sin or none at all.[24]

In common with proponents of sin accounts of depression such as Minirth and Meier, Pelagius emphasized the role of freedom in choosing faith in Christ. The anti-Pelagian party, headed by St Augustine of Hippo, instead taught that because of human brokenness we need divine grace to obtain the fullness of God's plan for us.[25] In particular, with respect to faith, we need grace to enable us to make particular decisions, including the decision to believe in Christ or to have faith. The Church ultimately favoured Augustine over the Pelagians, condemning the latter as heretics at the Council of Carthage. In so doing, the Church placed a greater emphasis on divine grace (and rejected the idea that we are saved through our own efforts), and accepted an ultimately gentler and less morally exacting approach to human frailty. Grace, on this view, is needed to enable human free will; people are not free to choose the good without it.

When considering Pelagianism and other forms of extreme voluntarism, including sin accounts of depression, it makes sense to ask: how much free will do we really have? This is a big and complex question, but let's take as a starting point the question of whether we have some choice and control over our emotions, since depression relates significantly and in different ways to emotional experience. Perhaps the philosopher most associated with the idea that we can choose our emotions is Robert Solomon, reacting against the idea that we are 'passion's slave' – in other words, powerless or passive in the face of our emotions. Solomon, like Pelagius, is keen to stress the role of choice in emotion because he thinks that denying the role of choice diminishes human responsibility.

In his most mature work, Solomon modifies his previous emphasis on choice to argue that emotions can be regarded as chosen, provided that we include within our understanding of 'choice' not only decisions that we make consciously and which take immediate effect, but also decisions that we make unconsciously and over time.[26] We might control our emotional life, not primarily in the way that we can switch on or off a light switch, but in the way that we might learn to dance or to drive a car – with consistent practice over time, until it becomes habitual to us. In this, Solomon is thinking especially of long-term emotions – he mentions long-term love of a partner – which we cultivate over time through the sharing of our lives and memories. Against Solomon, perhaps some people might say that long-term love is not best characterized as an emotion, even if it involves emotions. But we can think of other examples: for instance, long-term anger, which we cultivate over time by dwelling on ways in which someone has hurt us, could be seen as an emotion we choose in the sense of cultivating over time.

Is Solomon right, in his later and more moderate work, to suggest that there is a role for choice in emotion, where this is understood as the cultivation of emotional habits over time? It seems reasonable to think that emotions can be like that. Perhaps, for example, we might cultivate a kindly disposition towards others, by trying to see the best in them and thinking of possible mitigating circumstances when a stranger pushes into a queue in front of us, or drives in a fast and inconsiderate fashion. And yet surely there are instances when our emotions are more recalcitrant. Perhaps there are instances in which we fall in love with people we'd rather not, or fail to love people we want to love, in spite of our best efforts. Or perhaps the memory of a wrong done to ourselves or a loved one continues to play on our minds and makes us feel ongoingly angry, in spite of our best efforts to forgive. Or perhaps we can cultivate a kindly disposition towards others, but this might be overridden if we're feeling tired, or stressed, or down on that particular day.

The later Solomon agrees with this, conceding that in his earlier work he emphasized the role of choice too much. Emotions can be chosen and cultivated, he thinks, 'some of the time and to some extent'.[27] We might deliberately cultivate certain emotional habits over time, but sometimes certain emotions might simply happen to us, in spite of our best efforts to avoid them. Some voluntarism about emotion, then, is reasonable, provided we keep in mind Solomon's qualification, 'some of the time and to some extent'. In certain situations, emotions (as it were) 'happen' to us, in spite of our best attempts to control them. Our free will is real, but limited, and limited especially in particular situations or if certain conditions obtain.

In fact, it seems that depression can be one of the situations in which we have less free will. As philosopher Matthew Ratcliffe has shown, attention to people's descriptions of depression shows that depression characteristically involves diminished free will, or less free will compared to non-depressed human experience.[28] We can see this when we consider descriptions written by people with depression about the way in which their sense of possibilities is diminished when they are depressed:

> It is impossible to feel that things will ever be different (even though I know I have been depressed before and come out of it).[29]

> My father would assure me, smilingly, that I would be able to do it all again, soon. He could as well have told me that I would soon be able to build myself a helicopter out of cookie dough and fly it to Neptune, so clear did it seem to me my real life, the one I had lived before, was definitely over.[30]

> There was and could be no other life than the bleak shadow-land I now inhabited.[31]

The loss of free will and sense of possibility in depression relates not only to emotions and perceptions but also to behaviour. This is shown in the following vivid account written by another Solomon – Andrew Solomon – describing his experience of being unable to have a shower when he was depressed:

> I can remember lying frozen in bed, crying because I was too frightened to take a shower, and at the same time knowing that showers are not scary. I kept running through the individual steps in my mind: you turn and put your feet on the floor; you stand; you walk from here to the bathroom; you open the bathroom door; you walk to the edge of the tub; you turn on the water; you step under the water; you rub yourself with soap; you rinse; you step out; you dry yourself; you walk back to the bed. Twelve steps, which sounded to me then as onerous as a tour through the stations of the cross. But I knew, logically, that showers were easy, that for years I had taken a shower *every day* and that I had done it so quickly and so matter-of-factly that it had not even warranted comment. I knew that those twelve steps were really quite manageable. I knew that I could even get someone else to help me with some of them. I would have a few seconds of relief contemplating that thought. Someone else could open the bathroom door. I knew I could probably manage two or three steps, so with all the force in my body I would sit up; I would turn and put my feet on the floor; and then I would feel so incapacitated and so frightened that I would roll over and lie facedown, my feet still on the floor. I would sometimes start to cry again, weeping not only because of what I could not do, but because the fact that I could not do it seemed so idiotic to me. All over the world people were taking showers. Why, oh why, could I not be one of them? And then I would reflect that those people also had families and jobs and bank accounts and passports and dinner plans and problems, real problems, cancer and hunger and the death of their children and isolating loneliness and failure; and I had so few problems by comparison, except that I couldn't turn over again, until a few hours later, when my father or a friend would

come in and help to hoist my feet back up into the bed. By then, the idea of a shower would have come to seem foolish and unrealistic, and I would be relieved to have been able to get my feet back up, and I would lie in the safety of the bed and feel ridiculous.[32]

Attention to depression accounts, then, suggests that in depression people often experience a loss of possibilities, of agency, and so of free will.[33] Of course, voluntarists might object that a feeling of having lost free will does not necessarily match up to a real loss of free will. Perhaps the person really does have free will, for example to get out of bed and have a shower – they only feel that they do not. But this seems to separate the reality of free will too much from our experience of it. If a man believes he has been locked in a room, but in fact the door isn't locked, technically he has the freedom to walk out of it. But to all intents and purposes he is not free. He does not have the necessary conditions to utilize his freedom by walking out of the door. Free will is not some kind of metaphysical entity that exists independently and floats free of a person's ability to do a particular thing in a given situation.[34]

So far I've suggested that we have some, limited, free will, in relation to emotional experience and behaviour, and that free will is characteristically diminished in relation to depression. How about another voluntarist idea – the idea that we can choose to have faith in Christ?[35] Two quite different things might be meant by 'choosing to have faith in Christ'. One is that there's a decision to believe in Christ, where 'belief' means something like genuinely held assent to the proposition that 'Jesus is the Son of God'. This relates to what philosophers call 'doxastic voluntarism' – the idea that we can choose our beliefs more generally. We might say some similar things about doxastic voluntarism as we have said about emotional voluntarism. Sometimes we find it impossible to believe, even given our best efforts. Sometimes we might choose to put ourselves in certain situations (in the case of belief in Christ, perhaps going to church, socializing with other Christians, engaging in prayer) which help us to cultivate certain beliefs and make them habitual to us. But we are unlikely to be able to choose to believe in the way that we can turn on or off a light switch. The limits of choice and free will in relation to belief are well expressed in the Christian prayer based on the man's words to Jesus: 'I believe; help my unbelief!' (Mark 9.24). In depression, it seems that our capacity for belief can become more limited, just as it is more limited in relation to emotion, perception, behaviour and so on. So, for example, one person who suffers from depression writes that:

> In the middle of a depressive episode, it is impossible to believe it will pass. It is, oddly, a problem of believing that one is seeing the world 'as it really is' and is unable or unwilling to put a gloss on that perception.[36]

If belief that depression will pass, in spite of the evidence, typically becomes difficult in depression, it should be no surprise if other sometimes challenging beliefs, including belief in God and Christ, also become more difficult.

A second thing that can be meant by 'faith in Christ' is that one has an emotionally experienced personal relationship with Jesus. Much emphasis is put on this in some Christian traditions, where the individual rather than the community is the key focus. Indeed, so important has the experiential aspect of this been that accounts by people in these contexts have shown that they will worry extensively about not having strong feelings about Jesus.[37] That we do not always feel or have the emotional experiences we want to have, or that reflect our commitment to the Christian faith, is significant in the context of depression. For example, David Hilfiker, a Christian whose ministry includes extraordinary social activism, including founding and living in a shelter for homeless people, writes of his ongoing, intermittent experiences of depression. While Hilfiker's depression is atypical in some respects – for instance, he doesn't tend to experience a loss of energy – it does involve anhedonia or inability to feel happiness, as well as a sense of distance from others. He puts this in the following way:

My depression expresses itself in a limited sense of joy. Life is usually gray and, until I began to understand what was happening, filled with dread. I feel an almost constant emotional distance from others: from Marja, from my children, from my friends, and from God. My daughter, now twenty-seven, recalls a childhood Christmas when she presented me a handmade gift. I said I liked it, and I said I was grateful, but even at age eight she knew I was faking it. That would have been typical for me: hindered from the positive emotions of the moment, emotionally blocked from the love and togetherness offered me by others. And, not knowing what was going on, I felt constantly guilty about it.[38]

Perhaps unsurprisingly, Hilfiker's sense of distance includes not only his family, but also God:

I have never been fully able enter into the relationship with God, either. I don't experience God's presence as real; I don't experience joy in my relationship with God. At least in comparison to what I sense in others, my relationship with God has always seemed to lack something. I have tried to enter into the life of the church, done my best to follow Jesus. I have taken on our church's disciplines of membership: an hour of quiet time daily, tithing, weekly worship, silent retreat, and participation in corporate mission. I have been physician to the very poor and homeless, lived in our home for homeless men with AIDS. I have been an active preacher and worship leader.

But still, no experience of God. No real joy in my work. No sense of relationship with God.[39]

The disjunction between Hilfiker's commitment to and his feeling of God's love has sometimes made it impossible for him to remain in church. At times he has also worried that his inability to feel God's love reflects actual distance from God: 'I sometimes even kept myself outside of the faith community because I didn't *feel* the relationship with God and didn't want to be a hypocrite'; 'I've sometimes been unable to sit through church

... Sometimes, just being there was intolerable, and I would have to leave in the middle of the service.'[40] Continuation in Hilfiker's church life has ultimately been made possible by the support of the community. As one of the elders of his church put it to him:

> 'David, you may not feel you have a relationship with God, but God clearly has a relationship with you. Trust me: God has entered into your life, and you've responded to Him. You belong in this church as a member.'[41]

Hilfiker is not alone in experiencing an inability to feel in relation to God in the context of depression, and in spite of an evident commitment to the Christian faith. For example, the letters of Teresa of Calcutta (or 'Mother Teresa') show that she experienced severe and ongoing mental distress for most of her very long ministry to the poor of Calcutta. This included a sense of distance from God: 'In my soul I feel just that terrible pain of loss, of God not wanting me – of God not being God – of God not existing.'[42] According to voluntarists who see depression as a result of sin, Hilfiker and Mother Teresa remain depressed because they do not choose to have faith in Jesus, or a personal and felt relationship with him. But sometimes it might be impossible for us to feel a relationship with God, because we are depressed or for other reasons. The fruits of the Spirit include not only joy but also love, kindness, peace, forbearance and goodness. When we are depressed, we may need these to be recognized in us by others. Far from confirming our sense of alienation from God by telling us that we really are far from God, we may need someone to say, in the words of the elder in Hilfiker's church, 'you may not feel you have a relationship with God, but God clearly has a relationship with you'.[43]

Evaluating sin accounts of depression: are they helpful?

So far in this chapter, I have argued that a sin account of depression is implausible, focusing on the fact that it overestimates human free will and capacity for choice in relation to emotion, behaviour and beliefs. Even if this is true, might there still be a case for acting as though voluntarism is true, for example in relation to the advice we give to others?

Jay Adams seems to think so. Endorsing a sin account of depression, he writes that:

> The Medical Model destroys hope. Discouragement and despair permeate the concept of 'mental illness'. So to inform a Christian client in an early interview, 'Your problem seems basically to be the result of sin', does not discourage him, but rather gives him hope. Christians know that sin and its effects can be dealt with because God has said so in the Scriptures and Christ died to overcome sin. So when sin is mentioned, there is real hope.[44]

Adams and others might add that this is supported by one of my earlier arguments against voluntaristic accounts of depression. I said that in depression people often experience diminished free will, and that the experience of diminished free will corresponds to (actual) diminished free will. I drew an analogy to a man in a room who believed himself to be locked in, and said that he did not have the freedom to leave, even if the door was actually unlocked. By telling people that they are free (here, free not to be depressed), Adams, Minirth and Meier and others might be creating the conditions for freedom – they might be telling the man that the door is unlocked, and that in fact he's free to leave. In this way, a sin account of depression might in fact be liberating.

As I will show, this conclusion should be resisted for two reasons. First, while voluntarism might be empowering in some respects, those strengths are outweighed by the fact that voluntarism induces feelings of guilt and blame in people already vulnerable to those things. Feelings of guilt and worthlessness are already characteristic of depression, and increasing them is likely to make the person's depression much worse. Second, other theologies and therapies also have these hopeful elements, but do not come with the associated guilt and blame. We therefore have reason to prefer these theologies and therapies over ones that say depression is a choice and the result of sin.

Let's turn to the first of these. As psychiatrist and philosopher Thomas Fuchs has shown, while severe depression is often characterized by the loss of feelings and emotions, certain feelings such as guilt, anxiety and worthlessness remain. Such feelings alienate rather than connect us to others. These feelings don't occur as one-off emotions with particular objects but are embedded in the depressed mood so that they are directed both arbitrarily and at everything.[45] Feelings of worthlessness or excessive or inappropriate guilt are among the nine symptoms of major depressive disorder in psychiatric manuals. For example, DSM-5 explains that:

> The sense of worthlessness or guilt associated with a major depressive episode may include unrealistic negative evaluations of one's worth or guilty preoccupations or ruminations over past failings. Such individuals often misinterpret neutral or trivial day-to-day events as evidence of personal defects and have an exaggerated sense of responsibility for untoward events.[46]

In depression, it is often a non-specific feeling of guiltiness that comes first, and is the catalyst for the person seeking a reason, such as a wrong they have committed, for it. As one person puts it:

> It comes from below, from the gut, like a terrible oppression rising to the chest; then a pressure arises, like a crime that I have committed. I feel it like a wound on my chest, that is my tortured conscience ... then this attracts my memories, and I have to think again of all that I have missed or done wrong in my life.[47]

According to DSM-5, the feelings of guiltiness 'may be delusional' – in other words, 'fixed beliefs that are not amenable to change in the light of conflicting evidence'.[48] In normal, non-depressed experience we share a sense of reality with others that allows us, among other things, to take on the perspective of others in relation to ourselves. In normal, non-depressed experience we don't think about the shared sense of reality very much because it's in the background of, and the basis for, our lived experience; it's part of the 'bedrock of unquestioned certainties'.[49] In delusional depression, in contrast, we can lose this interpersonal sense of reality, giving rise to feelings of alienation and distance from others. In the case of depressive delusion, as Fuchs argues, this makes it impossible to take others' perspectives and 'to gain distance from oneself, thus forcing the patient *to completely equate himself with his current depressed state*'.[50] This is significant for inappropriate feelings of and delusions of guilt. As Fuchs puts it, drawing on examples of psychiatric cases:

> The delusional patient … is identified with his existential feeling of guilt to the extent that he is *guilty as such*. There is no remorse, recompense, or forgiveness, for the guilt that is not embedded in a common sphere that would allow for that … A state of self beyond the present one becomes unimaginable. It has always been like this, and it will stay like this for ever – to remember or hope for anything different is deception.[51]

The person with depression, characteristically, will already be feeling guilt and worthlessness. Furthermore, these feelings of guilt and worthlessness are frequently inappropriate and delusional or recalcitrant in the face of evidence. The feeling of guiltiness can occur prior to any evaluation that one is guilty of something, and the feeling of guiltiness can then lead the person to seek an object or reason for their sense of guilt. The person might completely equate themselves with their depressed state, and thus with their feelings of guilt. While it is possible for most non-depressed people to evaluate whether their feelings of guilt are appropriate by considering themselves from the perspective of others, the person with depression may feel alienated from others and no longer part of a world in which they can adopt another's perspective, communicate about their sense of guilt or accept understanding or forgiveness.

We have already seen that Hilfiker feared that his lack of feeling a relationship with God made him 'hypocritical' when attending church services. Actively increasing a person's feelings of guilt and worthlessness by holding them responsible for being depressed can have a terrible effect on them. This is shown in one person's account of his experience of attending two churches in Edinburgh:

> After moving house and changing church to a Baptist church the new minister's preaching was very much of the 'you must try harder' variety which made me feel really guilty as I was already running at full capacity just trying to function as a human being. He only had one sermon regardless of the text which was 'look at what God has done for you, so how much are you going to do in return'.
>
> Sad to say, if I had stayed away from that church I would have got better quicker.
>
> After withdrawing from church my condition did improve a lot and I made a good recovery followed by a few years of very good health when I was not attending any church. Then another bout of depression set in with quite serious self harm. By this stage I had started going back to church and had chosen the nearest church to my house. This was a pentecostal church. Goodness knows why I was going there. I suppose I went because they were very welcoming, but they had a very clear expectation that the normal Christian life was one of very fast transformation within six months or so of attending. Anything else was a sign of something being wrong with your spiritual life or the result of hidden sin. It was a guaranteed recipe for disaster with regards to my mental health.[52]

Conversely, release from sin accounts of depression is often experienced as therapeutic. For instance, Parker Palmer relates the case of a woman with depression who asks him why he thinks some people with depression die (by killing themselves) while others become better. At the time, Palmer racked his brain for a good answer but eventually confessed, 'I have no idea. I really have no idea.' In the days that followed, Palmer was haunted by the regret that he hadn't been able to come up with anything more helpful. However, when the woman contacted him again she said that of all the things in their conversation it was his 'I have no idea' that stayed with her the most:

> My response had given her an alternative to the cruel 'Christian explanations' common in the church to which she belonged – that people who take their lives lack faith or good works or some other redeeming virtue that might move God to rescue them. My not knowing had freed her to stop judging herself for being depressed and to stop believing that God was judging her. As a result, her depression had lifted a bit.[53]

Voluntarists who connect depression with sin argue that agreeing with someone that they have limited agency is only going to worsen their depression. In contrast to this, they say, voluntarism provides a form of support and encouragement to act, and especially to act in ways that are conducive to recovering from depression. But, as these accounts show, being told that depression is a result of sin or spiritual failure seems to worsen rather than help people with depression. This is particularly the case because of the role of guilt and blame in voluntarism, which confirms the feelings of guiltiness and worthlessness already characteristic of depression.

In addition to this, there are other theologies and therapies that provide a sense of hope at least as powerful as that given in voluntaristic accounts of depression, but do so without the accompanying sense of guilt or blame. One such therapy is behavioural therapy, when this is practised well. This tends to give analogous practical advice to people about behaviours that are conducive to good mental health (see friends; do exercise), but without attaching blame to people who can't follow it through. One example of a hopeful theology is a potential transformative view, which points to the ways in which some people have found that God brings good out of evil, including the experience of depression. I will consider a potentially transformative account in Chapter 5. It's enough for now to note that sin accounts of depression don't have a monopoly on providing hope: there are other accounts of depression than voluntarism, which provide hope without increasing a person's sense of guilt or worthlessness.

Sin accounts of depression can also be damaging in less direct ways. For example, they can deflect attention from the social and psychological causes of mental illness. They can discourage people from seeking medical and psychological help that may be therapeutic and even life-saving. That sin accounts of mental illness can function in this way, and the way they interact with other societal pressures, becomes clear in relation to the following account, involving someone who suffers from bipolar disorder:

> A few months ago an acquaintance told me about her mother-in-law, Cynthia … who had been found to have bipolar disorder in her late 50s. Always having been a competent person, Cynthia had a great deal of trouble coming to terms with this. She refused to accept the diagnosis or to take the medications prescribed by her doctor. She was hospitalized several times. Failing to cope, her life and her family's life was in turmoil.
>
> The evangelical faith she followed did not encourage her in her battle. The general opinion she had grown up with was that 'emotional problems' were an indication of not being right with God – the result of sin.
>
> In her mind, and in the minds of many others in her church, her illness was not a medical issue. They believed, as one author wrote, 'If a person has the "peace of God which passeth all understanding" (Philippians 4:7) in his life he cannot have emotional conflict. Ultimately symptoms are spiritual problems.' Cynthia's friend from church told her that taking medications demonstrated a lack of faith. The

friend advised her to throw away her pills. Not long after, Cynthia was found wandering the streets of another city, confused and in a daze. She had to be committed to hospital against her will. To this day, she is still in denial, feeling guilt and shame.[54]

Conclusion

In this chapter, I have argued against the claims of some Christians that depression is the result of sin, and that treating depression as the result of sin is a helpful response to depression. It might seem disconcerting that a book on depression and Christianity – on an ancient, psychologically and philosophically rich, religious tradition – begins by considering a crass and callous Christian response to depression. This beginning is necessary because sin accounts of depression continue to be widespread in some Christian communities, and the underlying voluntaristic ideas more common still.

This, of course, is not the only thing the Christian tradition has the resources to say in response to depression. Psalm 22 includes the verses:

> All who see me mock me;
> they make mouths at me, they shake their heads;
> 'Commit your cause to the LORD; let him deliver –
> let him rescue the one in whom he delights!'
>
> (Psalm 22.7–8)

Those who put forward sin accounts of depression are like the mockers in this psalm; far from providing encouragement to people who suffer, they call into question the sufferer's faith and relationship with God. They indicate that suffering is itself a sign that things are not right with the sufferer's spiritual life. But the words of the mockers need to be understood in the context of the psalm as a whole. The psalmist goes on to say that the Lord 'did not despise or abhor the affliction of the afflicted; he did not hide his face from me, but heard when I cried to him' (Psalm 22.24). And this psalm is in turn under-stood in the Christian tradition as being about the person and sufferings of Jesus. Psalm 22, then, read through a Christian lens, points to Christ's identification with sufferers in the face of people who increase their suffering by calling into question their relationship with God.

That the Christian tradition has much more fruitful things to say about depression than sin accounts suggest is indicated by the fact that Christian voluntarism has so much in common with Pelagianism, which is considered by the Church to be a heresy. We will discuss some of these more fruitful things in the coming chapters. First, though, I will look at an account of depression that needn't, but in practice often has, much in common with a sin account: the idea that depression is caused by demons.

Notes

1 E.g. Marcia Webb, Kathy Stetz and Kristin Hedden (2008), 'Rep-resentation of mental illness in Christian self-help bestsellers', *Mental Health, Religion and Culture* 11.7, pp. 697–717.

2 Rae E. Harcum (2010), *God's Prescription for your Mental Health: Smile if You Truly Believe Your Religion*, Hamilton Press; Frank Minirth and Paul Meier (1994), *Happiness is a Choice: The Symptoms, Causes and Cures of Depression*, Grand Rapids, MI: Baker.

3 This is worth mentioning, since some Christians have said, in con-versation, that their reason for preferring a sin account of depression is that it's distinctively Christian, whereas some other things we might say about depression are shared by Christians and non-Christians. Conversely, some non-Christians have said in conversation that they think a sin account (which they reject) is essentially and uniquely Christian or religious, and this is bound up for them with the rejection of Christianity in particular and religion more generally. For both of these reasons, I think it is worth highlighting that there are secular analogues of sin accounts of depression: they are neither distinctively Christian nor (as I shall go on to argue) Christian at all: they are part of a nexus of claims that orthodox Christianity rejects.

4 This is distinct from the claim that depression is caused by social sin (the structural injustices of our society), or original sin (that, like all illness, depression is the result of the Fall).

5 For a discussion of some other problems with a sin account of

mental illness, see Marcia Webb (2012), 'Toward a theology of mental illness', *Journal of Religion, Disability and Health* 16, pp. 49–73.

6 Unless part of a quotation by someone else, all biblical quotations are taken from the NRSV.

7 Jessy Grondin cited in Ken Camp (2009), 'Through a glass darkly: Churches respond to mental illness', available at www.baptiststandard. com/archives/2009-archives/through-a-glass-darkly-churches-respond-to-mental-illness/ (all websites in Chapter 1 notes accessed 13.12.19).

8 When I use the term 'free will' in this book I mean libertarian or incompatibilist free will. For recent defences of libertarian free will, see Helen Steward (2014), *A Metaphysics for Freedom*, Oxford: Oxford University Press, and Kevin Timpe (2012), *Free Will: Sourcehood and its Alternatives* (2nd edn), New York: Continuum. Importantly, these and other philosophical defences of libertarian free will do not argue for extreme voluntarism – on the contrary, they recognize the limitations of human free will.

9 Minirth and Meier, *Happiness*, pp. 58, 197. Since 2013, the book has been available as an audiobook: https://play.google.com/store/audiobooks/details/Happiness_Is_a_Choice_New_Ways_to_Enhance_Joy_and_?id=AQAAAADhX2JfkM&hl=en.

10 Harcum, *God's Prescription*, Preface.

11 Minirth and Meier, *Happiness*, 96.

12 Mathew Stanford (2007), 'Demon or disorder: A survey of attitudes toward mental illness in the Christian church', *Mental Health, Religion & Culture*, 10.5, pp. 445–9.

13 Minirth and Meier, *Happiness*; Jay Adams (1986), *Competent to Counsel: Introduction to Nouthetic Counselling*, Grand Rapids, MI: Zondervan; and Tim Wilkins, n.d., 'Homosexuality and clinical depression', *Cross Ministry*, available at www.crossministry.org/index. php?option=com_content&view=article&id=236:homosexuality-and-clinical-depression&catid=65:articles-by-tim&Itemid=278.

14 Kent Smithers, n.d., 'The fraud of modern psychiatry', available at www.bible.ca/marriage/mental-illness-nouthetic-psychiatry.htm.

15 Minirth and Meier, *Happiness*, p. 48, see also p. 124.

16 Trenholm, A. n.d., 'Depression – Is it Biblical?', available at www. earnestlycontending.com/KT/Studies/pdf/Depression.pdf.

17 Minirth and Meier, *Happiness*, p. 55.

18 Minirth and Meier, *Happiness*, p. 174.

19 Anon, n.d., 'Christian Depression', *Christianity Oasis*, available at www.christianityoasis.com/Keyword/Depression.htm.

20 Minirth and Meier, *Happiness*, p. 134.

21 Minirth and Meier, *Happiness*, p. 135; see also Mathew Stanford (2008), *Grace for the Afflicted: A Clinical and Biblical Perspective on Mental Illness*, Colorado Springs: Paternoster Press.

22 Minirth and Meier, *Happiness*, p. 136.

23 Maurice O'Connor Drury (2019), *The Danger of Words*, in *The Selected Writings of Maurice O'Connor Drury on Wittgenstein, Philosophy, Religion and Psychiatry*, ed. John Hayes, London: Bloomsbury, p. 327.

24 Pelagius, in B. R. Rees (2004), *Pelagius: Life and Letters* (rev. edn), Suffolk: Boydell Press, pp. 167–8.

25 A key issue in the debate between Augustine and the Pelagians was about what gets called 'original sin'. A reason for affirming original sin, as Augustine does, is to recognize the structural and dispositional aspects of sin. Because of the Fall, people do not begin as a *tabula rasa* and so cannot always freely choose the good rather than the evil. The concept of original sin can sound harsh to modern ears – and its mode of transmission bizarre – but the radical voluntarism of Pelagius (like modern-day voluntarists) leads to a harsher moral condemnation of those who fall short of Christian ideals. Thanks to Kevin Timpe for conversations about this.

26 Robert C. Solomon (2007), *True to our Feelings: What Our Emotions are Really Telling Us*, Oxford: Oxford University Press, p. 191.

27 Robert C. Solomon (2003), *Not Passion's Slave: Emotions and Choice*, Oxford: Oxford University Press, p. vii.

28 Matthew Ratcliffe (2015), *Experiences of Depression: A Study in Phenomenology*, Oxford: Oxford University Press.

29 Anon, cited Ratcliffe, *Experiences*, p. 67.

30 Andrew Solomon (2001), *The Noonday Demon: An Anatomy of Depression*, London: Vintage Books, p. 54.

31 Fiona Shaw (1997), *Out of Me: The Story of a Postnatal Breakdown*, London: Penguin, p. 25.

32 Solomon, *Noonday Demon*, pp. 52–3; see also p. 61.

33 See Ratcliffe, *Experiences*.

34 The philosopher Kevin Timpe agrees with my conclusion – that someone in the situation Solomon describes does not have free will to get out of bed – but would take a different route to it. Timpe has a reasons-responsive view of free will, according to which what you can do depends on what you recognize as reasons, and also how you weigh those reasons. Depression can affect both of these things. For example, depression might involve not being able to see the relevant reasons for getting out of bed. If someone can't see a good (motivational) reason for doing something, they are not free to do it in the relevant sense involved when we speak about 'free will'. Whether one adopts Timpe's or my view will depend partly on how one views free will – but, importantly, the conclusion that people with depression may have diminished free will is the same. For more on Timpe's view of free will, see Kevin Timpe (2013), *Free Will in Philosophical Theology*, New York: Bloomsbury, especially chapter 2. Thanks to Kevin Timpe for a discussion about this with me.

35 The idea that we can choose to have faith is also a long way from being the orthodox Christian line. For example, Thomas Aquinas regards faith (as well as hope and love) as an 'infused virtue' – one that is given by God rather than one we can form on our own. Aquinas sees faith not primarily as assent to a proposition (e.g. 'Christ is God'), nor as an emotionally experienced personal relationship with Jesus, but rather as a disposition to trust in God as the one who reveals truth. Thanks to Kevin Timpe and Simon Hewitt for conversations about this.

36 P. Burnard (2006), 'Sisyphus happy: The experience of depression', *Journal of Psychiatric and Mental Health Nursing* 13, pp. 242–6; p. 244.

37 See Webb, 'Theology'.

38 David Hilfiker (2002) (May and June), 'When mental illness blocks the spirit', available at www.davidhilfiker.com/index.php?option =com_content&view=article&id=33:when-mental-illness-blocks-the-spirit&catid=14:spirituality-essays&Itemid=24.

39 Hilfiker, 'Mental illness'.

40 Hilfiker, 'Mental illness'.

41 Hilfiker, 'Mental illness'.

42 Brian Kolodiejchuk (ed.) (2008), *Mother Teresa: Come Be My Light*, New York: Rider, p. 238.

43 Hilfiker, 'Mental illness'.

44 Adams, *Competent*, p. 139.

45 Thomas Fuchs (2013), 'Depression, intercorporeality, and inter-affectivity', *Journal of Consciousness Studies* 20, No. 7–8, pp. 219–38, available at www.klinikum.uni-heidelberg.de/fileadmin/zpm/psychiatrie/ fuchs/Literatur/Depression_Intercorporeality_and_Interaffectivity.pdf, p. 228.

46 APA (American Psychiatric Association) (2013), *Diagnostic and Statistical Manual of Mental Disorders 5th ed.* (DSM-5), Arlington: American Psychiatric Publishing, p. 164.

47 Anon, cited Fuchs, 'Depression', pp. 228–9.

48 APA, DSM-5, pp. 161, 87.

49 Ludwig Wittgenstein (1969), *On Certainty*, ed. G. E. M. Anscombe and G. H. von Wright, Oxford: Basil Blackwell; see Fuchs, 'Depression', p. 233.

50 Fuchs, 'Depression', p. 223.

51 Fuchs, 'Depression', p. 223.

52 Gordon Hudson (2011), Christian churches, mental illness and depression – my own story, available at www.ecalpemos.org/2011/02/ christian-churches-depression-and.html.

53 Parker J. Palmer (2000), *Let Your Life Speak: Listening for the Voice of Vocation*, San Francisco: Jossey-Bass, p. 59.

54 Marja Bergen (2007), 'Mental disorders: The result of sin?', available at www.heretohelp.bc.ca/visions/stigma-and-discrimination-vol2/mental-disorders-the-result-of-sin.

2

Demons

Introduction

A well-known British preacher stands behind a lectern in front
of a large group of people at an event in honour of his 80th
birthday. When he speaks, he talks to them about depression,
its demonic causes, and deliverance from it (or them). This, he
says, comes from personal experience – from his own struggle
with depression, prior to knowing it was demonically caused;
from his eventual deliverance from it; and from his ministry of
deliverance or exorcism to others with depression.[1]

'In the early years of my ministry I suffered from intense
depression that would come upon me and settle on me like a
dark cloud,' he says. 'I did everything, but I had no remedy.'
But then one day he read Isaiah 61.3: 'in place of the spirit of
heaviness, the garment of praise'. 'That's your problem,' he
believes he heard the Holy Spirit telling him: 'a spirit of heaviness or depression'. This he interpreted as meaning that the
depression was a spirit – or demon – of heaviness. He found
the idea that his depression was caused by a demon liberating:
when he realized he was dealing with a demon and not himself,
he says, he was 'about 80% to victory'.

All that was required to complete the therapy was revelation
through another part of Scripture. This came from Joel 2.32:
'It shall come to pass that whoever calls on the name of the
Lord shall be delivered.' So, he called upon the name of Jesus,
and was suddenly delivered from depression: 'This thing – it
was like a heavenly vacuum cleaner – came down over my
shoulders and just sucked this thing out.' Following that, he
relates, he never experienced depression again.

This preacher, Derek Prince, subsequently practised a ministry focusing on demonic deliverance to other people experiencing depression and other forms of affliction. He counsels the people listening to him at his birthday celebration that if they're depressed, once they realize they're dealing with a demon, 'you are about 80% to deliverance'. Elsewhere he advises that, while deliverance from a demon requires direct divine action, preventing demons from taking hold in the first place is something people can do for themselves, and which God therefore refuses to do for them. In particular, it is something that can be achieved by positive thinking: 'Every time a negative suggestion or reaction came to my mind, I had to meet it with something positive out of the Scriptures.'[2]

Demonic explanations for depression and mental illness will be news to people from some Christian traditions, but very well known to people from others. Most Christian Churches officially hold that demons exist. Most traditions (Orthodox, Catholic, Anglican, Evangelical and Pentecostal) will have some kind of deliverance or exorcism ministry. However, some Christian traditions are much more prone than others to talking about demons, and to ascribing particular experiences (including depression) to them.[3]

Within more demonically focused communities,[4] a demonic account of depression is often believed on the basis that, as Prince puts it, 'It's scriptural and it works.'[5] I will explore both of these claims. After sketching a demonic account of depression, I will look at the scriptural understanding of the demonic, particularly in relation to what we now call mental illness. I will argue that demonic explanations of depression tend to misread the New Testament in three ways. First, they see being afflicted by demons as a result of the individual's sin or sinfulness. Second, and relatedly, they tend to interpret spiritual warfare in a depoliticized way.[6] Third, and related to these first two points, they focus too much on the exorcism of demons in Jesus' ministry rather than seeing it as one aspect of a much larger ministry to do with liberation. In the course of exploring scriptural texts on demon possession and spiritual warfare, an account of demonic affliction will begin to emerge in this chapter that recalibrates these emphases.

I will then turn to the question of whether attributing depression to demonic influence 'works' or has therapeutic value. I will argue that while exorcism or deliverance ministry can be therapeutic and often has therapeutic aspects it can easily become pathogenic and a form of spiritual abuse, increasing guilt and low self-esteem, alienating people from their church communities, discouraging people from other therapeutic sources that may help them, and deflecting attention away from the social and political causes of mental illness. Whether we understand the demonic in terms of a personal agent such as a fallen angel or else as a metaphor for evil, there may be good reasons for using language about the demonic relation to mental illness. However, whether interpreted literally or metaphorically, language of the demonic needs to be understood in ways that include the systemic and political – as relating to the social structures that contribute to depression and other forms of human suffering. This is a more helpful way of understanding the demonic, as well as being more faithful to biblical language about spiritual warfare, demons and the devil.

What are demonic accounts of depression?

A demonic account of depression is usually part of (what gets called) a 'spiritual warfare' worldview. According to a spiritual warfare worldview, demons – who are personal beings who sinned and so fell from heaven – battle for the souls of individual human beings (for example, by tempting them to sin or to lose faith). One pastor explains this idea in his radio programme on spiritual warfare:

> You have this battle going on between the Spirit and the flesh, and there is a supernatural, angelic being, who fell from Heaven, who took a third of the angels with him, and his job, and his goal, and his strategy is to destroy your life, to murder you – spiritually, emotionally, relationally,

physically. He wants to take you out. He wants to ruin your life. He wants to ruin your marriage. He wants to ruin your children. He wants to split your church. He wants to have you overwhelmed, deceived, believing lies, and be rendered completely ineffective in this new relationship with Christ, so that the Church and the Gospel are discredited, and you become a miserable person, and all the work of God, and the work of the cross, and the Resurrection is for naught ... You can be aware of it, or you can not be aware of it, but you're in an invisible war.[7]

This battle is perceived as primarily or solely individualistic and psychological in nature: 'We are involved in a cosmic conflict that has eternal implications ... The battleground for this invisible war, this cosmic conflict, is largely between your ears. The attack is on your mind.'[8] Again: God permits demons 'to speak to human beings through the same channel the Holy Spirit uses to insert thoughts into our minds ... Demons know our fears, likes, and dislikes. They are masters at tempting and tormenting people.'[9]

Demonic explanations of depression vary considerably in how they see the relationship between the demonic and the medical. Some demon-focused Christian traditions argue that the term 'mental illness', which implicitly medicalizes experiences such as depression by describing them as illnesses, actually hides the real, demonic causes of these experiences and misleads people into treating them in inappropriate (e.g. medical or psychological) ways. Other traditions think that demons cause medical and biological problems, including (though not limited to) mental illnesses. Which of these views is adopted might determine to what extent these communities will think it's appropriate for someone with depression to see a medical professional or psychologist, and to what extent they think mental distress should be treated only in religious ways.

A further difference between demonic accounts of depression lies in whether all or only some instances of mental distress are thought to be caused by demons. An example of the latter view is expressed by Douglas Irvine, Convenor of the Church of Scotland's Deliverance Group.[10] More demonically focused communities, however, are likely to think that all or most mental distress is caused by demons. Again, which of these views are adopted will have practical implications. In communities where all depression is seen as demonically caused, medical and psychological intervention is likely to be discouraged in favour of religious forms of intervention (such as prayer, and perhaps an exorcism or a deliverance ritual). In communities where only some instances of mental distress are thought to be demonically caused, a pastoral response and medical and psychological treatment is more likely to be sought in the first instance.

The difference between these views can determine whether exorcism is a first or final port of call for someone manifesting signs of mental distress, and whether the advice of psychiatrists and others is sought and listened to. These views can therefore have a huge effect on people's lives. To take one example, in 2005 a young Romanian Orthodox nun, Irina Cornici, died after being gagged and chained to a cross and left in a cold room without food and water for three days at the hands of priests and fellow nuns. This was part of an attempt to exorcise her for what psychiatrists identified as schizophrenia. Following her death, the priest is reported to have said, 'God has performed a miracle for her; finally Irina is delivered from evil.'[11] This event is uncommon but not unique.[12] The victims of these events tend to be women or girls in vulnerable situations: Irina was an orphan and so the religious community was the only group of people who were there to care for her.[13] Such occurrences are less likely to happen in communities in which appealing to the demonic as an explanation is not the first port of call, or where medical and psychological help has been sought and listened to.

An often expressed distinction is made between demonic possession and demonic oppression. According to people who make this distinction, Christians cannot be demonically possessed (because they are possessed by the Holy Spirit), but only demonically oppressed. The difference is one of degree: someone who is possessed loses their agency and control over their actions much more than someone who is only oppressed by demons. For example, one ministry website explains:

> When we study what the Bible says about demons, it is very clear that Christians cannot be demon possessed. However, the Bible does say that a believer can be oppressed or influenced by a demon. What's the difference? Possession means that the demon has full control over the person ... Demon oppression is very different. If a person is oppressed by a demon, that demon influences the person toward sin.[14]

In the context of depression, this can be interpreted to mean that moderate depression is a symptom of demonic oppression, while severe depression, typically including suicidal ideation, is a symptom of demonic possession.

A common thought in demonic accounts of depression is that being demonically afflicted (whether possessed or oppressed) is the result of individual, personal sin. In sinning, it's argued, the person opens a door to demons. For instance, Prince relates the (hypothetical) example of a man who after a long and difficult day at work loses his temper at his wife (who has not prepared the dinner) and children (who are running around the house screaming). At that moment, says Prince, 'the demon of anger who has been following him about all day slips in, and after that he's a slightly different person'.[15] In this case, an initial act of sin (in the form of anger) allows the demon to enter the man so that he is then possessed by a demon of anger. Another preacher, Larry Wilson, writes that 'the door to demonic oppression opens when we knowingly and willingly choose to do wrong and violate our conscience'.[17] Typically on these accounts, when human free will is misused, a 'door' is opened, allowing a demon to enter, and from then on the person is demonically possessed or (if they are a Christian and so already 'possessed' by the Holy Spirit) demonically oppressed.

An absence of faith – usually conceptualized as an emotional, experiential and interior phenomenon – is often viewed as a form of sin (or even the arch-sin) within these religious traditions. It is not surprising, then, that an absence of faith is also regarded as a sin through which demons can enter:

Many people appear to have their lives in order. But in reality, they have not trusted Christ as Savior and Lord. Their souls are 'unoccupied' – that is, the Holy Spirit does not indwell them. Thus they are open to demonic invasion ... Indwelling by demons is only evidence of a lack of genuine salvation.[17]

It is easy to see the links between this view and the idea articulated in Chapter 1 that mental illness is a 'sign that you don't have enough faith': rather than being a completely different account, demons simply act as the 'middle man' between sin (including lack of faith) and mental illness. This kind of view is reported by Kay Redfield Jamison, who recounts that, following the publication of her autobiography *An Unquiet Mind* in which she details her experience of bipolar disorder:

I received thousands of letters from people. Most of them were supportive but many were exceedingly hostile. A striking number said that I deserved my illness because I was insufficiently Christian and that the devil had gotten hold of me. More prayer, not medication, was the only answer.[18]

As this suggests, there can be a strong relationship between demonic accounts of depression and the sin accounts of depression considered in the previous chapter. These demonic accounts are often an extension of sin accounts, rather than something completely different. As a result of the strong association between demonic affliction and sin (including absence of faith), it's often thought that thinking and behaving in allegedly correct Christian ways will prevent demonic affliction.[19]

Some communities use the term 'exorcism' to refer to the expelling of the demon from the person, while others prefer the word 'deliverance'.[20] Deliverance or exorcism will often involve a team of people praying over the person and commanding the demon to leave in the name of Jesus. Within these communities there are various debates, for example about what the form of wording should be, whether it is necessary to know the name and rank of the demon, whether some demons are associated with particular sins, and whether to allow the demons to 'manifest' during the deliverance.[21] Some deliverance sessions are likely to be dramatic, others might be low key. While an example of a 'typical' exorcism or demon deliverance in the context of more demonically focused traditions is difficult to find, accounts of two fairly characteristic deliverances in the Pentecostal tradition are available on YouTube.[22] Here, two young women, one of whom says that she has suffered from depression and schizophrenia, have hands laid on them by a team of people while a male pastor commands the demon to come out. After writhing around on the floor, shrieking, and in one case coughing up something (allegedly demonic), the young women say they feel better and believe themselves to be cured.

Are demonic accounts of depression scriptural?

It is not the purpose of this chapter to persuade you either to believe or disbelieve in demons. Rather, my aim in this section is to show how the demonic accounts of depression I have sketched above are unscriptural in some of their emphases, and to allow some other emphases to come to the fore. I argue that, contrary to these demonic accounts of depression, the Scriptures do not associate the demonic with personal sinfulness or lack of faith. Rather, language of the demonic and of spiritual warfare more generally is strongly political and social in character. Therefore, people suffering demonic affliction are much more likely to be particularly the victims rather than particularly the perpetrators of sin, and sin is to be understood primarily in social and systemic rather than individual terms. Relatedly, in the New Testament the demonic is only one part of a much wider narrative about liberation effected through the incarnation, teaching, healing, death and resurrection of Jesus.

As we have seen, demonic accounts of depression often presuppose individual sin: it is thought that the person might be depressed on account of being demonically afflicted, because they have committed some kind of sin. In the New Testament there is no association between demonic affliction (whether possession or oppression) and individual or personal sin. In fact, the first time we hear about the devil or demons[23] in the Synoptic Gospels (Matthew, Mark and Luke) is in the context of Jesus being tempted in the wilderness. The word used for 'being tempted' here, *peirazomenos*, can also mean to be tested, and testing is the main theme in each of the Gospel accounts. Matthew does this by evoking the similarities between Jesus' 40-day temptation in the wilderness and the 40-year trial of God's patience by the Israelites in the desert during the exodus from Egypt. Luke, who has the temptations occurring in a slightly different order from Matthew, emphasizes again their nature as tests in his Passion narrative, where Jesus encounters analogous tests to his mission (Luke 23.34b–39). In both cases, there's a Christological point (Jesus is the new Israel, the Son and Servant), and also an ecclesiological one (Jesus' faith and loyalty are the models for Christians facing conflict). This would be particularly important in the context of the early Church, when Christians faced persecution by the Roman empire – and so the theme of testing would be important to the audience for which the Gospels were initially written.

In none of the accounts of Jesus' affliction by the devil in the wilderness is there any sense that the encounter occurs because of Jesus' sin. Jesus is believed by Christians to be sinless (see Hebrews 4.15), and the event occurs immediately following Jesus' baptism during which Jesus received the Holy Spirit, and when we hear that God is 'well pleased' with his Son.

One might respond by saying that Jesus is a special case. But what about other people in the Gospels who are seen as being demonically afflicted or even possessed? Is there a sense that the reason they are demonically oppressed or possessed is that they have done something to 'open' themselves to 'demonic invasion', as modern-day demonic accounts often suggest?

There are five stories about people being possessed by demons, and exorcised by Jesus, that the Gospels recount in detail.

1 *Mark 1.21–28 and Luke 4.31–37.* Jesus is teaching in the synagogue in Capernaum when a man with an unclean

spirit or demon recognizes Jesus as the Holy One of God, and confronts him: 'Have you come to destroy us?' Jesus orders the unclean spirit out and the bystanders are amazed and recognize it as a sign of Jesus' authority. Luke differs slightly from Mark. In Mark the spirit convulses the man and comes out of him crying in a loud voice. In Luke the demon throws the man down and then comes out of him without having done him any harm, perhaps emphasizing that the demon became powerless to inflict further harm on the man.[24] In both cases the people who see it are amazed and note Jesus' authority and power.

2 *Mark 5.1–20, Matthew 8.28–34 and Luke 8.26–39.* In Mark, Jesus crosses the lake to the region of the Gerasenes. There he is greeted by a man with an unclean spirit. No one is strong enough to bind the man, who lives among the tombs and who cries out and cuts himself with stones. When he sees Jesus he recognizes him as Son of the Most High God and asks him not to torture him. When Jesus asks him his name, he replies, 'My name is Legion; for we are many.' The unclean spirit or spirits beg Jesus not to send them out of the area but instead to send them into a herd of pigs. When Jesus does so, the pigs rush down a steep bank and into the lake, where they are drowned. When the people come to see what has happened, they find the demon-possessed man clothed and returned to his senses (*sōphronounta*).

In Matthew, the story is different in that the demon-possessed are two men who are described as very dangerous. There is no mention of them crying out, or cutting themselves with stones, or being too strong to be bound. Luke's account is more like Mark's, though he notes that on many occasions the demon had seized the man, and though he was bound hand and foot and kept under guard, he would tear the bonds. He also notes that during this time the man was driven by the demon into the desert. In all three accounts the townsfolk seem to have become frightened and begged Jesus to leave.

3 *Mark 7.24–30 and Matthew 15.21–28.* In Mark's account, when Jesus enters a house in Tyre he is met by a Gentile woman whose little daughter is possessed by an unclean spirit. The woman falls at Jesus' feet and begs Jesus to expel the demon. Jesus replies that the children must be satisfied first, since it is not good to take the children's bread and to throw it to the puppies (*kunariois*). The woman retorts that even puppies eat the children's crumbs under the table. Jesus responds that because of her reply the demon has left her daughter. The woman returns to her daughter to find that this is the case. Jewish writers sometimes referred to Gentiles as 'dogs', and it seems that the 'children' refer to the Jews (who are the focus of Jesus' mission), while 'puppies' refers to Gentiles (perhaps 'puppies' rather than 'dogs' is intended to suggest a softness in Jesus' reply).[25] In Matthew, the debate about whether Jesus' ministry is also to the Gentiles is extended: Jesus explains to his disciples, 'I was sent only to the lost sheep of the house of Israel.' Jesus also notes that the woman's faith is great, before saying that he will heal her daughter.

4 *Mark 9.14–29, Matthew 17.14–21 and Luke 9.37–42.* In Mark, Jesus and his disciples are confronted with a boy who has a 'dumb spirit'. Whenever the spirit seizes the boy it tears at him, he foams at the mouth, grinds his teeth and becomes rigid. Jesus' disciples have been unable to expel the spirit. When the boy is brought to Jesus, the spirit throws the boy to the ground and the boy begins to foam at the mouth. The boy's father explains that the boy has been afflicted since childhood, and that the spirit has often thrown the boy into fire or water, which may kill him. He begs Jesus to help him and professes his faith in him. Jesus rebukes the unclean spirit, addressing it as 'dumb and deaf spirit', and commands it to come out of the boy and not to enter him any longer. After much crying and convulsing it comes out. The boy appears to be lifeless, and many think he has died – but Jesus takes him by the hand so that he stands up.

Matthew's and Luke's versions are similar, though briefer

than Mark's. Matthew's version describes the boy as 'moon-struck' (*selēniazesthai*), which usually refers to epilepsy.[26] Often epileptics are harmed not by the fits in themselves but by the fall – and so it makes sense that the boy's father worries about him falling into fire or water. Luke's account notes instead that the boy is bruised when the spirit departs from him, which is also consistent with epilepsy. The focus of the dialogues, especially in Matthew and Mark, is on the power of trusting faith.

5 *Matthew 12.22 and Luke 11.14.* In Matthew, Jesus is brought a demon-possessed man who is deaf and dumb. Jesus heals him, so that the man can speak and see. Luke's account is similar except that the demon is only mentioned as making the man mute. In both cases, the crowds are astonished, but some (in Matthew, the Pharisees) attribute demonic causes to Jesus' power.[27]

What are we to make of these accounts? Exorcising demons was seen in the ancient world as an expression of spiritual power. Ancient Judaism was no exception. The book of Tobit relates the story of the exorcism of Sarah by the archangel Raphael from the demon Asmodeus. In one of the Dead Sea Scrolls, which give us important information about Judaism during the time of Jesus' ministry and the first writings of the New Testament, Abraham exorcises Pharaoh.[28] In neither these nor the Gospel accounts examined above is there any sense that the afflicted or possessed person is afflicted or possessed because they have done something sinful or lacked faith. In fact, the possessed or afflicted person's faith and virtue are often emphasized. Consider the sympathetic account we get of Sarah in the book of Tobit:

> at Ecbatana in Media, it ... happened that Sarah, the daugh-ter of Raguel, was reproached by one of her father's maids. For she had been married to seven husbands, and the wicked demon Asmodeus had killed each of them before they had been with her as is customary for wives. So the maid said to

her, 'You are the one who kills your husbands! See, you have already been married to seven husbands and have not borne the name of a single one of them ...'

On that day she [Sarah] was grieved in spirit and wept. When she had gone up to her father's upper room, she intended to hang herself. But she thought it over and said, 'Never shall they reproach my father, saying to him, "You had only one beloved daughter but she hanged herself because of her distress." And I shall bring my father in his old age down in sorrow to Hades. It is better for me not to hang myself, but to pray the Lord that I may die and not listen to these reproaches any more.'

(Tobit 3.7–10)

As noted in Chapter 1, it's a common temptation to think that because someone has some affliction (whether demonic or not), they must have done something wrong. Yet this idea is something the Christian tradition repeatedly denies. When Jesus heals the man born blind, he is asked, 'Who has sinned that this man was born blind? The man or his parents?' Jesus responds that neither the man nor his parents have sinned – misfortune does not entail any personal (or generational) wrongdoing (John 9.1–3). If anything, suffering – including but not limited to affliction by demons – is linked to spiritual health and holiness rather than to spiritual illness and sin in the Christian tradition. So, for example, St Athanasius' *Life of St Anthony* relates several instances when Anthony of Egypt was afflicted by the devil, because 'the devil, who hates and envies what is good, could not endure to see such resolution in a youth'.[29]

What might be read as a hint that sin can 'let demons in' is a passage in 1 Peter: 'Discipline yourselves, keep alert. Like a roaring lion your adversary the devil prowls around, looking for someone to devour. Resist him, steadfast in the faith' (5.8–9a). However, it is important to read scriptural passages with an ear both to the wider text and to the context in which the passages were written. Here, the author has in mind the persecution of Christians, which may lead some

Christians to apostasize (or renounce Christianity) rather than to remain steadfast in their faith. The tense used for 'Discipline yourselves, keep alert' demands immediate attention: these are sudden cries suggesting that the devil isn't always prowling around but is especially doing so at that point. That persecution is in the background here becomes clearer in light of what comes next: 'you know that your brothers and sisters in all the world are undergoing the same kinds of suffering' (1 Peter 5.9b). Sermons and commentaries designed for preaching have generalized this passage to include temptation in the Christian life more generally, which is understandable given the risk that the text becomes redundant once Christians are no longer facing state persecution. However, remembering the original context and that the persecution being referred to is political rather than individual and psychological is an important corrective to the association between demonic affliction and sinfulness, and to spiritual warfare worldviews more generally.

What kinds of affliction are indicated by the Gospel's demon possession accounts? Some scholars see the demon possession accounts as ancient descriptions of what today we would simply regard as illness. On this view, it is notable that there is not a particular association between demonic affliction and what we now call mental illness.[30] In the exorcism narratives discussed above, the only narrative that seems to be about what we now call mental illness is the story of the Gerasene demoniac (2). This story involves the man crying out, living apart from others, and self-harming (cutting himself with stones). In addition, Mark 5.15 uses the word *sōphrovounta*, which means 'being in one's right mind' or 'being sober-minded', suggesting that he was thought to be out of his right mind before that time.[31] Some people have gone further and seen a link between the fact that the demon or demons refer to themselves as 'Legion' as an indication that the man is suffering from schizophrenia or multiple personality disorder. However, this seems extremely tenuous since the man's behaviour doesn't reflect these disorders. Nevertheless, in very general terms the man's experience is reminiscent of what today we might call mental illness.

The other exorcism narratives do not suggest anything that should make us think they are about mental disorder. (1) and (3) don't specify what form the demon possession takes, while (4) suggests epilepsy and (5) suggests being mute and perhaps deaf. This is also true of the Jewish literature written before or around the same time that would reflect similar ideas about demonic possession. In the book of Tobit, Sarah's problem is that the demon kills her husband every time she gets married – it's hard to see any similarity with mental illness here. The Genesis Apocryphon says that Abraham heals Pharaoh and his servant and exorcises a 'pestilential spirit' who seems to be responsible for what sounds to modern ears like some kind of ulcerative skin disorder.[32] This point that demonic affliction is not particularly associated with what we now call mental illness is worth making: while many phenomena are attributed to the demonic by some Christians, mental illness seems to be especially demonized or to get the lion's share of the attention.[33]

I want to suggest an account of the demon possession narratives that is slightly different from the idea that they are simply ancient ways of describing illnesses. The Gospel writers clearly regarded demon possession as distinct from the illnesses Jesus healed: they are described differently and Jesus responded to them in a different way. This raises the question, how should we understand the distinction between the states Jesus responded to with healing, and those he responded to with exorcism? One promising answer to this lies in the idea that the states described as demon possession were not reducible to illnesses, even if they involved them. Rather, demon possession was a culturally specific manifestation of the trauma and distress caused by social and political oppression, including though not limited to the Roman occupation. It was therefore a distinct kind of experience or condition to that of illness, though not incompatible with it.

Why might we think this? One reason is that it's usually a mistake to think that ancient people – including the Gospel writers and Jesus' contemporaries – were stupid or less intelligent than people today. The claim that the demon possession narratives are simply ancient, mistaken ways of describing some illnesses amounts to a claim that people in the ancient world simply failed to notice the similarities between the experiences they described as demon possession (on the one hand) and illness (on the other) and so misdiagnosed the latter as the former. The philosopher Ludwig Wittgenstein argued that religion should not be treated as an attempt at science because as science it misses the mark by too much. As he put it, 'For a blunder, that is too big.'[34] In other words, simply mistaking some illnesses for demon possession is so large an error that one should look for other explanations for the ancient writers' language about the demonic.

Another reason is that there are hints that political oppression might be part of the story in the texts themselves. For example, in the story of the Gerasene demoniac, the demon(s) refer to themselves as Legion – a word that has strong associations with the Latin word *legio*, referring to the legions of the Roman army. In addition, demonic affliction may have been associated with manifestations of the experience of living under political oppression more generally. For example, in Tobit, Sarah and her family are Jews who have been deported to modern-day Iran, and the exile and oppression of Jewish people and practices is a theme of the book as a whole.

New Testament scholar José Pagola expresses this understanding of the Gospel demon possession accounts:

It is probably more correct to see demon-possession as a complex strategy, used in a dysfunctional way by oppressed people to protect themselves from an unbearable situation. When they have no other way to rebel, individuals can develop a separate personality that permits them to say and do what they could not under normal circumstances, at least not without some great risk. Was there some connection between the oppression of Palestine by the Roman Empire, and the simultaneous phenomenon of so many people possessed by the devil? Was this a dysfunctional way to rebel against their subjection to Rome and the domination of the powerful? ... It is hard to imagine today the terror and frustration that the Roman Empire inspired in people who were absolutely defenseless against its cruelty. There was also plenty of conflict and oppression within the peasant families, with their rigid patriarchal structure ... For victims of this, too, possession was a defense mechanism that enabled them to get attention, defend themselves from the people around them, and exercise a kind of power.[35]

On this account, descriptions of demon possession such as those we find in the Gospels are not merely reducible to illness accounts. Rather, they refer to a culturally formed and culturally specific response to political and social oppression and distress.

This view resonates with the way in which spirit possession is treated in DSM-5, the chief manual used to diagnose psychiatric disorders today (along with ICD-10). For example, in the context of discussing Acute Stress Disorder, DSM-5 has a section on Culture-Related Diagnostic Issues, in which it notes the following:

> The profile of symptoms of acute stress disorder may vary cross-culturally, particularly with respect to dissociative symptoms, nightmares, avoidance, and somatic symptoms (e.g., dizziness, shortness of breath, heat sensations). Cultural syndromes and idioms of distress shape the local symptom profiles of acute stress disorder. Some cultural groups may display variants of dissociative responses, such as possession or trancelike behaviors ...[36]

Similarly, in relation to Dissociative Identity Disorder, DSM-5 says:

> Many features of dissociative identity disorder can be influenced by the individual's cultural background ... In settings where normative possession is common (e.g., rural areas in the developing world, among certain religious groups in the United States and Europe), the fragmented identities may take the form of possessing spirits, deities, demons, animals, or mythical figures.[37]

Notably, both Acute Distress Disorder and Dissociative Identity Disorder are also strongly correlated with experiences of trauma, oppression and abuse, suggesting that these things are among the causes of these states.

This understanding of demon possession, as arising as a dysfunctional psychological mechanism for coping with situations of political and social stress, oppression and trauma, does not determine whether one believes in the reality of demons themselves. It is possible to think that demons cause the necessary conditions for possession (oppression, affliction), or that demons opportunistically take advantage of experiences of oppression and affliction, or else that the experience of (perceived) demonic possession is solely a psychological response to stress and oppression. When thinking about mental illness and the demonic, the account I am proposing suggests that the (real or imagined) experience of demon possession may coincide with mental illness, particularly as oppression and trauma are aetiologically related to both. However, it also suggests that the experience of demon possession may occur independently of mental illness, or of illness more generally. This coheres with the Gospel accounts.

A final scriptural text needs to be considered in relation to the demonic. This passage is a key source for spiritual warfare worldviews, and thus for those churches that talk a lot about the demonic and in which exorcism or deliverance ministries play a central part:

> Finally, be strong in the Lord and in the strength of his power. Put on the whole armour of God, so that you may be able to stand against the wiles of the devil. For our struggle is not against the enemies of blood and flesh [*aima kai sarka*], but against the rulers, against the authorities, against the cosmic powers of this present darkness, against the spiritual forces of evil in the heavenly places. (Ephesians 6.10–12)

Proponents of a spiritual warfare worldview tend to see the dichotomy in dualistic terms, as being between 'blood and flesh' and 'spiritual forces': 'this real struggle ... isn't against physical, material adversaries, but against a hierarchy of demonic forces doing battle in the spiritual realm'.[38] But this flesh–spirit dichotomy is not true to the text: 'blood and flesh' is a term used to mean the whole human being (see Galatians 1.16; 1 Corinthians 15.5).[39] Rather than opposing the spiritual and the material, this passage is saying that the enemy is not a human person or people (e.g. the pagan hordes), but unseen, systemic structures and powers that make living in the Roman empire so full of possible pitfalls – such as persecution-driven apostasy – for Christians.[40] That this is closer to the author of Ephesians' intentions is indicated by the fact that they mention rulers, authorities and powers of this present darkness world alongside the spiritual forces of evil in the heavenly places. These all seem to refer to the same or closely related entities, rather than being a list of different ones.[41]

What is the point of these exegetical niceties? Churches who have a spiritual warfare worldview derive this belief principally from a particular reading of this text. According to them, a Christian is perpetually fighting off the spiritual forces of evil, which are constantly tempting them to sin – and then perhaps entering and possessing them in the way we saw Prince describe in the case of the husband losing his temper. But attention to the original Greek and to the Pauline writings more generally shows that spiritual warfare is not about this depoliticized and individualistic understanding of sin. Rather, spiritual warfare is about not seeing other human beings as the enemies, but taking seriously systemic evils – for example, oppressive political structures and social inequalities. These, of course, are much more difficult to focus on and deal with, because if we live in socially and politically unjust and oppressive societies these forms of injustice and oppression are so pervasive that they are invisible to us. We are like a sheep in the Yorkshire Dales that doesn't know it's in the Yorkshire Dales because it's never been to Derbyshire, or a town, or the sea. A challenge to the early Christians for whom the letter to the Ephesians was written was to begin to see the culture and society they lived in and had been formed by through a Christian rather than a Roman lens – which involved seeing oppressive aspects of it in a way that hadn't until then been visible to them.

So far, I've explored Prince's claim that demonic accounts of depression (and mental illness more generally) are scriptural. I've argued that they are scriptural, though not in the way that demonically focused communities think. When compared with the New Testament writings on demon possession and spiritual warfare, these churches depoliticize the experience of the demonic. Far from making sense of these along the lines of the oppressive systems that were foremost in the experience of early Christians – and that continue, in different forms, today – they regard demon possession purely in terms of the individual, cut off from any political and social context. Furthermore, they frequently, and unbiblically, associate demonic affliction and especially possession with the person's own sin.

A final, simple point needs to be made. Demonically focused Christian communities often see deliverance from the demonic as a primary focus of Christian ministry, and see demons in a huge array of different activities and experiences, including depression and other forms of mental illness. But demon exorcism was only one part of Jesus' own ministry: a wider ministry of liberating love. This ministry mainly involved teaching and healing, breaking conventions by socializing with sinners and, at the end of his earthly ministry, a political execution that was the outworking of his compassion. In all this, exorcizing demons was only one part – and a part that seems to have been regarded as no more exceptional from the Evangelists' points of view than Jesus' ministry of healing. In the context of the ancient world, the exorcism of demons was not an uncommon sign of someone's spiritual power, and there would have been nothing uniquely or distinctively Christian about the practice of exorcism. It seems out of sync with the Gospels, then, to regard the exorcism of demons as the focal point of Christian ministry. A similar point might be made about the language of spiritual warfare, which doesn't occur as a phrase in the New Testament, and which is based only on Ephesians 6.10–18 and a few other scattered texts.

Are demonic accounts of depression helpful?

How about the 'they work' bit of Prince's argument for believing demonic accounts of mental illness? Whether or not demons exist, and whether or not they cause (some or all) mental illness, it would be unlikely that exorcisms or deliverances *never* have therapeutic value. Our knowledge of the placebo effect tells us that merely the belief that something will work greatly increases its therapeutic value, even if it is not effective for the reasons people think it is.[42] Furthermore, responses to perceived demon possession such as exorcism or deliverance often involve ritual, and ritual in itself can have therapeutic power. This may be because in ritual, as Claude Lévi-Strauss argues, an affliction is mapped on to a mythic landscape. The metaphorical journey from illness to health causes changes in attention, cognition and experience, through which healing can occur.[43] Rituals may be effective precisely because they are formed around narratives, and involve our bodies, our imaginations and our senses.[44]

Andrew Solomon discusses the impact of an exorcism ritual – here, to deliver him from a sexually jealous spirit rather than an evil demon – in his search for a cure for his depression. This exorcism, which was called the *ndeup* and took place in Senegal, involved the community slaughtering a ram and some cockerels and smothering Solomon in the animals' blood before tying him up with their intestines. At a particular point, Solomon recounts that:

> I had to say something. And what I had to say was actually incredibly, strangely touching in the middle of this weird experience. I had to say, 'Spirits, leave me alone to complete the business of my life and know that I will never forget you.' And I thought, *What a kind thing to say to the evil spirits you're exorcising: 'I'll never forget you.'*[45]

Solomon does not attribute his recovery from depression to this experience, but he does view it in positive terms therapeutically, partly because of the dramatic, performative aspects of the experience. As he puts it, 'the effect of any ritual – being covered in the mixed blood of a ram and a cockerel or telling a professional what your mother did when you were small – is not to be underestimated'.[46]

Solomon's experience and reflections on it highlight another reason why demonic accounts of depression might sometimes be therapeutic. This is that demonic and spirit possession accounts of depression often externalize the problem: the problem is not the person, but a distinct and separable spirit or demon. As Solomon puts it:

> The *ndeup* impressed me more than many forms of group therapy currently practised in the United States. It provided a way of thinking about the affliction of depression – as a thing external to and separate from the person who suffers.[47]

In this respect, demonic accounts of depression are similar to the way in which medical diagnoses are experienced by some (though by no means all) people who are told that they have depression. Externalizing an experience such as depression, whether by perceiving it as an illness or as a demon, can be liberating. Solomon discusses this in the context of medical diagnosis when he relates the experience of a woman called Lolly who suffers from depression:

> The labelling of the complaint was an essential step towards her recovery from it. What can be named and described can be contained: the word *depression* separated Lolly's illness from her personality. If all the things she disliked in herself could be grouped together as aspects of a disease, that left her good qualities as the 'real' Lolly, and it was much easier for her to like this real Lolly, and to turn this real Lolly against the problems that afflicted her. To be given the idea of depression is to master a socially powerful linguistic tool that segregates and empowers the better self to which suffering people aspire.[48]

Perhaps demonic accounts of depression might have therapeutic value, then, because they allow the sufferer to distinguish their real self from their negative feelings and self-perceptions.[49]

However, I think we should be cautious about drawing this conclusion too hastily or without qualification, for several reasons. First, that demonic accounts will enable people to distinguish their real self from their negative feelings and self-perceptions is far less likely to be the case if, as in demon possession accounts put forward by some churches, demon possession is associated with individual or personal sin. If demon possession is associated with personal sin, demonic accounts of depression are likely to reinforce the negative feelings about the self (feelings of guiltiness, low self-esteem) that the person is already feeling.[50] Studies already point to the harmful effects on mental health of belief in the demonic[51] – at least in certain contexts and where these beliefs are likely to play a central role in the worldview of the person.[52]

Second, while *over*-identification with the negative feelings and self-perceptions involved in depression may be harmful, a psychologist might question whether complete separation from these things (such as we saw in Solomon's characterization of Lolly's attitude) might in fact be a way of avoiding understanding of and reconciliation with those aspects of ourselves that we would rather not own.[53] A person's initial feelings about a potentially therapeutic event are only one source of information about how therapeutic the event actually was. We would also want to know how they evaluated it some time afterwards, and how their friends, family, therapists and doctors perceived its effect on them. Relatedly, the idea of an instant or fast cure, such as that promised by an exorcism, might allow the person to avoid the fact that recovery is in fact painful and takes time.[54]

Third, the idea that one is demonically possessed may be particularly dangerous if the person is susceptible to audio or visual hallucination, as can happen in the case of depression and other mental disorders. The pathogenic (or illness-causing) potential of demonic accounts of mental illness is evident in the following account, written by a woman suffering from bipolar disorder:

[My Christian counselor] revealed to me she had the gift of discernment, which meant she could identify good or evil spirits. She then told me I was possessed by demons ... So she got a priest from a very traditional Catholic parish to come to the next session, and he did an exorcism. It wasn't like you see in the movies; it consisted of prayers and anointings with holy water and oil.[55] Afterwards, I thought perhaps all my troubles would be gone.

But my emotional problems – bipolar disorder – were still with me. I still felt awful, and I still couldn't shake it. I went back to her for the next session and told her how terrible I still felt. She then told me that I was still filled with demons, the exorcism hadn't worked, and she had done all she could for me. She refused to see me any more. I was devastated! ...

I write this partly because I mentioned this experience in another Forum post, and partly because I was looking at some of the articles in this site, and one of the items under a list of misunderstandings about bipolar disorder was the idea that the disorder is caused by demons, and if you were a better Christian, or prayed harder, or served God better, you wouldn't have those awful feelings and strange thoughts. As the article said, this is wrong! ... However, I have never fully been able to get over the awful experience with this counselor. That is how badly it harmed me. During a time when I had some psychotic symptoms, I saw demons all around. The counselor's words came back to me, and I felt the guilt and dirtiness of being told that I was possessed.[56]

Demonic accounts of mental illness can be pathogenic, then, because they can cause a person susceptible to hallucination to see or hear demons and to be terrified by the experience.

A further effect of demonic accounts of mental illness, particularly when they are associated with personal sin, is that they result in stigma and the person being alienated by the religious community that should be one of their foremost pillars of support. For instance, a pastor's wife who suffered from depression writes that:

> Several church people told my husband that I did not have
> enough faith or must have a poor relationship with God or
> that my mental illness was a form of 'demon possession'.
> Because of attitudes that still prevail, I am cautious about
> sharing my experiences. I fear people will consider me a
> lesser child of God.[57]

Religious communities can be a valuable source of support
for people with mental health problems, but associations with
sin and the demonic can instead mean that people are stigmatized and alienated from their communities. In addition to
this, like sin views, demonic accounts of mental illness can dis-
suade people from seeking psychological and medical forms
of support that many people find helpful and are for some
people life-saving. The demonic accounts of depression I have
been discussing are also strongly individualistic: they see the
individual person as the locus of the problem, rather than considering the wider context. As a result, demonic accounts often
deflect attention away from the social and political causes of
depression. Understanding the demonic individualistically is
to depoliticize the demonic – which is another way of saying
'to make it politically conservative'. This applies in a Western
context today just as much as it applied in the Eastern context
in which Indian theologian T. K. Thomas was writing 40 years
ago:

> We have freedom in many Asian countries to preach the
> gospel, to speak in tongues, to conduct healing ministries,
> and even to cast out evil spirits – as long as the gospel does
> not disturb, the tongues do not make sense, the healing does
> not extend to the diseases of the body politic, and the spirits
> are the ones with no visibility. We rejoice, against Jesus'
> explicit injunction, that the spirits are subject to us and leave
> the principalities and powers strictly alone.[58]

In individualizing the demonic, these accounts of depression,
then, in fact remove the Gospel's liberative power.

A final consideration when discussing whether demonic
accounts of depression and corresponding exorcisms or deliver-

ance sessions 'work' or have therapeutic value relates to the televised exorcisms we find on YouTube and religious television shows. These usually show a pastor exorcising a demon from someone who is then briefly interviewed about their experience. In these interviews, the exorcised person usually explains what the problem was and says they now feel better. This is depicted as occurring immediately after the exorcism. These recordings are designed to show the effectiveness of the exorcism or deliverance, but we shouldn't set too much store by them. That the interview occurs directly after the exorcism or deliverance means that we don't have much information about the longer-term effects of the ritual. Furthermore, the pastors and churches in question decide which events to publicize and which to omit. Religious studies scholar Adriaan van Klinken relates an occasion on which he attended a Pentecostal church in Kenya when conducting research into African Christianity. This service involved a prophetess, who claimed that she could discern an evil spirit in van Klinken's life, and ordered him to come to the stage, where she laid hands on him and began to pray over him. During this episode, he wondered, 'Should I let my body collapse and fall on the floor? Should I start crying? How to create the impression that I was indeed being delivered? Could I fake deliverance?' Instead, he made no outward movement, and she gave up. Later van Klinken returned to the church in order to get a copy of the recording that had been made of the service, so that he could use it for teaching students about Pentecostal churches in Africa back in the UK. When he eventually obtained a copy, however, he discovered that the recording included the whole service except for the failed exorcism by the prophetess.[59] If the history of exorcisms is written by exorcists, we have to wonder which cases make it into the history books, and which do not.

Concluding reflections

An Anglican priest who was a diocesan deliverance minister (the Anglican name for an exorcist) explained to me how he went about his job. 'If someone thinks they've got a demon or a ghost,' he said, 'I start by giving them pastoral counselling. I also check their lightbulbs and bleed their radiators. That fixes most of the problems. Perhaps I'll also pray with them and bless them. What gets called "exorcism" is hardly ever needed, and it's only ever a last resort.' He had a number of good anecdotes about his job, which he regaled with good humour. 'Once I was called to a Hindu family who thought they had a house-ghost,' he recalled. 'That's fine – but just out of interest, why did you call a Christian priest?' he asked. 'Well,' they replied, 'we thought if there's a ghost, it must be an English ghost – so it's much more likely to listen to a priest of the English religion.' He himself seemed to be agnostic about the existence of demons, ghosts and other entities. 'I'm a practical person,' he said. 'I don't have any kind of theory for it, but occasionally strange things happen, and for whatever reason sometimes it's a deliverance or requiem mass that solves the problem. But much more often it's the radiators.'[60]

This grounded, non-sensationalist approach is a far cry from the demonic focus of some Christian communities, including those who are most likely to attribute mental illness to the demonic. The demonic focus of these communities is danger-ous, since they can cause or reinforce feelings of guilt among people who are most vulnerable to it, cause or justify abuse of people in vulnerable situations, isolate and alienate people from potential forms of support, discourage people from seek-ing psychological and medical help they may need, and deflect attention away from the social and political causes of mental illness.

What are we to make of scriptural language of the demonic and spiritual warfare in the light of all this? In this chapter I have focused on correcting some emphases, and so my argu-ments have been largely negative: demonic affliction should not be associated with individual or personal sin; individual deliverance from demons is not the most important part of Christian ministry; spiritual warfare should not be seen as an individual battle against the devil or some demons vying for our souls. These ideas have much more in common with elements of contemporary US pop culture than they do with the gospel.[61]

However, in the course of correcting certain views and recalibrating particular emphases I hope some more fruitful lines of thinking about the demonic have emerged. Jesus' ministry was one of liberation. Where liberation from the demonic is described as part of this, the demonic seems to be understood both in terms of illness and in terms of political and social oppression. People are demonically possessed rather than merely ill because they are suffering the effects of the political and social oppression to which they are subjected. Furthermore, Jesus' exorcism ministry – his liberation of people from demons – is not something separate from his disruption of the status quo – his willingness to heal on the sabbath, his teaching about the coming of the kingdom of God – but is part and parcel of the same thing. If we wish to have a scriptural understanding of the demonic, then, we need to attend to the demonic not solely in psychological and individualistic terms – though the demonic will involve people and their psychological states – but with attention to the way in which these are part of a wider story about the political and social systems with and in which we live.

I will return to these themes in Chapter 8. In the next chapter I want to consider an interpretation of depression that is emerging especially in Christian communities that have held sin and demonic accounts of depression in the past, but are becoming critical of them. Reacting against the (negative) spiritualization of mental illness, these communities are now emphasizing instead that depression is an illness, and in particular that depression is biologically caused and so should be biologically treated.

Notes

1 Derek Prince (2014), 'How demons cause negative thinking', *Derek Prince Ministries*, available at www.youtube.com/watch?v=lnr 97uGmIc8 (all websites in Chapter 2 notes accessed 13.12.19).

2 Derek Prince (2016), 'The struggle against depression', *Derek Prince Ministries*, available at www.youtube.com/watch?v=JK5wx2 tQR5M.

3 See Kristine Hartog and Kathryn Gow (2005), 'Religious attributions pertaining to the causes and cures of mental illness', *Mental Health, Religion & Culture* 8.4, pp. 263–76, and Edna Hunneysett (2006), *Christian Congregations and Mental Illness: A Survey of Contemporary Attitudes in their Historical Context*, North Yorkshire, UK: Fryup.

4 Broadly speaking, these tend to be some Evangelical, Pentecostal and Charismatic communities. Anglican and Catholic Churches have deliverance ministries, which can in rare cases include exorcism, but for the most part they are not demonically focused. For an overview of Anglican deliverance ministry, see Pat Ashworth, 17 February 2017, "Deliver us from evil', *Church Times*, available at www.churchtimes. co.uk/articles/2017/17-february/features/features/deliver-us-from-evil.

5 Prince, 'Demons'.

6 By this, I mean that they detach it from the political and social causes of affliction, including what is described in the Gospels as demon possession. Although this is depoliticizing in some ways, it is political in another, since by deflecting attention away from social and political oppression it serves to maintain the status quo, and so is politically and socially conservative.

7 Chip Ingram (n.d.), 'Spiritual Warfare 101: What is the invisible war?', *Living on the Edge with Chip Ingram*, available at https://living ontheedge.org/broadcast/spiritual-warfare-101-what-is-the-invisible-war-part-1/daily-radio#.XDNbhGngrIU.

8 Ingram, 'Spiritual Warfare'.

9 Larry Wilson (2017), 'Demonic possession – how demons take control', *Wake up America Seminars*, available at www.wake-up.org/ demonic-possession/demonic-possession-how-demons-take-control-part-2.html.

10 Douglas Irvine, cited in: Eunice K. Y. Or (2004), 'Deliverance Group recommends the Church of Scotland a cautious approach to exorcism', *Christian Today*, available at www.christiantoday.com/article/ deliverance.group.recommends.the.church.of.scotland.a.cautious. approach.to.exorcism/536.htm.

11 Anon (2005), 'Crucified nun dies in "exorcism"', *BBC News*, available at http://news.bbc.co.uk/1/hi/world/europe/4107524.stm.

12 See, for example, Anon (2017), 'Nicaragua woman burnt on a fire in an exorcism ritual', *BBC News*, available at www.bbc.co.uk/news/ world-latin-america-39123952 and Anon (2001), 'Cleric said Climbié was possessed', *BBC News*, available at http://news.bbc.co.uk/1/hi/ uk/1586816.stm.

13 To my knowledge there hasn't yet been a study looking at the

gender balance of people regarded as demonically possessed, but they seem more frequently than not to be female.

14 Anon (n.d.), 'Deliverance ministries', *All about God*, available at www.allaboutgod.com/deliverance-ministries.htm; see also e.g. Matt Slick (n.d.), 'Can demons cause possession?', *Christian Apologetics and Research Ministry*, available at https://carm.org/can-demons-cause-depression.

15 Prince, 'Demons'.

16 Wilson, 'Demonic possession'.

17 John MacArthur (2019), 'Can Christians be demon-possessed?', *Grace in You*, available at www.gty.org/library/questions/QA191/can-christians-be-demonpossessed.

18 Kay Redfield Jamison (2006), The many stigmas of mental illness, *Lancet*, pp. 533–4.

19 Slick, 'Demons'.

20 In the demonically focused traditions being discussed here, deliverance refers to exorcism. In some other Christian traditions – for example, the Church of England – 'deliverance' is a wider ministry responding to the demonic, which involves not only exorcism but more common practices such as prayers and blessings.

21 See James K. Beilby and Paul Rhodes Eddy (2012), 'Introduction', *Understanding Spiritual Warfare: Four Views*, ed. J. K. Beilby and P. R. Eddy, Grand Rapids, MI: Baker Academic, especially pp. 37–8.

22 www.youtube.com/watch?v=f3yMoaJBwfI.

23 Proponents of spiritual warfare today tend to speak of 'demons'; in the past they would have referred to 'devils'. Several words are used in the New Testament: *diabolos* or devil (which has become a personal name for Satan by the time of the New Testament); *daimon* or demon; *pneumati akathartō* or unclean spirit; *peirazōn* or tempter; *Satana* or Satan, and *Beelzebub*. In pre-Christian Judaism, Satan was sometimes seen as an adversary or tester in the heavenly court, rather than a fallen angel (see Job), but by the time of the New Testament it seems likely that he was regarded as the head of the fallen angels. In keeping with what seems to me to be the most likely New Testament usage, I shall use 'devil' as a personal name for 'Satan', which I shall assume is a personal name for the head of the fallen angels or demons. I will presuppose that Beelzebub is another name for Satan, and that 'unclean spirit' refers to a demon. This usage reflects that of most spiritual warfare proponents.

24 Robert J. Karris, OFM (1997), 'The Gospel according to Luke', in *The New Jerome Biblical Commentary*, ed. Raymond E. Brown, Joseph A. Fitzmyer and Ronald E. Murphy, London: Geoffrey Chapman, p. 691.

25 Daniel Harrington, SJ (1997), 'The Gospel according to Mark', in *The New Jerome Biblical Commentary*, p. 612.

26 Mark Ahonen (2014), *Mental Disorders in Ancient Philosophy*,

London: Springer, p. 32: 'The rare word *selēnblētos* ("moonstruck") and related words (such as *selēniazesthai*) seem to refer to epilepsy.' According to Ahonen, the words *epilēpsis* and *epilēptos* seem to have originally denoted a seizure caused by a divinity, and were appropriated for medical use to mean a disease later on.

27 Some twin Luke 11.14 with another very brief demon possession account in Matthew (9.32), where the man is mentioned as being mute. There are some other reasons for the pairing I adopt here, but which pairing is correct isn't important for current purposes.

28 IQGA20. See James Dunn and Graham Twelftree (n.d.), 'Demon-possession and exorcism in the New Testament', *Churchman*, available at https://biblicalstudies.org.uk/pdf/churchman/094-03_210.pdf.

29 *Life of St Anthony* 5, available at *New Advent*, www.newadvent.org/fathers/2811.htm.

30 See Marcia Webb (2012), 'Toward a theology of mental illness', *Journal of Religion, Disability and Health*, 16, pp. 49–73.

31 I'm indebted to Paul Middleton for a conversation about this (personal correspondence, 7 January 2019).

32 IAQG 20.16ff.

33 See Webb, 'Theology'.

34 Ludwig Wittgenstein (1970), *Lectures and Conversations on Aesthetics, Psychology, and Religious Belief*, Oxford: Basil Blackwell, compiled from Notes taken by Yorick Smithies, Rush Rhees and James Taylor, pp. 61–2.

35 José A. Pagola (2009) (Eng. trans.), *Jesus: An Historical Approximation*, Miami, FL: Convivium Press, p. 170.

36 Anastasia Philippa Scrutton (2011), *Thinking through Feeling: God, Emotion and Passibility*, New York and London: Continuum, p. 285.

37 APA, DSM-5, p. 295.

38 Ingram, 'Spiritual Warfare'.

39 Joseph A. Fitzmeyer (1997), 'Pauline Theology', in *The New Jerome Biblical Commentary*, p. 1406.

40 Beilby and Eddy, 'Introduction'; Paul Middleton, personal correspondence, 7 January 2019.

41 See Harold W. Hoehner (2002), *Ephesians: An Exegetical Commentary*, Grand Rapids, MI: Baker Academic, p. 828.

42 There is even some evidence to indicate that the placebo effect works, even if people know that the treatment is (only) a placebo.

43 Claude Lévi-Strauss (1967), 'The effectiveness of symbols', *Structural Anthropology*, New York: Basic Books.

44 Anastasia Philippa Scrutton (2017), 'Grief, ritual, and belief', *Continuing Bonds in Bereavement: New Directions for Research and Practice*, ed. Dennis Klass and Edith Steffen, London: Routledge.

45 Andrew Solomon (2008) (29 October), 'Notes on an exorcism',

The Moth, available at http://themoth.org/posts/stories/notes-on-an-exorcism.

46 Andrew Solomon (2001), *The Noonday Demon: An Anatomy of Depression*, London: Vintage Books, p. 170.

47 Solomon, 'Notes on an exorcism'.

48 Solomon, *Noonday Demon*, p. 342.

49 Thanks to Beth Seacord for raising this as a possibility.

50 Thanks to Simon Hewitt for making this point.

51 For example, Fanhao Nie and Daniel Olson undertook a pair of studies involving a longitudinal telephone survey of 3,290 young Americans between 2003 and 2008, which strongly suggest two things. First – at least as far as young people in the US go – while there is a positive correlation between mental health and much religious belief, there is a significant negative correlation between mental health and belief in demons. Second, because the study was longitudinal, the causal direction seems to run from belief in demons to poor mental health, rather than the reverse (Fanhao Nie and Daniel Olson (2017), 'Demonic influence: the negative mental health effects of beliefs in demons', *Journal for the Scientific Study of Religion* 55.3, pp. 498–515). Notably, this study is typical of religion and mental health studies since these focus overwhelmingly on the USA (and to a lesser extent Western Europe), and this should be borne in mind when considering religious beliefs, practices, etc. in other contexts and cultures. See Simon Dein (n.d.), 'Religion and mental health: Current findings', *Royal College of Psychiatrists*, available at www.semanticscholar.org/paper/Religion-and-Mental-Health-%3A-Current-Findings-Dein/6ce5e674fe6c952a2ac2f55fc23113f77c0ace52.

52 Beliefs can play different roles in people's lives. For example, someone might assent to a belief in demons because it's part of the doctrine of their church, without giving much thought to demons or seeing them behind every bush. Not only whether but also how demons are believed in may affect their relationship to a person's mental health. The context and cultural milieu in which a belief occurs will significantly affect this. See Anastasia Philippa Scrutton (2015), 'Why not believe in an evil God? Pragmatic encroachment and some implications for philosophy of religion', *Religious Studies: An International Journal for Philosophy of Religion* 52.3, pp. 345–60.

53 My thanks go to Jo Buglass for raising this point. For more on this idea, see John Monbourquette (2001), *How to Befriend your Shadow: Welcoming your Unloved Side*, London: Darton, Longman and Todd.

54 Thanks to Rebekah Latour for this point. See also Judith Herman (1997), *Trauma and Recovery: The Aftermath of Violence – From Domestic Abuse to Political Terror*, New York: Basic Books.

55 This priest may have been a freelance rather than an authorized exorcist, since this is not in keeping with Catholic exorcist practices.

56 Wonder (2006), 'Counselling from Hell', available at https://web.archive.org/web/20111013112248/http://bipolar.about.com/cs/choosepdoc/a/9910_counshell.htm.

57 Norma Swetman, cited in Kathleen Greider (2007), *Much Madness is Divinest Sense: Wisdom in Memoirs of Soul-Suffering*, Ohio: Pilgrim Press, p. 191.

58 T. K. Thomas, *One World* 38 (July–August 1978), p. 18, cited in Kenneth Leech (1981), *The Social God*, London: SPCK, pp. 95–6.

59 Adriaan van Klinken (2019), *Kenyan, Christian, Queer: Religion, LGBT Activism, and Arts of Resistance in Africa*, University Park: Penn State University Press, 'Prophetess'.

60 Sadly, he died some time after meeting with me. Thanks to his wife for allowing me to recount our meeting here.

61 See Robert A. Guelich (1991), 'Spiritual warfare: Jesus, Paul, and Peretti', in *Pheuma: The Journal for the Society of Pentecostal Studies* 13.1, pp. 33–64.

3

Biology

Introduction

> This has nothing to do with whether I believe in Jesus ... This
> does not have anything to do with whether or not I am read-
> ing my Bible or how hard I am praying. I can pray 24 hours
> a day, seven days a week, and I'm still going to have to take
> that little white pill every single day.

These are the words of Carlos Whittaker, an Evangelical
musician and writer who suffers from anxiety.[1] Whittaker
is part of a wider rejection of, and campaign against, the sin
accounts of mental illness we've examined already. In rejecting sin and demon accounts, Whittaker and others instead
emphasize that mental illness is an illness and in particular that
it is physical or biological. Thus, for example, responding to a
question about sin and depression, the evangelist Billy Graham
replies:

> If you broke your arm in an accident, do you think your
> friend would claim it was a sin for you to have a broken arm,
> and all you needed to do was pray? I doubt it. Neither is it
> a sin for you to seek treatment for a chemical imbalance in
> your brain.[2]

Similarly, anti-stigma campaigns beyond the Church describe
depression as a 'biological, medical illness', in order to combat
moralization and consequent alienation.[3] Depression, these
movements within and outside the Church emphasize, is a
disease, not a sin. Consequently, both the causes and the effective treatment of depression are biological.

This biological turn in understanding depression and mental illness more broadly is to be applauded in several ways: it must come as a welcome relief to people who have been given the impression that their depression is the result of sin or moral failure. It also may well have encouraged people to seek medical help that is life-changing or even life-saving. But there are more nuanced, and more helpful, interpretations of depression available. The best evidence for depression suggests to us a biopsychosocial model, both in relation to the causes of depression and in relation to the best treatment. The well-intentioned emphasis on the biological in anti-stigma campaigns can easily become an overemphasis, so that in place of the biopsychosocial model we have the older biomedical (for which read 'bio-bio-bio') model of mental illness, which has room only for biological causes and treatments for depression. This is problematic since it ignores the other causes of mental illness, deflecting attention away from the social causes of depression, and tacitly discouraging psychological interventions (e.g. counselling, psychoanalysis, mindfulness) in favour of medications alone. And so, while the shift away from 'sin' accounts is to be applauded, falling headlong into a biomedical model in response is dangerous and flawed.

So far, I've suggested a negative sort of thesis: we should rein in the overemphasis on the biological in the (much needed) anti-stigma campaigns about mental illness in favour of a biopsychosocial model. There is nothing very original or even controversial about this in theory, but it nevertheless needs saying: there is a tendency within some churches to focus on the biological to such an extent that sight is lost of important social issues relating to mental health. This is particularly a worry since the Christian tradition has important and distinctive things to say and do regarding these social issues, and so it should concern us if these are watered down or lost. In addition to this, medical professionals sometimes adopt a biopsychosocial model in theory but a biomedical model in practice, particularly when faced with limited resources and time. As one psychiatrist put this to me, 'We're biopsychosocial at our most reflective, but biomedical when we're short of time.'[4]

Underlying biopsychosocial and biomedical models of depression are different anthropologies (or 'theories of what a human person is'). The biomedical model is reductively physicalist. At its most extreme, proponents of physicalism hold that all aspects of reality ultimately reduce to physical realities. Thus my desire for coffee is not only correlated with the change in my brain that takes place when I want coffee: my desire for coffee actually *is* the change in my brain that takes place.[5] Not all proponents of the biomedical model of mental illness will be physicalists about the whole of reality, however. For example, Christians who adopt a biomedical model will typically think that non-physical realities exist (perhaps God, angels, demons and/or souls), but they will still think that all aspects of depression reduce to biological realities. For this reason they may end up being dualists, and positing a physical realm (in which depression exists) and a separate mental or spiritual realm (which is the domain of God and souls).

The biopsychosocial model has a different anthropology from either a physicalist or a dualist anthropology. While it holds that humans are biological, it also holds them to be psychological and social creatures. These three are not separable components, but interdependent aspects of the person that affect one another in different ways. While both physicalism and dualism jar with traditional Christianity, as I shall argue, the biopsychosocial model and Christianity (at least potentially) have much more in common.

In addition to arguing for a biopsychosocial model and against a biomedical one, on theological and other grounds, in this chapter I want to build on some anthropological ideas to explore one way in which Christian theology can contribute positively to our understanding of the biological in the context of depression. Christianity has often been muddled up with Gnosticism, both internally and perhaps especially in terms of how it is seen by others. And so, sometimes with good reason, Christianity has been thought to deny our animality in favour of emphasizing our spiritual nature, or instead see our animality as a bad thing or a lesser good. I want to draw attention to significant aspects of Christianity where this is not the case, where our biological nature and kinship with the rest of the animal world are affirmed and celebrated. I will do this by looking at what I take to be two examples of this: the idea of the new creation and resurrection of the body, and stories of saints with animals. While perhaps not obviously related to mental health, I will argue that in recognizing our animality they help us, individually and collectively, to combat alienation, which is a major cause of depression. They also have important implications in terms of how we relate to our world and see ourselves within it.

That's what I'm going to do; here's how I'll do it. First, I'll explain in more detail what biopsychosocial and biomedical models are, and why we should prefer the former to the latter, in practice as well as in theory. Then, I'll get on to talking about Christianity, the resurrection of the body, some saints who knew animals, depression, and our animality. This chapter therefore falls into two parts, though these two parts are united by the theme of a proper appreciation of the biological in the Christian tradition, in relation to depression and more generally. My thesis is that a genuinely Christian anthropology or understanding of the human person – one that recognizes the animal (biological, psychological and social) needs of humans – is better suited to creating a society conducive to mental health than is a society in which we try to escape or ignore core aspects of our animality, such as our vulnerability, and our needs for stability and the companionship of others.

What are the biomedical and biopsychosocial models of depression?

In her brilliant autobiographical comic strip and film *Persepolis*, Marjane (or Marji) Sartrapi tells of a severe depression into which she fell when she returned home to her family in politically turbulent Iran, after an equally turbulent and alienating few years living in Vienna.[6] When she returns Marji expects to find peace, but instead feels like an outsider, and says she no longer knows who she is. She tries psychoanalysis, which she finds unhelpful, and medication, which she finds effective until the pills 'wear off', and which also comes with trance-like side effects. Significantly overdosing on antidepressants, Marji attempts suicide but survives, for which her otherwise atheist therapist says he can find no explanation except divine intervention. Accepting his interpretation, she infers that she is not meant to die, and discovers new reasons for living.

Marji attributes her recovery, at least primarily, to her belief that she survived suicide for a reason, and to the new sense of purpose that gives her. She also strongly suggests that social and psychological causes were at the root of her depression: 'I thought that by coming back to Iran, everything would be fine. That I would forget the old days. But my past caught up with me. My secrets weighed me down.'[7]

Marji's emphasis on the social and psychological aspects of both depression and recovery is at odds with a biomedical model, which would regard her depression solely as a brain disease caused by neurotransmitter dysregulation, genetic anomalies, and defects in her brain's structure, curable through medication and/or electro-convulsive therapy. In response to attempts to point to psychological and social causes (for example, negative thinking about the future caused by the ongoing stress of the past), a proponent of the biomedical model would insist that the underlying biological reality to which negative thinking corresponds will become clear once we have better neuroscience, and that no further explanations are required.[8] Ultimately, according to this model, the causes of depression all lie within the brain, or at least within the person's physical body.

In contrast, a proponent of the biopsychosocial model would take the context of Marji's depression – her experience of trauma and instability – much more seriously. While we can never know for sure the root causes of a particular person's depression, a proponent of the biopsychosocial model would describe the trauma and instability she experienced as among the likely social causes of depression, which they might relate to psychological causes – perhaps, in Marji's case, coping strategies such as keeping weighty secrets about what she has gone through, which could become unhealthy over time. However, this model would not see social and psychological kinds of cause as mutually exclusive of biological causes. It is not about saying that if someone's depression is 65 per cent biologically caused, then only 35 per cent can be social and psychological causes. Rather, it could be said that biological, psychological and social causes are complementary. One kind of cause does not push out another. This is because biological, social and psychological causes correspond to different levels of causation.

What do I mean by 'different levels of causation'? Imagine a person, Sally, who lights a match to build a fire. We might ask whether the match being lit caused the fire. In one sense it did: without the match being lit there would be no fire. But we might say that other things caused the fire: Sally caused the fire because she lit it; Sally's friends coming round caused the fire because she lit it for their comfort; the bringing together of some flammable material with oxygen and heat caused the fire, and so on.[9] What explanation is given is likely to depend on who's asking and in what context: is it Sally's young daughter, who has a burgeoning interest in chemistry, or Sally's penurious father, concerned about why wood has been burned so early in the year? Significantly, these causes aren't equivalent factors all contributing to there being a fire, but quite different kinds of causation that affect one another at different levels. It would be sufficient to say that there was a fire because 'Sally lit it because her friends were coming round' or else that there was a fire 'because heat and oxygen came into contact with a flammable material', without appeal to any of the other explanations.

In the case of depression, biological, psychological and social causes may relate to one another in various ways. Here's one of many possible examples. While the term 'biological causes of depression' is sometimes assumed to refer only to genetic predispositions to depression, in fact it also refers to other aspects of our bodies, including the ways in which our brains change over time, and especially during the earlier parts of our lives.[10] Our brain development might be affected by traumatic events or ongoing stress, bringing on an early depressive episode, and/or making a later depressive episode more likely.[11] Social causes of depression – such as poverty or abuse or isolation or instability – can refer to contingent social and political factors that affect us biologically.[12] A social and political phenomenon like the rise of casualized job contracts (to take one of many possible examples) can mean that family life is less stable and secure and more stressful, and that the family is less able to 'put down roots' in a particular place. As a result, family members may become alienated from one another and from the wider community. This can create long-term changes in the brain that can cause[13] depression in one or more members of the family at a time, and/or that can make a child in the family more prone to depression when they are older.

While we can't be sure, it seems unlikely that the social conditions in Iran, and Marji's experiences in Vienna, were totally unrelated to Marji's depression. On the other hand, we shouldn't be surprised if her depression had a biological cause or causes as well, whether this relates to congenital factors, the way her brain has developed over time, or even (as some research suggests) gut bacteria.[14] We are not spiritual or mental beings placed in a body but unaffected by it, a 'ghost in the machine',[15] but are biological creatures through and through.

As we saw in relation to Sally and the fire, whether it is biological, social or psychological causes that are more talked about can often depend on context, and who is doing the talking. Consider the differences between a person with depression discussing with their counsellor or psychologist which experiences played a part in getting depression, a mental health activist talking to a politician in the context of a campaign to combat homelessness, and medical researchers weighing the chemical imbalance theory of depression in relation to other neurological causes of depression.[16] In these examples, the people are (all quite rightly) talking about psychological, social and biological causes of depression without much attention to the other kinds of cause or level of explanation. We might be given the impression that there is only one kind of cause if we are used to thinking and talking about only one level of explanation, but we need to remember this would be a partial rather than a full view of the matter.

So far, I've talked about how the biomedical and biopsychosocial models differ when it comes to understanding the causes of depression. They differ, in related ways, in terms of treatment as well. For a biomedical model, the appropriate treatment is solely the 'little white pill' Whittaker mentioned at the beginning of this chapter (or, in more extreme cases, electro-convulsive therapy): a biological cause should be met with a biological treatment. Biopsychosocial models are much more likely to suggest a combination of approaches: perhaps antidepressant medication, counselling, and lifestyle changes such as increased exercise – while also recognizing that some of the causes might be beyond the person's or their doctor's control (e.g. poverty, unemployment, instability caused by having asylum-seeker status).

According to a proponent of the biopsychosocial model, because the relationships between the biological, psychological and social are complex, the effective treatments for any given person's depression will not necessarily match up neatly to the originating causes. For example, when antidepressants work, it is often assumed that the originating causes of depression must have been primarily biological. But even if we knew that in fact the medication was the most effective treatment for Marji's depression, that would not tell us much about its ultimate cause. Several therapies (for example, cognitive behavioural therapy) treat depression by addressing its correlates (for example, negative thoughts and behaviours) without it being required that these correspond to the originating or ultimate cause of the depression, rather than a later aspect of it. In treating the biological correlates of depression, medicines may likewise be effective in providing the conditions for a non-depressed state to 'kick in', regardless of whether biology was an initial or originating cause. Of course, it is also possible that medications work because the root cause of the person's depression, or at least one of the causes, is biological. We are animals, and so it should not surprise us if our bodies (which include our brains) sometimes go wrong.

Why should we prefer a biopsychosocial model to a biomedical one?

At one level the biopsychosocial model doesn't need arguing for, since it seems that the majority of mental health professionals sign up to it.[17] It's the model that is taught to students with a career in mental health in mind, while the biomedical model is mentioned as its flawed predecessor.[18] However, there is some evidence to suggest that popular conceptions of mental illness – what sometimes gets called 'folk psychiatry' – is at odds with mental health professionals in being more likely to overemphasize the biological causes and treatments for depression.[19] If correct, this is likely to influence the anti-stigma campaigns in churches and beyond.

In addition to this, it seems that while most mental health professionals sign up for the biopsychosocial model in theory, sometimes it's only the biological that is focused on in practice.[20] This may well be, as some have argued, due to an unwillingness to pay anything more than lip service to a biopsychosocial model[21] – but if this is so this unwillingness should be understood at a systemic level. At the level of individual health professionals, it is much more likely to be a reflection of what powers they have available to help someone: a doctor can prescribe fluoxetine, and maybe at a push get her patient some cognitive behavioural therapy sessions; she can't make his job or housing more secure. There are therefore practical reasons for why mental healthcare often defaults to the biological.

Furthermore, in countries like the USA where healthcare is privatized and insurance companies have to be convinced about, or goaded into, paying for healthcare, doctors may need to emphasize that mental illness is 'real', where 'real' is quickly mistakenly equated with 'physical' or 'material'. Again, the reasons for the tendency towards the biological within healthcare are systemic rather than at an individual level. The privatization of healthcare is not the fault of individual healthcare professionals who work within that system. But the fact that it's not something that's the fault of individual health professionals, nor something within their power to redress at an individual level, doesn't mean that it's the way things have to be, or that we should turn a blind eye to it. Rather, it means that we can and must do something about it, but at a collective and systemic rather than merely individual level. For all these reasons, we need to rehearse some of the reasons why we should prefer a biopsychosocial model of depression to a biomedical one.

One reason lies in what we know about cases of depression when we look at many cases together. It would be possible to look at Marji's depression as entirely unrelated to her experience of trauma and alienation, and to regard it as purely a biological aberration. But, looking at demographics of people who report depression, we know that there are higher levels of diagnosed mental illness among people who experience or have experienced poverty, oppression, torture, abuse, violence, instability and so on.[22] It is difficult to explain these correlations without seeing them as evidence for the social causes of depression.

Our theories about depression are often based on what works best. Our best evidence suggests that a combination of approaches – perhaps antidepressants and a talk therapy – is the most effective treatment for severe depression, more effective than a single kind of treatment.[23] Again, this lends support to a biopsychosocial model. If clergy and pastors in churches follow through on the biomedical model put forward by Billy Graham and others, they are likely to recommend to someone who comes to them with depression a trip to the doctor with a view to obtaining some prescribed antidepressants. They are less likely to ask questions about the person's current situation, or about things that have happened to them in the past that might continue to affect them. The biomedical model therefore gives churches one less reason to take social injustice seriously: it is no longer thought to be a significant contributor to people's mental health.

As this suggests, a serious problem with a biomedical model is that it ignores and deflects attention away from the social causes of depression, turning a blind eye to abuses and injustices and becoming politically apathetic or quietistic. A biomedical model allows churches to preach an individualized and interiorized simulacrum of the gospel. In addition, a biomedical model may encourage people to overlook psychological causes of depression – for example, lurking features of their earlier experience that they may need to reflect on and find some resolution for.

A further reason to be suspicious of a biomedical model is that it relies on a faulty anthropology or view of the human person. I have already said that we are biological creatures through and through. In this there is some partial agreement between me and physicalist anthropology, at least against a dualistic anthropology that sees us as souls or spirits temporarily located, quite superficially, in bodies, such that our souls and spirits can come apart. But this similarity between my view, which is in keeping with a biopsychosocial model on the one hand, and a physicalist anthropology on the other, is only superficial. By 'biological through and through' I mean that everything we do and experience and are, we do and experience and are as biological (and also as psychological, and as social) creatures. We don't do (and experience and be) some things as biological creatures and other things as psychological or social or some other kinds of being. But when a biomedical model speaks of being 'biological' beings, it means rather that we are reducible to biology: there is no significant aspect of us not explicable in biological terms, such that when our scientific knowledge is complete, we will know everything we need to know about the human person.

So far, I have outlined biomedical and biopsychosocial anthropologies, shown how these relate to views about and treatments for depression, and given some (theological and other) reasons for preferring the biopsychosocial to the biomedical view. This is intended as a (gentle) corrective to the biomedical views put forward by Carlos Whittaker, Billy Graham and others, cited at the beginning of this chapter, and evident in churches and wider society. Whittaker's and Graham's emphasis on the biological nature of depression is a vast improvement on teaching that depression is the result of individual sin. And yet we can do better than this: a biopsychosocial rather than biomedical model reflects our best understanding of human creatures, and is more in keeping with the Christian tradition.

Having qualified the role of the biological by arguing that humans are not *only* biological, and that depression should not be seen *solely* as a biological phenomenon, in the second half of this chapter I want to say something more constructive about the biological. In particular, I want to talk about the ways in which the Christian tradition speaks of humans as biological and even as animals, and of the implications and possibilities this raises for how we approach depression, and mental illness and health more generally.

Christianity and animality

Earlier in this chapter I took casualized employment and consequent loss of stability, community and rootedness in place as an example of one of the social causes of depression. This, I suggest, is related to a cultural propensity to deny our animality, and thus to deny that we need these things, in favour of holding up self-sufficiency, including a capacity to live and function without significant communities and homes, as ideals. This denial of our animality is something nature writer Richard Mabey writes about, lamenting that:

> The list of our disastrous failures, from forest obliteration and oceanic pollution to the raising of the extinction rate a thousandfold, bears all the marks of a species which no longer believes itself to be part of the animal world at all.[24]

Recounting his own depressive episode, Mabey relates finding a swift fledgling and launching it into the air to enable it to fly (swifts can't take off from the ground, and so being 'beached' can be fatal). Reflecting on the fact that the swift would embark on a long journey to Africa before returning to 'race recklessly about the sky just for the sheer hell of it' the following May, Mabey recalls that:

When that May came round I was blind to the swifts for the first time in my life. While they were flying *en fête* I was lying on my bed with my face away from the window, not really caring if I saw them again or not. In a strange and ironic turn-about, I had become the incomprehensible creature adrift in some insubstantial medium, out of kilter with the rest of creation. It didn't occur to me at the time, but maybe that is the way our whole species is moving.[25]

Our society inclines us to reject our animality. This is perhaps because denying our animality means that we can, at least for a while, deny our bodiliness, our vulnerability, and ultimately our mortality. Yet friendships with particular non-human animals can reunite us with our sense that we ourselves are also animals. My dog, Lola, requires companionship, physical affection, regular walks and play. By attending to these needs, I realize that I do too, and in a deeper way than I had realized before. This is an antidote to ways in which we are encouraged to present ourselves as humans, especially but not only in the professional sphere. Our society can give us the impression that we should be independent, self-sufficient, serious, and as close as we can to being 'brains in vats'. Our relationships with non-human animals remind us not only of our similarities with them but also of the distinctive differences of our own species. Unlike dogs, we experience the world primarily through sight, not sound or smell. Unlike dogs, we are complex language-users, and experience the world in ways only language-users can: through propositions, beliefs, narratives, and so on. And so, non-human animals also remind us of what it is to flourish not only as animals but as that-kind-of-animal-called-'human'.

What has all this to do with Christianity? Christianity is often associated with a separation of humanity from other animals, and with the idea that we are not essentially physical beings, but spiritual beings who happen to be travelling for a while in temporary physical bodies. I will show that this is not, in fact, true to the Christian tradition, focusing on the biblical teaching about the resurrection of our bodies, and the renewal of the created world. Then I will point to strands of later Christian tradition that speak promisingly of friendships between humans and non-human animals, focusing on stories about saints and their inter-species friendships.

The resurrection of the body and new creation

In one of the university philosophy of religion courses I teach, the students and I think about different theories of the afterlife. Right at the beginning, I ask them to name some different kinds of afterlife. Heaven and hell, and perhaps purgatory and reincarnation, are the most common responses. It's fairly rare that students say 'bodily resurrection' or 'the resurrection of the dead'. Sometimes students who are Christians or who have been brought up in Christian traditions will react to the notion of a bodily resurrection – a resurrection not just of Jesus' but also of our own bodies – with a sense of unfamiliarity or even surprise. In spite of its place in historical Christianity, and in the Creed today ('we believe in the resurrection of the dead, and the life of the world to come'), much contemporary Christianity, at least in the West, is not associated with the idea of bodily resurrection. The idea of a disembodied heaven as a final resting place has taken its place as the primary understanding of the afterlife in Christian thought.

While what form the afterlife might take might seem a distant and rather theoretical concern to many of us, theories about the afterlife have significant practical implications in the here and now. For example, the (Platonic and Gnostic) dualistic conception of the human person suggests that we are spiritual beings simply travelling through a (lower if not evil) material world on our way to our proper and permanent spiritual or heavenly abode. This might well lead to apathy about or even the legitimization of actions that are disastrous to the ecological system and to non-human animals. If the current world is merely a place we higher beings pass through, we are less likely to genuinely love it or the other creatures who inhabit it. And so this dualistic anthropology and otherworldly view of the afterlife is not only at odds with biblical Christianity; it is also politically and socially problematic. As New Testament scholar Tom Wright puts it:

> That is a peculiarly modern form of would-be Christian negativity about the world, and of course its skin-deep 'spiritual' viewpoint is entirely in thrall to the heart-deep materialism of the business interests that will be served, in however short a term, by ... hazardous [ecological] practices.[26]

So, what is the Christian idea of bodily resurrection? In a nutshell, it's the idea that God is going to raise people from the dead, or do for people what he did for Jesus at Easter: 'For as in Adam all die, so will all be made alive in Christ' (1 Corinthians 15.22).[27] St Paul describes Jesus using the imagery of the 'first fruits', recalling the Jewish festivals of Passover and Pentecost at which the first crops of the harvest were presented to God (1 Corinthians 15.23). These festivals were a sign of the great (agricultural) harvest still to come, and also a remembrance of God's promise to liberate Israel.[28] This bodily resurrection of humans is part and parcel of a bigger picture: a transformed created order – not only humans but the whole of creation is caught up in this renewal of life. Thus, the whole of 1 Corinthians 15 echoes Genesis 1—3: 'It is a theology of new creation, not of the abandonment of creation.'[29]

The idea of bodily resurrection often gets missed today partly because as moderns we read the Bible through the lens of dualism, which is deeply ingrained in our culture and thus tends to separate what is physical from what is spiritual. Faulty translations of the Bible sometimes perpetuate our deafness to language about the resurrection of the body. And so, misleadingly, some English translations of the Bible render the terms *psychikon* and *pneumatikon* in 1 Corinthians 15.44 'physical body' and 'spiritual body'. To our ears, because we have a cultural inclination to dualism, it is hard not to hear this as referring to 'a body made of physical stuff' and 'a body made of spiritual stuff', with the latter perhaps referring to a non-physical afterlife (such as heaven). But in fact the contrast is between the present, corruptible body and the future, incorruptible body. 'Physical' does violence to the word *psychikon* (*psychikon* is related to the word *psyche*, or 'soul', after all). Moreover, the Greek adjectives ending *-ikos* do not describe the material out of which things are made, but the power or energy that animates them: 'The contrast is not between what we call physical and what we call non-physical, but between corruptible physicality on the one hand and non-corruptible physicality on the other.'[30]

The idea of bodily resurrection being the ultimate afterlife state (or, as Wright puts it, 'life after life-after-death') is also found in Jesus' teachings, where Jesus reflects the contemporary mainstream Jewish view of the afterlife (see Luke 20.27–40, which is about an intra-Jewish debate about the resurrection of the dead). Jesus' main focus is on bringing about the kingdom of God. This is of apiece with the resurrection of the body and the creation of the new earth. Bringing about the kingdom of God – for example, by healing the sick and bringing liberation to the oppressed – is not just something Jesus did and calls us to do in order to make the present reality slightly less unbearable.[31] Rather, it is a part of helping to bring about the new earth, 'where righteousness is at home' and 'mourning and crying and pain will be no more' (2 Peter 3.13; Revelation 21.4).

While New Testament Christianity holds that heaven exists as an intermediate state, between this life and the resurrection of the body, it does not see salvation as an individualistic event to do with getting to go to a disembodied heaven when one dies. Instead, it is about creation being raised to a new life in God's new creation. Nor should we assume that only humans will be part of the new creation. This is likely to be bad news for people inclined to tell grieving pet-lovers that it is ridiculous or inappropriate to hope to see their pet again. The categorical 'no pets in the afterlife' kind of view arises only from a dualistic framework with its ultimate rejection of the physical and animal world from the story of salvation, and this is in fact a misunderstanding of the Christian tradition as we find it in the New Testament. In fact, we find that St Paul speaks of the whole of creation as groaning with labour pains and waiting with eager longing for the resurrection that has begun with Jesus (Romans 8.19–25).

What has all this got to do with the first half of this chapter, which was about biomedical and biopsychosocial models of depression? Christian thought is sometimes perceived in dualistic terms, as regarding the spiritual and physical as separable. When seen from a dualistic framework, depression and other forms of mental illness tend to be viewed either as spiritual problems (as in the case of the sin accounts in Chapter 1), or as physical problems (as 'just like a broken leg' in the anti-stigmatizing church campaigns discussed at the beginning of this chapter). But this kind of dualism is in fact foreign to Christianity. The doctrine of the resurrection of the body and new creation points us firmly in a different direction: that we are bodily through and through, not in the reductive, physicalist sense but in the sense that our bodies are part of who we are, and are going to be an important part of the picture when it comes to salvation, depression, or indeed anything else. The anthropology at the heart of the doctrine of bodily resurrection, then, is a corrective against the tendency to view the biological in reductive terms, but also against the tendency to separate the biological and the spiritual.

In addition to this, the doctrine of the resurrection points to the fact that we are also inherently and fundamentally social creatures, creatures whose salvation is bound together rather than discrete, and suggests to us that the alienation we experience as a result of the dualism and (relatedly) individualism of our culture is not natural to us but something that has gone wrong. Combatting alienation is hugely significant in preventing and recovering from depression. This is well recognized by mental health professionals, even if they often lack the power to do anything much about it. As professor of psychiatry Keith Meador says, 'I can't explain how many times I have yearned, though the worst of the patient's depression might be over, what I really wanted to do is write a prescription for a community, a place to belong.'[32]

In pointing to our non-reductively biological and social natures, the doctrine of the resurrection of the body shows us that Christian anthropology is neither reductively physicalist nor dualist. It shows us that in spite of alienation and the fallenness of creation, and even in spite of death, humans were created to be (biologically, socially and psychologically) whole, and gives us hope that we will be again.

Saints with animals

Earlier in this chapter I talked about how the attempt to deny our biological natures – perhaps an unconscious and collective attempt to deny our mortality – leads us to alienation from the non-human animal world, and also a denial of the needs we have as the kind of animal that we are (for example, like dogs, but not like snakes, humans need the companionship of others). Both of these things – our alienation from the non-human animal world and the denial of the needs we have as the kind of animal that we are – are detrimental to our mental health.

Growing up and living for most of my life in the north of England, the Christianity I'm familiar with is imbued with stories of Northumbrian saints – like Aidan, Bede, Hilda, Oswald and Cuthbert – and a love of places associated with them – Whitby, Durham, York and Lindisfarne. The last of these, Lindisfarne, or Holy Island, is a tidal island: twice a day, visitors can cross on foot or by car, but for the rest of the time it is cut off from the mainland. It is where in AD 635 St Aidan chose to found his monastery and where, between around 715–720, the Lindisfarne Gospels were written. If you approach Lindisfarne on foot when the tide is out you make the crossing via the medieval Pilgrim's Way. You see ahead of you a long stretch of vertical poles showing the way through the sand and mud to the island, which you spot glimmering in the distance. You hear only the sound of the birds circling above you, and perhaps also the distant 'ooo-ooo' of seals on the nearby other Farne islands. Lindisfarne and the saints who lived there cross ecclesial boundaries: it is loved not only by Catholic Christians but by Christians in Protestant traditions, including traditions in which people don't usually show much interest in saints.

One of the most famous saints who lived in Lindisfarne is Cuthbert. Cuthbert seems to have lived in Lindisfarne from 665 until 686, first as a prior and later as bishop. Cuthbert's remains were removed from Lindisfarne when the monastery was attacked by Danes, and carried by monks first to Chester-le-Street and then (following another invasion) to Ripon. Eventually they found a home in the White Church in Durham and are now in Durham Cathedral, which was built on the same site in 1093.

A legend about St Cuthbert tells of his propensity to leave the monastery every night and not return until morning prayer. On one occasion, an intrigued fellow monk sneaks out stealthily to see where he will go. He follows Cuthbert from the monastery to the sea; there he sees Cuthbert wading into the water up to his arms, chanting prayers across the sea. As dawn approaches, Cuthbert wades back to the beach, kneels, and again starts to pray. As he does, four otters run up to him and try to warm his feet by panting on them, and to dry his feet with their fur. We do not hear whether the otters' attempts at warming and drying are successful, but only that Cuthbert blesses them, and they return to the water.[33] Other stories tell us of St Cuthbert's friendship with ravens.[34]

We can put forward arguments – for example, that we should relate to animals in friendship rather than exploitatively. That, we might say, can give us something like propositional knowledge: we would be able to say 'we should relate to animals in friendship rather than exploitatively' and give reasons for this. But stories, including that of St Cuthbert and the otters, can give us what philosophers call 'knowledge by acquaintance': a non-propositional 'picture' so that we grasp intuitively what relating to animals in friendship is like, and perhaps even why it is valuable. Stories such as that of Cuthbert and the otters tell us not that friendships with animals should involve w, x, y and z, where these are propositional descriptions of the properties of friendships with animals, but that friendships with animals are 'like this'. Such stories and indeed images of saints involve our imaginations, and (whether or not we regard them to be historically true – to get caught up in this question is to miss their point), they can make a deep imprint on our view of the world.

Saints with animals is a common theme in hagiographical literature and art, whether we hear about St Anthony of Egypt who healed and whose primary companion was his pig; the injured wolf St Francis of Assisi convinced to stop eating townsfolk in exchange for being regularly fed; the deer St Giles had as his only companion and for whom he sustained an injury, or the lion whose paw the otherwise tetchy and cantankerous St Jerome healed and who became the saint's greatest friend. These stories speak to us of the proper nature of the relationship between humans and non-human animals, which will be restored in the kingdom of God, and of which (like miraculous healings) the saints' relationships with animals are a sign and a foretaste. They call to mind biblical passages about the messianic age: 'The wolf shall live with the lamb, the lion shall lie down with the kid, the calf and the lion and the fatling together, and a little child shall lead them' (Isaiah 11.6). So, our alienation from and exploitation of the non-human animal world, which is bound up with our attempt to deny our vulnerability and mortality, is not just something of which the contemporary ecological movement speaks – though this has important things to say, and it is important it does speak. It is also a thread found running through the heart of the Christian tradition.

Conclusion

> Then I saw a new heaven and a new earth; for the first heaven and the first earth had passed away, and the sea was no more. And I saw the holy city, the new Jerusalem, coming down out of heaven from God, prepared as a bride adorned for her husband. And I heard a loud voice from the throne saying:
> 'See, the home of God is among mortals.
> He will dwell with them;

they will be his peoples;
and God will be with them;
he will wipe every tear from their eyes.
Death will be no more;
mourning and crying and pain will be no more,
for the first things have passed away.'

(Revelation 21.1–4)

This passage from Revelation gets to the heart of many of the things I want to say about our biological nature: Christianity is not dualistic, but holds us to be bodily through and through, though not in a reductive way. Our cultural denial of our animality means that we are alienated from our own animal needs – say, our need for companionship; our dependence upon others. In addition to this we are also alienated from non-human animals and from the rest of our world. Our mental health suffers as a result of all these things.

The anthropology suggested by the Christian doctrine of the resurrection of the body and the new creation is not the anthropology of the biomedical or 'bio-bio-bio' model of depression. Some churches, understandably pulling away from the often dualistic sin accounts of depression we saw in Chapter 1, opt for biomedical narratives about the causes and cures of depression in an attempt to get away from the judgemental attitudes embedded in sin accounts. But the underlying physicalist and dualist anthropologies are a long way from the Christian gospel and its hope for the resurrection of the body and the transformation of the earth. In departing from the Christian gospel in this way they are also dangerous. In particular they deflect attention away from the social causes of depression and present an apolitical form of the gospel that is a tamed and diminished copy of the real gospel.

Closer to Christian anthropology is the biopsychosocial model I outlined in the earlier part of the chapter. This affirms that we are thoroughly biological and animal creatures, while also holding that there are other aspects of the human person, including the psychological and the social. A good biopsychosocial model will not see these as different parts, or the biological, psychological and social as competing explanations: it will regard us as biological, psychological and social through and through, and the different causes as interdependent. Christian theology complements the anthropology of this sort of biopsychosocial model. Themes within Christian theology such as the resurrection of the body, and saintly friendships with animals, also enrich the biopsychosocial model by telling us more about the way our animal natures are supposed to be, and giving us hope that they will be again.

I will return to some of these themes in Chapter 8. In the meantime, I'm going to turn to a very different interpretation of depression from those explored so far. This is the idea that some quite select instances of (what looks like) depression are not mental illnesses at all. Rather, it is argued, these states – usually experienced by people regarded as saintly in the Catholic tradition – are in fact dark nights of the soul, sent by God as a sign of the person's holiness in order to bring them even closer to God.

Notes

1 Cited in Amanda Holpuch (2014) (13 November), 'Christians and mental health: "This has nothing to do with whether I believe in Jesus"', *Guardian*, available at www.theguardian.com/world/2014/nov/13/evangelicals-increasingly-putting-faith-in-medicine-to-treat-mental-health-issues (all websites in Chapter 3 notes accessed 13.12.19).

2 Billy Graham (2017) (9 January), 'Answers', *Billy Graham Evangelistic Association*, available at http://billygraham.org/answer/is-it-a-sin-to-be-depressed-the-doctor-says-i-have-a-chemical-imbalance-that-can-be-treated-with-medication-but-my-friend-says-i-just-need-to-pray-and-have-more-faith/.

3 National Alliance on Mental Illness (2012), cited in E. P. Kvaale, W. H. Gottdiener and N. Haslam (2013), 'Biogenetic explanations and stigma: A meta-analytical review of associations among laypeople', *Social Science and Medicine* 96, pp. 95–103.

4 Thanks to David Sims, 27 June 2019.

5 Alternatively they might be an epiphenomenalist, and so see the desire as separate from but arising out of the brain state. See E. J. Lowe (2000), *An Introduction to the Philosophy of Mind*, Cambridge: Cambridge University Press.

6 A PDF of the comic strip is available at https://rhinehartadvanced english.weebly.com/uploads/2/2/1/0/22108252/the-complete-perse polis-by.pdf. Marji's episode of depression is recounted in the section called 'Skiing'.

7 See Sartrapi, *Persepolis*, 'Skiing'.

8 See Brett J. Duncan (2013), 'The biomedical model of mental disorder: A critical analysis of its validity, utility, and effects on psychotherapy research', *Clinical Psychology Review* 33, pp. 846–61, available at http://jonabram.web.unc.edu/files/2013/09/Deacon_biomedical_model_2013.pdf.

9 Aristotle distinguishes between four kinds of cause. See Andrea Falcon (2015), 'Aristotle on Causality', *The Stanford Encyclopedia of Philosophy*, available at https://plato.stanford.edu/archives/spr2015/entries/aristotle-causality/. Thanks to Simon Hewitt for a discussion about this.

10 See, for example, Jacquelyn Cafasso, 'What is synaptic pruning?', available at www.healthline.com/health/synaptic-pruning. Thanks to David Sims for a discussion about this.

11 Benjamin G. Shapero, Shimrit K. Black, Richard T. Liu, Joshua Klugman, Rachel E. Bender, Lyn Y. Abramson and Lauren B. Alloy (2014), 'Stressful life events and depression symptoms: The effect of childhood emotional abuse on stress reactivity', *Journal of Clinical Psychology* 70.3, pp. 209–23; abstract available at www.ncbi.nlm.nih.gov/pubmed?Db=pubmed&Cmd=ShowDetailView&TermToSearch=23800893.

12 See e.g. Andrea Schmitt, Berend Malchow, Alkomiet Hasan and Peter Falkai (2014), 'The impact of environmental factors in severe psychiatric disorders', *Frontiers in Neuroscience: Systems Biology* 8:19, available at www.frontiersin.org/articles/10.3389/fnins.2014.00019/full#B131.

13 These changes in the brain are usually spoken of as 'causes', though arguably it's more correct to say that they 'implement' depression – they are depression, at the neurological level.

14 See e.g. Sarah Dash, Gerard Clarke, Michael Berk and Felice N. Jacka (2015), 'The gut microbe and diet in psychiatry: Focus on depression', *Current Opinion in Psychiatry* 28.1, pp. 1–6.

15 This way of characterizing a dualistic view of a human person was first used by philosopher Gilbert Ryle, who argued that dualism is 'entirely false, and false not in detail but principle. It is not merely an assemblage of particular mistakes. It is one big mistake and a mistake of a special kind. It is, namely, a category-mistake' (Gilbert Ryle (1978/1949), *The Concept of Mind*, Harmondsworth: Penguin, p. 17).

16 At the time of writing, the explanation that depression is caused by a chemical imbalance in the brain has some evidence but isn't proved. On the one hand, there is indirect evidence for it because antidepressants

seem to work by acting on particular chemicals or neurotransmitters (serotonin, dopamine, noradrenaline). On the other hand, there is no direct evidence for depression being caused by a chemical imbalance because it is very difficult to measure the level of a neurotransmitter in someone's brain. If proved, it is only one of several different neurological causes of depression, and neurological causes are only one of several type of cause. See Rashmi Nemade, 'Biology of depression: Neurotransmitters', *Gracepoint Wellness*, available at www.gracepointwellness. org/5-depression-depression-related-conditions/article/12999-biology-of-depression-neurotransmitters.

17 See, for example, Carmine Pariante (2018) (10 January), 'As a psychiatrist, I know that Johann Hari is wrong to cast doubt on anti-depressants', *Independent*, available at www.independent.co.uk/voices/johann-hari-depression-anti-depressants-psychiatrists-pills-therapy-change-lifestyle-job-psychology-a8151606.html.

18 For example, Frederick Toates, Chapter 1: Explanations in mental health, in *SDK228 The Science of the Mind: Investigating Mental Health Science: Level 2: Core Concepts in Mental Health*, Milton Keynes: Open University, pp. 12–19.

19 See, for example, Kvaale, Gottdiener and Haslam, 'Biogenetic explanations'.

20 See Johann Hari (2018), *Lost Connections: Uncovering the Real Causes of Depression and the Unexpected Solutions*, London: Bloomsbury, p. 7; Duncan, 'Biomedical model'.

21 See e.g. Duncan, 'Biomedical model'.

22 See, for example, Iris Elliott (2016), *Poverty and Mental Health: A Review to Inform the Joseph Rowntree Foundation's Anti-Poverty Strategy*, London: Mental Health Foundation, available at www.mentalhealth.org.uk/sites/default/files/Poverty%20and%20Mental%20Health.pdf; Ko Ling Chan, Ruby Lo and Patrick Ip (2018) 'From exposure to family violence during childhood to depression in adulthood: A path analysis on the mediating effects of intimate partner violence', *Journal of Interpersonal Violence*, https://doi.org/10.1177/0886260518790596; Tanja Frančišković, Ljiljana Moro and Ana Kaštelan (2001), 'Depression and torture', *Military Medicine* 166, pp. 529–33.

23 See, for example, Treatment: Clinical Depression, *NHS*. Available at www.nhs.uk/conditions/clinical-depression/treatment/; Kate Loewenthal (2007), *Religion, Culture and Mental Health*, Cambridge: Cambridge University Press, p. 59; P. Cuijpers, A. van Straten, L. Warmerdam, G. Andersson (2009), 'Psychotherapy versus the combination of psychotherapy and pharmacotherapy in the treatment of depression: A meta-analysis', *Depression and Anxiety* 26.3, pp. 279–88.

24 Richard Mabey (2005), *Nature Cure*, London: Vintage, p. 14.

25 Mabey, *Nature Cure*, pp. 3–4.

26 Tom Wright (2007), *Surprised by Hope*, London: SPCK, p. 103, my parentheses.

27 See Wright, *Hope*, p. 104.

28 See Wright, *Hope*, p. 109.

29 Wright, *Hope*, p. 167.

30 Wright, *Hope*, p. 168.

31 Wright, *Hope*, p. 205.

32 Cited in Holpuch, 'Christians and mental health'.

33 See Helen Waddell (trans.) (1934), *Beasts and Saints*, London: Constable, pp. 59–61.

34 Waddell, *Beasts and Saints*, pp. 62–7.

4

The dark night of the soul

Introduction

In 2007, ten years after her death, a small portion of the letters of St Teresa of Calcutta (or 'Mother Teresa') were published. These revealed that Mother Teresa suffered something that at least *looked* a lot like severe depression for most of her very long ministry.[1] Responses to the letters were fast and furious, expressing strong opinions about the nature of Mother Teresa's mental distress, and providing a litmus test for people's different, often unconscious beliefs about mental illness and distress.

These responses are split roughly three ways. The first type of response assumes that Mother Teresa had depression, and regards the letters as evidence of an absence of faith, reflecting Christian – and secular[2] – versions of the idea that mental illness relates to personal sin or is a kind of 'spiritual illness'. Having discussed and rejected this view of depression in Chapter 1, I won't give it more time here.

The second and third types of response are in some ways the polar opposite of this, in that they see Mother Teresa's mental distress as a kind of spiritual health rather than a kind of spiritual illness. The second type of response regards Mother Teresa's mental distress as a period of spiritual growth and purgation in the mystical tradition of the dark night of the soul. Furthermore, it sees the suggestion that Mother Teresa experienced depression or another psychiatric disorder as a mistaken medicalization of a religious phenomenon. I will call this view the 'either-or' view, since it treats a period of mental distress either as depression, or else as a dark night of the soul.

The third type of response regards Mother Teresa's mental distress as properly diagnosable as depression, and *also* as a dark night of the soul. On this view, a dark night and depression can coexist. Perhaps even more than that, 'a dark night' and 'depression' might refer to one and the same experience, with the medical and religious terminology being different lenses through which mental distress is both viewed and shaped.[3] I will call this the 'both-and' view, since according to this view a period of mental distress might properly be described and treated both as depression and also as a dark night of the soul.

Which of these views one adopts is not merely a matter of theoretical concern. It's practically important in relation to how we perceive and respond to mental distress that has a strongly spiritual or religious component, and in particular that is redolent of dark night of the soul accounts. Should people experiencing mental distress that takes on a particular religious form consider medical and psychological treatment and so, ultimately, recovery? Or is doing so a kind of denial of or resistance to an experience sent by God for a spiritual purpose? Conversely, how do our answers to this question affect our theological understanding of the mental distress of Christians who seem to be depressed but whose mental distress is *not* reminiscent of a dark night of the soul?

In this chapter I will argue in favour of the 'both-and' view and against the 'either-or' one – that someone might experience both a mental illness and a dark night of the soul at the same time. I will begin by looking at the seminal texts on the dark night of the soul written by St John of the Cross, arguing that a 'both-and' view is in keeping with his account of the dark night. Then I will provide some further reasons for preferring the 'both-and' view to an 'either-or' one. Finally, I will consider whether and how St John's account of the dark night is relevant to thinking theologically about depression today. While St John's account is to be distinguished from the less specific, more popular usage that 'dark night' has come to have today, we may take from St John's account the idea that periods of mental distress, including though not limited to depression, may be occasions of divine grace. In arguing this,

I will prepare the ground for Chapter 5, which discusses ways in which depression can come to have spiritual meaning or be potentially transformative.

What is a 'dark night of the soul'?

In general conversation, and some popular self-help and/or spirituality literature, a 'dark night of the soul' has an astonishingly wide range of meanings.[4] Perhaps most often, 'dark night' is used to mean a period of mental distress, and especially one that gives rise to personal, moral or spiritual growth. In the Christian mystical tradition, the phrase has a related meaning to this, but with an important difference. In this tradition, 'dark night' refers primarily to the kind of experience thought to be described in a short poem written by the sixteenth-century Carmelite mystic St John of the Cross, and to two book-length commentaries he wrote on the poem, *The Dark Night* and *The Ascent of Mount Carmel*. In the poem, St John tells of the soul's yearning, and its journey to and union with God, in terms reminiscent of erotic love.[5] The commentaries were written several years after the poem in order to explain the poem's religious significance and provide spiritual guidance to others. In *Ascent*, St John writes about the active purgation or purification of the soul. In *Dark Night*, St John writes about the passive purgation of the soul. In other words, *Ascent* is about the task of disposing oneself to divine action, and *Dark Night* is about the effect of this divine action on the person.

When St John describes the dark night of the soul in *Ascent*, he regards it as relating generally to the life of the faith, and talks about 'darkness' and 'light' in relation to knowledge and perception: the life of faith is darkness from the perspective of the soul because the soul is blinded by a light too great for its visual faculties.[6] In *Ascent*, where the focus is on active purification, the darkness is about giving up reliance on one's own intellectual faculties (and more generally, natural reason, or knowing things through the senses), which is ultimately of little value in relation to union with God.[7]

Given that the dark night is a description for the life of faith in general and given St John's emphasis on the perceptual and epistemic dimensions of the darkness in *Ascent*, it might seem strange that 'dark night of the soul' has become so strongly associated with psychological struggle or mental distress. The reason for this becomes much more apparent in *Dark Night*, where the focus is on the dark night as passive, purgative, privative and painful.[8]

Spiritual direction was at the heart of St John's ministry or vocation, and *Ascent* and *Dark Night* were written with spiritual direction in mind. St John was troubled by the fact that many people failed to advance spiritually on account of insufficient understanding of the trials of faith. In *Ascent*, St John expresses concern that those who want to 'lean on some light of their own' will become blind, and so will be held back from the road leading to union with God.[9] In *Dark Night*, he laments that if there is no one who understands people going through a dark night:

> they either turn back and abandon the road or lose courage, or at least they hinder their own progress because of their excessive diligence in treading the path of discursive mediation. They fatigue and overwork themselves, thinking that they are failing because of their negligence or sins.[10]

St John distinguished between two kinds of dark night. The first dark night is the purification of the senses. Since prayer and contemplation give rise to joy and satisfaction for spiritual beginners and God desires to lead them on to a higher degree of divine love – one where there is not instant gratification for prayer and contemplation – God withdraws in order to liberate them from the 'lowly exercise of the senses and of discursive meditation, by which they go in search of him so inadequately'.[11] Consequently:

> it is at that time that they are going about their spiritual exercises with delight and satisfaction, when in their opinion the sun of divine favour is shining most brightly on them, that God darkens all this light and closes the door and the spring

of sweet spiritual water they were tasting as often and as long as they desired.[12]

As a result, they experience spiritual dryness: they no longer get pleasure or satisfaction from their prayer and good works, but even find these things distasteful and bitter. Not much time usually passes before beginners start to enter this dark night, and the majority do enter it: it is very common for spiritual directors to see people suffer this.

After the dark night of the senses, a person may undergo the second kind of dark night: the dark night of the spirit. St John spends some time talking about the intermediate state between the dark night of the senses and the dark night of the spirit – presumably this is also important to spiritual directors. The soul does not enter the dark night of the spirit immediately after the dark night of the senses; rather there are usually several years in which the person who will experience the dark night of the spirit 'goes about the things of God with much more freedom and satisfaction of spirit' than they did before entering the dark night of the senses.[13] During this time of serenity, certain needs and also dryness, darkness and conflict are felt. These are often more intense than those experienced during the dark night of the senses, and are like omens of the coming night of the spirit.[14]

In the second kind of dark night, the dark night of the spirit, the person thinks that they are unworthy, and that there are no more blessings for them.[15] The person feels abandoned by God, and this is the worst part of the suffering, since they are a person of faith for whom union with God is their primary desire. Saying all this is important if St John is to advise spiritual directors to encourage and comfort people experiencing the dark night of the spirit. Without encouragement, people can mistake purgation for real divine absence and mistakenly think that they are not on the right path. At the same time, it's important for the person not to be caught up with the thought that they're spiritually advanced. The spiritual director therefore needs to encourage the person so that they don't despair, while not leading them to become proud or arrogant.

In order to be effective, St John writes, the dark night of the spirit is likely to last for some years, although there will be intervals during which 'this dark contemplation ceases to assail the soul in a purgative mode and shines upon it illuminatively and lovingly'.[16] This illumination is a sign of the health of the purgation, and also a foretaste of the future.

Drawing on the poem's image of a ladder, St John describes ten distinguishable steps of the dark night of the spirit, in order to help spiritual directors gauge where their spiritual charges are on their journey towards union with God.[17] These are: being unable to find satisfaction, support, or consolation (on the first step); searching for God unceasingly (on the second); being motivated to various good works while thinking one does very little (on the third step); experiencing a habitual suffering on account of loving God (on the fourth); an impatient desire and longing for God (on the fifth); an impatient running towards and experience of God (on the sixth); and an ardent and daring boldness imparted by God (on the seventh). On the eighth step, the soul lays hold of God without letting go. The soul satisfies its desires on this step, though not continuously.[18] On the ninth step, the soul burns gently with love for God, and there are many goods and riches of God that the person enjoys.[19] The tenth step is no longer of this life, and consists in complete union with God.[20]

What does St John say about the dark night and depression?

The similarities between depression and dark night experience are numerous, and it's easy to understand why people have often linked the two, or else sought to find ways to distinguish them. The word 'depression' wasn't in use at the time, but St John makes a few scattered remarks about the relationship between dark night and melancholy. 'Melancholy' is, very roughly speaking, the precursor of 'depression', and so we might take what St John says about melancholy as relevant to depression.

It is important in trying to understand what St John says here to bear two things in mind. First, that St John does not say a lot about melancholy is itself worthy of mention. Distinguishing between a spiritual experience and a mental disorder is not St John's concern. What *is* his concern is ensuring that people who are experiencing the kinds of spiritual struggles he himself was familiar with are not discouraged through a lack of awareness that these experiences are part and parcel of faith, or at least of a certain kind of spiritual journey.[21]

Second, St John was an early modern, and had a corresponding view of melancholy. Views about melancholy were split between what we might call the biological and the sin-related. The sin-related associated melancholy vaguely with sin, which was sometimes construed in terms of personal sinfulness. The biological view saw melancholy as having a primarily physical cause – most often an imbalance of one of the four humours. Melancholy was treated medically, primarily with oral remedies thought to alleviate an excess of one of the humours – such as bile. The question of whether depression or melancholy should be treated as a physical complaint or as something to do with sin is one the substance of which St John would probably be familiar with.

When St John does write of melancholy, he is keen to distinguish it from associations of personal sinfulness. Thus, in the Prologue of *Ascent of Mount Carmel*, he cautions that:

> It will happen to individuals that while they are being conducted by God along a sublime path of dark contemplation and aridity, in which they feel lost and filled with darknesses, trials, conflicts, and temptations, they will meet someone who, in the style of Job's comforters ... will proclaim that all of this is due to melancholy ... or to some hidden wickedness, and that as a result God has forsaken them. Therefore the usual verdict is that these individuals must have lived an evil life since such trials afflict them.[22]

St John goes on to say that some spiritual directors will tell people they are falling back since they no longer find consolation in God, and that this only doubles the trials of a poor soul, since 'when this soul finds someone who agrees with what it feels (that these trials are all its own fault), its suffering and distress grow without bounds'.[23] The spiritual director might urge the person to go over their past and think about their sins, and does not understand that 'now is not the time for such activity. Indeed, it is a period for leaving these persons alone in the purgation God is working in them, a time to give comfort and encouragement.'[24] In fact, quite a lot of St John's commentary concerns not giving damaging advice to people, for example by telling them that their distress is the result of sin, but allowing divine grace to work in them.

Some people have seen in this passage a sharp distinction between a dark night on the one hand and melancholy or depression on the other, according to which an experience is either depression or a dark night, supporting an 'either-or' account of mental distress.[25] However, attention to the wider textual context shows that in fact St John is here expressing concern about a 'sin' account of mental distress, and advising a kind of pastoral gentleness and sensitivity to timing that may be thought to include people experiencing depression as well as a dark night, since depressed people often have an exaggerated sense of guilt.[26]

In another important passage on melancholy, St John distinguishes purgative dryness from superficially similar phenomena that derive from sin or imperfection, tepidity or lukewarmness, 'or some bad humour or bodily indisposition'.[27] St John provides several ways of knowing that the experience is a genuine dark night of the senses rather than the result of sin or tepidity, some of which also distinguish the dark night from 'indisposition or melancholic humour', which, he repeats, are quite different from sin or tepidity.[28]

One notable way of distinguishing a dark night from melancholy lies in the experience's effects: whether it purifies the person (as in the case of the dark night) or whether it only does harm to the person. Here St John expresses more explicitly the view that a dark night and melancholy can be compatible in the sense of being able to occur simultaneously:

Even though the dryness may be furthered by melancholy or some other humor – as it often is – it does not thereby fail to produce its purgative effect in the appetite, for the soul will be deprived of every satisfaction and concerned only about God. If this humor is the entire cause, everything ends in displeasure and does harm to one's nature, and there are none of these desires to serve God that accompany the purgative dryness.[29]

We might wonder why St John only expresses a 'both-and' view in terms of a dark night and melancholy being able to coexist, rather than in terms of them being different lenses through which to view the same experience, as others have interpreted this view.[30] Considering the reasons why St John does not articulate this view in these terms helps us to appreciate what he meant by a 'dark night of the soul', when compared with its meaning in more recent popular literature and conversation.

A significant reason why St John does not regard a dark night and melancholy as different aspects of the same experience is that he views melancholy as negative – as something for which a cure is sought – whereas he is keen to emphasize that while aspects of a dark night may be unpleasant, and even terrifying, we should see it as wholly good. St John regards his own dark night as being 'great happiness and a sheer grace for me'.[31] He worries about the negative influence of spiritual directors who tell their charges that they must be regressing in the spiritual life because of psychological struggle, when in fact the converse is the case. A dark night is, for St John, a very specific experience of divine grace, and is good through and through. This is quite different from one more recent usage of 'dark night', where the phrase tends to mean any negative experience, and draws attention to the way in which negative experiences (perhaps through divine grace) can have positive aspects or consequences.

A further reason for not describing a dark night and melancholy as different aspects of the same experience is that St John clearly thinks that although a dark night might involve psychological struggle, a person might have a dark night without having melancholy or depression. By speaking of melancholy and a dark night as different aspects of the same experience, St John would give the impression that melancholy is necessary in order to have a dark night and in order to reach union with God.[32] Again, this highlights a difference from recent popular usage of 'dark night' where it is associated much more strongly with periods of mental distress such as depression and other mental disorders. Melancholy or depression is in no way central to St John's understanding of a dark night, though he recognizes that some people will experience depression or melancholy at the same time as experiencing a dark night. It is quite possible for the two experiences to come apart.

Relatedly, for St John a dark night involves experiences such as a loss of hope and spiritual dryness – which might be similar to symptoms of depression – but also other experiences such as voluntarily ceasing to rely on natural reason, and running to God, which are not especially characteristic of depression. Again, this highlights a difference from the more recent popular use of 'dark night', where the focus is primarily on experiences characteristic of depression. St John was not trying to write a theology of melancholy or depression. Given St John's understanding and use of 'dark night' it would not make much sense for him to talk about them as different aspects of the same experience, or different lenses through which to view the experience. That makes more sense in the context of recent, popular understandings of 'dark night' where what is meant by 'dark night' is any mental distress that has transformative spiritual value.

Reasons for preferring a 'both-and' account

It seems from St John's scattered comments about melancholy that a 'both-and' view is in keeping with the dark night tradition – St John affirms that a dark night and melancholy or depression can coexist. And yet, a 'both-and' account is at odds with some discussion of a 'dark night' in psychiatric literature on the topic. For example, drawing on the work of

Jordi Font i Rodon, a Jesuit psychiatrist and theologian, psychiatrists Gloria Durà-Vilà and Simon Dein distinguish between salutary religious depression (or a dark night of the soul) and pathological religious depression (which is in the domain of psychiatry). They argue that these two have a number of similarities, which are familiar to anyone acquainted with psychiatric descriptions of depression: low mood, anhedonia, loss of interest, volition, appetite and weight, low self-evaluation, insomnia or hypersomnia, and so on. However, Durà-Vilà and Dein argue, there are also significant differences between salutary and pathological religious depression. While pathological depression is unhealthy and excessive, salutary depression involves healthy guiltiness that causes loving feelings to repair the evil caused. Salutary depression involves a clear wish to recover completely, whereas pathological depression does not. In pathological depression people become reclusive, whereas in salutary depression people continue social interaction and maintain their community life. Unlike in pathological depression, in salutary depression people do not become less active in relation to their good works or their prayer, and never cease to feel hope. In salutary depression people don't regard themselves as pathological, but consider their experience as a natural process of maturation of the spiritual life.[33] A dark night of the soul and depression are therefore presented as comparable experiences that can be distinguished from one another.

At the heart of Durà-Vilà and Dein's study are the clinical implications that arise from seeing some instances of depression as salutary or as dark nights of the soul. They argue that:

> the psychiatric conception of depression as due to a chemical disturbance of the brain relieves the patient of personal responsibility, and deprives the individual experience of any meaningful significance, possibly leading to greater isolation.[34]

They are concerned that people whose depression may have personally and especially religiously transformative elements will lose these through a process of psychiatric diagnosis and treatment. And so, they argue:

once the feelings of sadness and dissatisfaction are defined in existential terms – as is the case for people undergoing the *Dark Night* – it can cease to be pathological and it may even be resolved through the attribution of meaning, allowing the individual to reflect on the negative aspects of their life.[35]

They conclude that: 'By giving a diagnosis of a depressive episode to the *Dark Night of the Soul* psychiatrists may hold up – or even prevent – the attribution of meaning to take place.'[36] This is because the attribution of meaning to experiences of mental distress is important for the person's spiritual growth. In contrast, persuading someone that they are suffering from a depressive episode is to dismiss a person's religious interpretation of their experience.[37] Therefore, they argue, 'It is imperative that health professionals ensure that people who experience an eruption of the supernatural in their life are not treated for a biogenetic brain disease rather than a spiritual "illness".'[38]

There are some things in Durà-Vilà and Dein's argument that are absolutely right. It's important that mental health professionals take account of their patients' religious contexts, try to understand the interpretations religious communities give to particular experiences, and don't negate the good that can come from religious meaning-making narratives.

But Durà-Vilà and Dein draw an unnecessarily and dangerously sharp distinction between pathological and salutary depression, or between depression that should be treated psychiatrically and depression that should be allowed to have religious meaning. We do not know whether Mother Teresa's mental distress would have responded to psychological or medical help such as counselling, psychoanalysis or medication, for example to help her deal with her father's sudden and violent death, or the possibility of compassion fatigue[39] – but it is possible that it would. It's possible that Mother Teresa's distress would not have been virtually permanent had her spiritual directors encouraged her not only to see her suffering in dark night terms but also to seek psychological and medical help. And this applies not just to Mother Teresa in the past but to people now or in the future who might experience mental distress, and who might be told that it is a dark night of the soul and that they should therefore not seek medical or psychological help for it on the basis of this kind of view.

Conversely, it would be sad if someone who experienced mental distress were told that their depression is pathological and not salutary. There is some evidence to suggest that positive meaning is more readily available to experiences such as mental distress if the person's context and the interpretations they have available to them allow for the possibility of positive meaning.[40] As we shall see in the following chapter, some spiritual autobiographies attest that depression can and often is experienced as both pathological and salutary – as in need of cure yet also as potentially transformative; as having biological, social and other natural causes, and yet also having religious or spiritual meaning.

I think Durà-Vilà and Dein's concern to separate the dark night and pathological depression might relate to a worry sometimes expressed that medical care might somehow 'block' divine grace. Grace, on this view, is intermittent rather than continuous, and consists in occasional interventions from on high rather than being infused in the human person.[41] On this view, something is either an instance of divine grace or else a natural experience or phenomenon: both cannot work together. Durà-Vilà and Dein's worry also presupposes a latent dualism – that the things of the spirit are not the same as the things of the flesh, and so the two should be treated separately.[42] Thus, where mental distress is an 'eruption of the supernatural' in someone's life, it is a 'spiritual' event, and so cannot also be a 'biogenetic brain disease'.

This view of grace is less common in Catholic theology and we do not find it in St John's thought. St John also does not have a dualistic anthropology. And so, for example, St John's language of the purgation of the senses is not about the person being purged from the senses but the senses themselves being purged – in other words, refined and enlivened through divine grace. And the senses are not the physical aspect of the person but, like the spirit, a part of their soul. This is not obvious to modern readers, since the language of the purgation of the senses and the distinction between the senses and the spirit are often misunderstood in dualistic terms because of the pervasive dualism of our culture.

In his 2004 book *The Dark Night of the Soul*, psychiatrist and theologian Gerald May also reaches a 'both-and' conclusion, though in an earlier work he seemed to lay the ground for an 'either-or' view. I think he is right in his later work:

> In my earlier book, *Care of Mind, Care of Spirit*, I attempted to clarify the distinction between dark night and depression in modern psychological terms. I said, for example, that a person's sense of humor, general effectiveness, and compassion for others are usually not impaired in the dark night as they are in depression ... But it is not quite so simple. Perhaps the distinctions I have made ... might help distinguish depression from the dark night of the soul when there is no overlap. But my experience is that people often experience depression and the dark night at the same time. To say the least, the dark night can be depressing. Even if most of the experience still feels liberating, it still involves loss, and loss involves grief, and grief may at least temporarily become depression. Conversely, a primary clinical depression can become part of a dark-night experience, just as any other illness can.
>
> ... I want to restate this, because it can prevent unnecessary suffering and in some respects even be life-saving. If someone is experiencing symptoms of significant depression, it is important that those symptoms be recognized and acknowledged ... It's wonderful if the same person happens to be experiencing something of the dark night of the soul as well, but the presence of the dark night should not cause any hesitation about treating depression.[43]

Here, May agrees with St John: depression and the dark night are not two comparable but mutually exclusive experiences that differ with respect to whether they have natural or divine causes. Relatedly, medical treatments for depression would not 'block' divine grace or interrupt the dark night process.

Is St John's dark night of the soul relevant to thinking theologically about depression today?

Today, the term 'dark night of the soul' has taken on numerous new meanings outside theological and historical discourse. In a more popular or everyday context 'dark night of the soul' frequently refers to a distressing experience, often psychological, that has transformative potential – for example, by offering the person an opportunity to become wiser, more compassionate, more insightful, or in some other way to grow spiritually or morally. In this context, it makes some sense to view 'depression' and 'dark night' as different lenses through which to view the same experience. The term 'depression' might refer to an illness or disorder for which a cure is (rightly) sought. A 'dark night' might refer to the same experience or set of experiences, but allude to the fact that in addition to being an illness for which a cure is sought it might also have some positive meaning, for example by enabling the person to grow in various ways.

St John of the Cross was writing at a particular time and in a particular context – for sixteenth-century monastics in the Carmelite tradition whose spiritual formation would have involved quite specific things. It is easy to see why it is tempting to extend the rich and suggestive language of the dark night of the soul to psychological struggle understood religiously or spiritually more generally. At the same time, in extending 'dark night' language in this way there is a risk of conflating depression and a dark night in a way that is at odds with St John's own account. In addition, it may lead us to think that we can simply transplant St John's thought into a very different context and produce (what we take to be) the same effects. Religious traditions aren't only about individuals and beliefs (though they typically involve these things). They are also about communities and practices and specific times and places. We shouldn't assume a dark night approach would make sense or 'work' in a different context, especially if we are not sensitive to the original context, its theology and anthropology, and our own very different assumptions about these things.

That said, taking into account St John's context, purpose, and background theology and anthropology, I think we can take the following insights from St John as important for thinking theologically about depression. First, it seems clear from St John's account that someone might both be depressed and be having a dark night of the soul. Second, in such cases people should be encouraged to seek medical and/or psychological help for their depression. Seeking a cure for depression does not negate the fact or possibility that they are having a dark night of the soul, or block the work of divine grace within them. Third, a dark night is ultimately a work of divine grace upon the person. While the person's response to grace and the support of those around them is important, St John's emphasis on grace forms an important corrective to self-help literature in which (as one might expect from the genre) an individual's choice is overemphasized. St John is important in thinking theologically about depression since, in contrast to accounts that see depression as a sign of spiritual illness (such as sinfulness or lack of faith), he points to the fact that mental distress, which might involve depression (but doesn't have to), carries no implications of personal sinfulness, and may in fact be an indication of and occasion for spiritual health.

I think we might go beyond St John's account of the dark night and say that there are ways in which periods of mental struggle or distress, including depression, might be transformative in ways that are not described in his work on the dark night of the soul. That the transformative potential of experiences such as depression is not described by St John need not worry us: it is not surprising, given that St John was not trying to write a theology of depression or melancholy. My aim in the next chapter is to develop this idea in conversation with more recent spiritual autobiographers who have written about their experiences of depression. In so doing, I don't want to impose a 'dark night' paradigm on these writers or their experiences. Rather, I wish to develop an account of the way in which experiences such as depression can be 'potentially transformative' – in other words, intrinsically negative or undesirable, but nevertheless occasions of divine grace. This seems to me to be in keeping with St John's core insights in relation to the dark night and melancholy, and also to move beyond it in being relevant to more diverse contexts and experiences of depression.

Notes

1 Brian Kolodiejchuk (ed.) (2008), *Mother Teresa: Come Be My Light*, New York: Rider.

2 For example, the vehemently anti-Teresa New Atheist Christopher Hitchens wrote: 'So, which is more striking: that the faithful should bravely confront the fact that one of her heroines all but lost her own faith, or that the Church should go on deploying, as an icon of favorable publicity, a confused old lady whom it knew had for all practical purposes ceased to believe?' (Christopher Hitchens (2007) (10 September), 'The dogmatic doubter: The nun's leading critic argues that the psychic pain revealed in a new book was a byproduct of her faith', *Newsweek*, p. 41).

3 S. Taylor Williams (2004), 'Illness narrative, depression and sainthood: An analysis of the writings of Mother Teresa', *Journal of Religion and Health* 53, pp. 290–7; pp. 295–6.

4 For example, googling 'dark night of the soul' yields one website that asks: 'Are you experiencing loneliness, isolation, and depression? Do you seem to be developing new perspectives and views regarding life? If so, you may be experiencing a Dark Night of the Soul. Take our unique Dark Night of the Soul test to discover your unique percentage score here' (https://lonerwolf.com/dark-night-soul-test/). Another website relates the dark night to New Age psychospiritual categories (https://fractalenlightenment.com/28187/spirituality/7-signs-you-may-be-experiencing-a-dark-night-of-the-soul) (all websites in Chapter 4 notes accessed 13.12.19).

5 Available at www.poetseers.org/spiritual-and-devotional-poets/christian/the-works-of-st-john-of-the-cross/dark-night-of-the-soul/.

6 *Ascent* 2.3.1. St John probably has in mind here Aristotle: 'For as the eyes of bats are to the blaze of the day, so is the reason in our soul to the things which are by nature most evident of all' (*Metaphysics* 2.1). In *Dark Night*, St John makes a similar claim that 'the clearer and more obvious divine things are in themselves, the darker and more hidden they are to the soul naturally', which he ascribes to 'a certain principle of the Philosopher' (*Dark Night* 2.5.1). St John goes on to make a similar analogy to the bat one: 'The brighter the light, the more the owl is blinded; and the more one looks at the brilliant sun, the more the sun darkens the faculty of sight, deprives and overwhelms it in its

weakness' (*Dark Night* 2.5.3). Unless otherwise stated, all quotations by St John of the Cross are taken from Kieran Kavanaugh and Otilo Rodriguez (eds and trans) (1991), *The Collected Works of St John of the Cross*, Washington, DC: Institute of Carmelite Studies.

  7 *Ascent* 2.4.3. St John has Thomist/moderate empiricist leanings: 'The intellect knows only in the natural way, that is by means of the senses' (*Ascent* 2.3.2).

  8 *Dark Night* 2.5.1.

  9 *Ascent* 2.4.7.

  10 *Dark Night* 1.10.2.

  11 *Dark Night* 1.8.3.

  12 *Dark Night* 1.8.3.

  13 *Dark Night* 2.1.1.

  14 *Dark Night* 2.1.1.

  15 *Dark Night* 2.5.5.

  16 *Dark Night* 2.7.4.

  17 *Dark Night* 2.19; 2.20.

  18 *Dark Night* 2.20.1.

  19 *Dark Night* 2.20.4.

  20 *Dark Night* 2.20.5.

  21 *Ascent* 2.4.7; *Dark Night* 1.10.2.

  22 *Ascent*, Prologue, 4.

  23 *Ascent*, Prologue, 5.

  24 *Ascent*, Prologue, 5.

  25 For example, Phyllis Zagano and Kevin Gillespie (2010), 'Embracing darkness: A theological and psychological case study of Mother Teresa', *Spiritus: A Journal of Christianity Spirituality* 10.1, pp. 52–75, p. 57.

  26 For example, one of the symptoms of Major Depressive Disorder in DSM-5 is 'feelings of worthlessness or excessive or inappropriate guilt' (APA (American Psychiatric Association) (2013), *Diagnostic and Statistical Manual of Mental Disorders 5th ed.* (DSM-5), Arlington: American Psychiatric Publishing, p. 161).

  27 *Dark Night* 1.9.1.

  28 *Dark Night* 1.9.2.

  29 *Dark Night* 1.9.3. The second way of distinguishing a dark night from melancholy, St John says, relates to whether the person experiences a powerlessness, in spite of her efforts, to meditate and make use of the imagination. This is because St John thinks that in the case of melancholy inability to meditate might only be short term since, he says, if the dissatisfaction derived solely from a bad humour, 'people would be able with a little care to return to their former exercises and find support for their faculties when that humor passed away, for it is by its nature changeable'. This is only sometimes true to our experience of depression, and perhaps highlights that we shouldn't think of St John

as an infallible guide in relation to mental disorder, or that melancholy maps precisely on to depression.

30 For example, Williams, 'Illness narrative', argues that this is how we should see the relationship between depression and a dark night.

31 *Dark Night* 4.2.2.

32 St John distinguishes between melancholy and a dark night in terms of aetiology, aspects of the experience, and teleology – for example, a humour might be the entire cause of dryness, and in this case it will not be accompanied by desire to serve God, and will not have a purgative effect on the appetite. And yet a dark night and melancholy can coexist, and an experience of spiritual dryness or mental distress might, and 'often is', both a dark night and melancholy caused by a humour.

33 Gloria Durà-Vilà and Simon Dein (2009), 'The Dark Night of the Soul: Spiritual distress and its psychiatric implications', *Mental Health, Religion and Culture* 12.6, pp. 543–59.

34 Durà-Vilà and Dein, 'Dark Night', p. 556.

35 Durà-Vilà and Dein, 'Dark Night', p. 556.

36 Durà-Vilà and Dein, 'Dark Night', p. 557.

37 Durà-Vilà and Dein, 'Dark Night', p. 557.

38 Durà-Vilà and Dein, 'Dark Night', p. 558.

39 Compassion fatigue is a condition affecting people who work with victims of illness and trauma, such as healthcare professionals. Symptoms include feelings of hopelessness, anhedonia, anxiety and insomnia.

40 See C. Heriot-Maitland, M. Knight and E. Peters (2012), 'A qualitative comparison of psychotic-like phenomena in clinical and non-clinical populations', *British Journal of Clinical Psychology* 51, pp. 37–53.

41 Thanks to Peter Kevern for helping me to develop some of these thoughts in relation to grace.

42 See Gerald May (2004), *The Dark Night of the Soul: A Psychiatrist Explores the Connection between Darkness and Spiritual Growth*, New York: Harper Collins, p. 159.

43 May, *Dark Night*, pp. 155–7.

5

Can depression help us grow?

Introduction

It certainly was a time of purification for me. My heart, ever
questioning my goodness, value, and worth, has become
anchored in a deeper love and thus less dependent on the
praise and blame of those around me. It also has grown into
a greater ability to give love without always expecting love
in return ... What once seemed such a curse has become a
blessing. All the agony that threatened to destroy my life now
seems like the fertile ground for greater trust, stronger hope,
and deeper love.[1]

These are the words of Henri Nouwen, a psychologist and
Roman Catholic priest, looking back on the diary he kept
during a major depressive episode he experienced between
1987 and 1988. Nouwen's understanding of his depression
exemplifies what I will call a 'potentially transformative' view:
that through the experience of depression a person might grow
or be transformed psychologically, morally and spiritually.

The idea that depression can be transformative is not
uncommon among people who have experienced depression,
Christian or otherwise. For example, Andrew Solomon writes
that, if you yourself have been depressed you 'lose some of
your fear of crisis' and are more likely to help others who have
depression:

If you have been through such a thing, you cannot watch it
unfold in the life of someone else without feeling horrified.
It is easier for me, in many ways, to plunge myself into the

sorrow of others than it is for me to watch the sorrow and stay out of it ... Not interfering is like watching someone spilling good wine all over the dinner table. It is easier to turn the bottle upright and wipe up the puddle than it is to ignore what is going on.[2]

Other people talk about the way in which depression has, after the event, given them a heightened appreciation of beauty, and especially the beauty of the natural world. For example, one person writes that following the sudden death of her husband:

> The shock and deep depression took some years to live through, but gradually my mind became conscious of ... a more acute sense of the beauties that are around us and a thankfulness which I was not aware of before.[3]

As this suggests, people understand their experience of depression to have been transformative in different ways: because it provides them with insight that makes them happier with themselves and better at relating to others (Nouwen), more compassionate and courageous (Solomon), or more able to appreciate beauty and to give thanks for it.[4]

In this chapter, I'll explore and argue for a potentially transformative view of depression. In order to avoid a caricature of the view, I'll focus on the life and thought of Henri Nouwen, and the influences on him from the Christian and psychological traditions that helped him to see his experience of depression as transformative. I will then clarify how a potentially transformative view differs from the 'either-or' dark night idea of mental distress rejected in the previous chapter. I will argue that a potentially transformative view of depression is valuable in that it can give hope to people with depression that some good can come out of an otherwise distressing event, and so facilitate a richer therapeutic process than some other interpretations of depression (including sin, demonic and biomedical ones) are able to do.

Some serious objections have been levelled against a potentially transformative view of depression and other kinds of suffering. In the second part of the chapter, I will defend a potentially transformative view from four of these objections: (1) that a potentially transformative view can become voluntaristic and so burden people with the pressure to find positive things in negative experiences; (2) that a potentially transformative view can encourage glib and insensitive responses to people's experiences of suffering, and can portray something that is an evil – suffering[5] – as a good; (3) that a potentially transformative view can encourage apathy in the face of political and social injustice; and (4) that a potentially transformative view doesn't apply to all cases of depression, and (in particular) that it is less likely to apply to severe, permanent cases of depression. In responding to these objections, what a good potentially transformative view looks like will become clearer, and some core emphases for Christian theology will emerge.

Henri Nouwen: a case study

I began this chapter with a quotation from Henri Nouwen, a Dutch Roman Catholic priest who described his own experience of depression as 'fertile ground' for greater trust, stronger hope and deeper love. Nouwen has been one of the most popular Christian spiritual writers of the last century, alongside C. S. Lewis, Thomas Merton and others, and was known for speaking and writing with passion and energy about the unconditional love of God. In spite of his faith in God's love, he is also someone who experienced terrific loneliness and anxiety about whether he was loved by others, particularly in the earlier part of his life. Nouwen's biographer Michael Ford, drawing on interviews with Nouwen's friends and family, observes that: 'Almost as soon as Henri was able to talk, his questions revolved around whether or not he was loved. Among his first words from the playpen were, "Do you really love me?"'[6] These anxieties were projected on to God, and also became a pervasive aspect of later friendships. Nouwen's friend Jean Vanier noted that 'Aristotle said that if you are not loved, you seek admiration, and you saw with Henri that double movement: the sense of not being loved and the feeling of loneliness – and a terrific need for admiration.'[7] Other friends recount that Nouwen would often phone friends during the night, discussing his deep-seated unhappiness and feelings of loneliness.[8]

The expression of Nouwen's loneliness reached its peak in the mid-1980s, when Nouwen was in his fifties. At this time his need for affection was tapped into by an increasingly close friendship with a colleague that triggered a profound emotional response that was 'to affect him at his deepest and most painful level of need for the rest of his life'.[9] Nouwen hoped that his new friend would be his companion in life, who would ensure that he would never be alone in his struggle.[10] The sudden interruption of this friendship was the catalyst for his episode of severe depression that began in 1987. As he later reflects with his characteristic openness and honesty:

> Going to L'Arche (a community which includes people with mental disabilities) and living with very vulnerable people, I had gradually let go of my inner guards and opened my heart more fully to others. Among my many friends, one had been able to touch me in a way I had never been touched before. Our friendship allowed me to encourage myself to be loved and cared for with greater trust and confidence. It was a totally new experience for me, and it brought me immense joy and peace. It seemed as if a door of my interior life had been opened, a door that had remained locked during my youth and most of my adult life.
>
> But this deeply satisfying friendship became the road to anguish, because soon I discovered that the enormous space that had been opened for me could not be filled by the one who had opened it. I became possessive, needy and dependent, and when the friendship finally had to be interrupted, I fell apart. I felt abandoned, rejected, and betrayed.[11]

Nouwen was a celibate Catholic priest, and he was also gay – something he was aware of from an early age but was only able to come to terms with towards the end of his life.[12] In his earlier writings, Nouwen puts forward the idea that human relationships can't fulfil a person's deepest desires, and that to put faith in them as a source of fulfilment or solution to loneliness is to set oneself up for a disappointment. For example, in 1972 he wrote:

> We ignore what we already know with a deep-seated intuitive knowledge – that no love or friendship, no intimate embrace or tender kiss, no community, commune or collective, no man or woman, will ever be able to satisfy our desire to be released from our lonely condition.[13]

In the early 1980s, Nouwen was frightened that his homosexuality would be revealed. He described homosexuality as a handicap and as 'an evil state of being'.[14] During this time he is reported to have taken Catholic doctrine about homosexuality, as one person puts it, 'in a very Northern European way, interpreting it literally and basically crucifying people on it'.[15]

Nouwen's experience of depression and recovery from it seems to have made a big difference to his evaluation of human relationships and his response to homosexuality and sexuality more generally. And so, for example, in a 1992 BBC interview Nouwen said that he wanted to write more explicitly about sexuality, but that he wanted to write about it in the language of mysticism as well as of morality. He goes on to say:

> Every human being leads a sexual life, whether you're celibate, married, or whatever. Sexual life is life, and it has to be lived as a life that deepens our communion with God and with our fellow human beings. If it doesn't, then it can be harmful. I haven't found the right language for it yet but I hope I will one day.[16]

Nouwen's new understanding of sexuality, not just as a physical need but as connected to spirituality and as part of who we are at a profound level, is accompanied by a reassessment of the body. In the journal he kept during his depressive episode,

Nouwen begins to speak of the way in which people need to love and befriend their bodies, in opposition to the view that the body is something that needs to be conquered. This possibility can be realized by allowing the body to participate in the deep desire to receive and offer love, including desire 'to be held and to hold, to be touched and to touch'.[17] The aim is to 'bring the body home', which means moving towards 'integration and intimacy'.[18] Nouwen is explicitly critical of spiritual writers who 'speak about the body as if it cannot be trusted', which is true only if one's body 'has not come home'.[19]

Nouwen's own experience in this regard, as well as his thought on the topic, was undoubtedly helped during his depressive episode by the therapy he received. This included being held physically:

> It responded to a craving within him to be held ... The sessions took place fully clothed on a bed for comfort's sake, but in the context of an office. There, in the arms of his male therapist, in a primal state, he could be held very tightly and weep, scream, writhe, and be caressed, all the things a parent does when holding an infant or small child. He was held unconditionally with an enormous amount of nurture and tenderness, which was for him very healing.[20]

The pastoral counsellors who cared for Nouwen at the start of his depressive episode recall that there were aspects of Nouwen's personality that were undeveloped – his ability to trust love, to believe in his value regardless of his talents and, relatedly, to have non-manipulative friendships.[21] As one of them put it, 'here was a wounded little child, not a six-year-old, but a two-year-old or an 18-month-old who needed to be held'.[22] Nouwen's depressive episode seems to have been fertile ground for addressing these aspects of his personality and resolving his feelings of lack of self-worth, and the therapy he received seems to have provided a helpful context for doing so.

In addition to a shift in Nouwen's understanding of (his own and others') sexuality and the body, Nouwen seems to have begun to think differently about his understanding of human relationships. Whereas in the past he had talked about how human relationships cannot ultimately address our deep-seated loneliness and will disappoint us, after his depressive episode he talked about how human relationships reveal divine love and are mediated by it. So, for example, in an audio recording of a talk he made after his depressive episode, Nouwen reflects that:

> It is a fact that we live because of being touched by the love of parents and others that is only a reflection of an even greater love ... It seems to me that it is the limited experience of un-limited love that awakens us to the deep inner cry for some-one to love us unconditionally.[23]

Nouwen's depressive episode, then, seems to have been a catalyst for addressing underlying loneliness, low self-esteem, and in-ability to trust in the love of others, and through it Nouwen came to a new assessment of sexuality, bodiliness and human relationality. This helps make sense of why he talked about his depressive episode, several years afterwards, as something that seemed like a curse but had become a blessing, and as 'fertile ground for greater trust, stronger hope, and deeper love'.[24] In keeping with these things, it also prepared the ground for his ministry for people with HIV/AIDS and, towards the end of his life, his support of gay people in relationships.

Influences on Nouwen's interpretation of his depression

Nouwen's understanding of his depression was the result of his experience of depression, the loneliness and lack of self-worth he felt before it, and the healing he experienced during recovery from it. His understanding was also influenced by interpretations of suffering he had available to him through both the Christian and the psychological traditions in which he was embedded.

Within the Christian tradition, the idea that God brings good out of evil and suffering is well established. A recurring

theme in Christian worship is that the Fall of Adam and Eve
– the introduction of sin and suffering into the world – can be
described as a 'happy accident', since without these the incarnation, death and resurrection of Christ – and thus our own
redemption – would not have happened. Thus, for example, in
Milton's *Paradise Lost*, Adam exclaims that the good resulting
from the Fall is 'more wonderful' than the goodness of the
initial creation:

> Oh goodness infinite, Goodness immense!
> That all this good of evil shall produce,
> And evil turn to good; more wonderful
> Than that which creation first brought forth
> Light out of Darkness![25]

The Gospels tell the story of Jesus' own torture and execution
– a death that was considered politically expedient because
Jesus' ministry of compassion disrupted the status quo. Yet
out of the evil of Jesus' suffering and death came liberation
and new life.[26] Particularly in some strands of the Christian
tradition, it has been by (in different ways) identifying with the
suffering Christ and participating in his sufferings that we also
participate in Christ's resurrection and are redeemed.

As one might expect, Nouwen reflected deeply on the passion
and resurrection of Christ. In developing his Christology,
he referred to a Talmudic legend that speaks of the Messiah
being known by the fact that he would be sitting among the
poor covered with wounds. The legend continues, 'The others
unbind all their wounds at the same time and bind them up
again. But he unbinds one and binds it up again, saying to himself, "Perhaps I shall be needed: if so I must always be ready
so as not to delay for a moment".'[27] Nouwen argued that, like
Jesus, all healers are wounded and their woundedness is a part
of their healing power. The healer is called 'not only to care for
his own wounds and the wounds of others, but also to make
his wounds into a major source of his healing power'.[28]

Nouwen was both a priest and a psychologist, and the
Christian theology of suffering here resonates with themes in

psychology. Carl Jung famously said that 'only the wounded physician heals', which Nouwen interprets in terms of the way in which suffering can reveal insights to the wounded healer, and can increase her capacity for empathy.[29] Jung also suggests to Nouwen that through ministering to others the healer also ministers to herself. This idea was taken up particularly by psychologist James Hillman, on whom Nouwen draws extensively in his book *The Wounded Healer*, which he wrote long before his depressive episode but where he expresses ideas about the value of suffering that paved the way for his assessment that his depression was 'fertile ground'.[30] Hillman writes about how the healer is constantly striving to heal the 'wounded child' in himself in the course of healing the wounds of others.[31] Nouwen reflects this idea in his own writings. For example, on the cover of the 1972 edition of *The Wounded Healer* Nouwen writes of how, in the process of attending to the wounds of others, the 'personal interrelationship will affect the life of the minister himself'.

Another figure who brought together theology and psychology, Anton Boisen, was influential in this aspect of Nouwen's life and thought. Boisen was a chaplain to people with mental illness and became the father of the clinical pastoral education movement.[32] Boisen regarded his own sufferings as the source of his ability to help others, and wrote of how his own psychotic episode had 'broken an opening in the wall which separated religion and medicine'.[33] Boisen thought that there was no separation between the abnormal mental states we call 'insanity' on the one hand and valid religious experience on the other. Rather, what distinguishes different experiences 'is not the presence or absence of the abnormal or erroneous, but the direction of change which may be taking place'.[34] Nouwen didn't engage with the debate about the difference between pathological and religious experience. However, like Boisen, he emphasized the transformative potential of experiences of mental illness, rather than focusing only on their pathological nature: like Boisen, his emphasis was on the teleological and not just the ontological. Nouwen visited Boisen a year before Boisen's death, and reflected that: 'Seeing a man so closely and being able to experience how a deep wound can become a source of beauty in which even the weaknesses seem to give light is a reason for thankfulness.'[35]

How does a potentially transformative view differ from the view rejected in Chapter 4?

In the previous chapter, we saw the way in which some people interpreted the depression (or depression-like distress) of Mother Teresa of Calcutta as a dark night of the soul, caused by God, for which a cure should not be sought – least of all through secular interventions such as psychology or medication. I called this the 'either-or' view of the dark night of the soul, because it holds that people might either be having a dark night of the soul, or else be depressed, and I argued against it.

A potentially transformative view, such as the one Nouwen applied to his own experience of depression, is similar to the either-or dark night view in some respects. In particular, they both regard even experiences that involve significant suffering as having some potential value, rather than necessarily being totally meaningless. In this, they are both opposed to a purely biomedical account of and response to depression, according to which depression is only a problem to be solved, rather than having any possible meaning beyond that.

However, a potentially transformative view and the either-or dark night view have significant differences. For Nouwen, the suffering and distress involved in depression are only *potentially* transformative, rather than intrinsically or necessarily so. This allows for the suffering and distress itself to be seen as intrinsically negative and undesirable, and so we do not end up treating something that is an evil – suffering in general and the suffering involved in depression in particular – as a good. God brings good out of evil because God cannot be checkmated by evil;[36] but this does not stop evil from being evil.

This difference provides an overwhelming reason to prefer the potentially transformative view of Nouwen to the either-or dark night view when thinking about how to interpret depression and other kinds of mental distress. Regarding suffering as a good is not only a theoretical error: it leads to the practical idealization of suffering, to the tolerance and justification of the social conditions that give rise to suffering, to the diminishment of people's motivation to recover, and to the justification of the removal of resources such as medicines and therapies that can help people to recover. By regarding suffering as something good we idealize suffering and justify both its causes and its continuing presence, even when it is something that could be addressed.

It is worth spelling out the differences between the potentially transformative view of Nouwen and the either-or dark night view attributed by some to Mother Teresa's mental distress a little further, since these two views often get conflated. Related to the idea that on Nouwen's view depression and suffering more generally are only *potentially* transformative is the fact that depression can be seen to have natural rather than supernatural causes. A potentially transformative view, then, has space for biological, psychological and social causes and treatments. The underlying idea is that God can bring good (growth and transformation) out of evil (suffering; specifically depression). This is distinct from the idea implicit in the either-or dark night view that God causes something we usually (and rightly) assess as evil – namely, suffering and distress.

A potentially transformative view sees depression both as an illness for which a cure should be sought and also as a 'fertile ground' for a deeper kind of healing than a mere reversion to the previous, non-depressed state of existence.[37] Consequently, a potentially transformative view is open to the possibility of medicines and psychological therapies being used in the treatment of depression, while (as we saw in the case of Mother Teresa) once the experience of mental distress has been labelled a 'dark night' on an either-or view of the dark night, therapies aimed at recovery and cure are ruled out.

An either-or dark night view also means that we draw a sharp line between people whose mental distress is thought to be pathological – some kind of mental illness such as depression – and people whose mental distress is thought to be religious and to have spiritual value. Perhaps the worst affected by this are likely to be people in the latter group, who might be denied medical and psychological help for their distress. But it might also be detrimental to those in the former group, whose mental distress is regarded as pathological and not as having religious and spiritual value. A potentially transformative view is more in keeping with many people's experience, in which they find that depression is both a negative, undesirable state for which they seek recovery and also a time in which they address and resolve underlying issues so that they flourish to a degree that had not been possible before. By regarding someone's depression as only pathological and not as having potential spiritual value, an either-or dark night view may be depriving people of a helpful lens through which to view their experience.[38]

Four objections to a potentially transformative view

As Nouwen's account of his depression suggests, a potentially transformative view of depression can reflect people's real experiences, can facilitate good things coming out of evil, and can provide people with a sense of meaning and purpose while they are suffering. However, significant objections have been put forward against a potentially transformative view. I will consider and respond to the four I take to be most serious here: that a potentially transformative view can become voluntaristic and place pressure on people to find aspects of their experience transformative; that it can encourage glib and insensitive responses to suffering; that it can encourage apathy in the face of evil; and that a potentially transformative view doesn't apply to severe and permanent cases of depression.[39] Because the objections are closely related to one another, I will outline all four objections before I then go on to respond to them. Defending a potentially transformative view against these objections will ultimately show the viability of a potentially transformative view. It will also allow a pastorally helpful and theologically nuanced expression of the potentially transformative view to come to the fore.

Objection 1: Choice and blame

A potentially transformative view can go horribly wrong. Consider the words of one self-help book writer, Thomas Moore:

> Even if the source is external – a crime, rape, an abortion, being cheated, business pressure, being held captive, or the threat of terrorism – you can still discover new resources in yourself and a new outlook on life.[40]

Moore regards this kind of situation as an example of a 'dark night of the soul', but as we saw in the previous chapter this kind of view has very little in common with St John's understanding and use of the term, and is in fact much closer to a potentially transformative view. Worse than this error by far, however, is the crassness and insensitivity of telling someone that a horrendous experience such as rape is an 'opportunity to discover new resources in yourself'; the voluntarism involved in such a claim; the way this claim implicitly justifies the continuing existence of evils such as patriarchy and sexual violence; and the burden this places on people who have had horrendous experiences to find meaning in them.

Here, a potentially transformative view that should be the opposite of a 'sin' view of depression in fact becomes very close to it. In no small part this is because of the voluntarism, the emphasis on choice, that arises not only in the context of sin accounts of depression but also at times in potentially transformative accounts. This can be accompanied by pressure and a sense of blame if the person does not appear to have made the correct choice in how she responds to her suffering.

Objection 2: Glib and insensitive responses

The example of Moore's advice highlights that a potentially transformative view might not only be voluntaristic; it might also encourage glib, insensitive responses to experiences of extreme suffering. Such insensitive responses are regrettably easy to find. The risk of encouraging insensitive responses to suffering is highlighted in theologian John Swinton's *Raging with Compassion: Pastoral Responses to the Problem of Evil*. Swinton discusses theodicies (or explanations of why God allows or might allow suffering to happen) and their potential for insensitive responses to people's suffering. Among these is a 'soul-making' theodicy, which argues that God allows suffering because suffering is necessary for people to grow morally and spiritually. A soul-making theodicy holds that it is necessary to have some suffering in order for people to become compassionate, courageous, self-sacrificing, and so on, and that these characteristics are sufficiently important that God allows evil and suffering to occur in order to allow people to develop these virtues. Soul-making theodicy is different from a potentially transformative view such as Nouwen's because it is aetiological: it says not only that suffering can help us grow but also that this is the (or at least a) reason for why God allows suffering. A potentially transformative view of depression does not include this aetiological element: it talks about God bringing good out of evil, but doesn't extend this to explain why God allows evil in the first place. Nevertheless, the central thought – that psychological, spiritual and moral goods can arise out of situations of suffering – are common to both a potentially transformative view and a soul-making theodicy. Swinton's criticism of soul-making theodicy and the examples he gives of how this can encourage insensitive responses to evil are therefore also relevant to a potentially transformative view of suffering.

Swinton relates the following incident:

Her story was tragic and disturbing. Six months prior [to her coming] to me for personal guidance, her seven-year-old daughter had died of a brain aneurysm on a Sunday evening while she and her husband were attending a service in their church. The child had been left at home with a babysitter and they were summoned out of the service by paramedics who responded to the call for help. Tragic as this sudden death was ... what happened next was disturbing and the cause of outrage directed against God. The funeral service for her little girl was held in the church with the pastor officiating. During the service, in an attempt to bring some meaning and comfort to the parents, he suggested that God wanted to bring spiritual renewal to the members of the church and had selected one of their most prominent families and had taken their daughter to be at home with the Lord, where she was much better off than to live in this world. God's purpose in doing this, the pastor went on to say, was to cause the members of the church to reflect on the brevity of life and to call them to repentance and renewed commitment to the Lord. He then gave an invitation to those who wished to acknowledge their new commitment to Christ to come forward for a prayer of dedication. Following the service she never went back to the church.[41]

It is easy to see how something like this terrible response to the couple's suffering might occur in the context of depression. Imagine being told, in the midst of depression, that your suffering is (in Moore's words) an opportunity for a new outlook on life, or to discover new resources in yourself. Imagine the way that an autobiographical account such as Nouwen's could be misused to suggest that you, like Nouwen, should be able to find insights about yourself and should regard your distress as a 'precious time' or a 'blessing'. Swinton is surely right when he says, 'To tell a mother whose baby is dying of starvation that it is really for the good and that she will learn valuable lessons through the experience is to develop a ... theory that is ... in practice evil.'[42]

Objection 3: Social and political apathy

In addition to encouraging insensitive responses to suffering, a potentially transformative view may also justify evil and encourage apathy in relation to political and social justice. No baby should die of starvation. There are sufficient resources for no one to be hungry, but these are not fairly shared: the rich become much richer while the poor become poorer, even to the point of dying because of poverty. By telling a mother to focus on positive outcomes such as the valuable lessons she will learn through the experience, the speaker is deflecting attention away from the evil itself, and also from the avoidability of the evil. The speaker is in effect saying, 'Don't be angry and don't try to change society: instead, find some positive thing about the situation so that you can accept the situation lying down.'

This may sound far-fetched, but there's ample evidence to show that this is how the imperative to find and focus on some positive dimension of a negative experience (sometimes called 'bright-siding') works in practice. Barbara Ehrenreich relates the response she received when, diagnosed with breast cancer, she wrote a post about how angry she felt at a number of things, including the environmental carcinogens that contribute to the chances of people getting cancer in industrialized societies but which are allowed because of the profits they yield to the most powerful people in those societies. Responses rebuked her for her 'bad attitude' and for failing to 'enjoy life to the fullest'.[43] Ehrenreich concludes that:

> Breast cancer, I can now report, did not make me prettier or stronger, more feminine or spiritual [some of the 'positive benefits' other people posited]. What it gave me, if you want to call this a 'gift', was a very personal, agonizing encounter with an ideological force ... that I had not been aware of before – one that encourages us to deny reality, submit cheerfully to misfortune, and blame only ourselves for our fate.[44]

Swinton, too, makes this point well in the context of theodicy. As he puts it, 'If the Holocaust was a good thing because it provided opportunities to be caring, then why would we contemplate social and political actions that might prevent similar occurrences?'[45] If our primary response to depression is to point to ways in which it is or might be an opportunity for personal growth, we deflect our own and others' attention from the social causes of depression – causes such as poverty, oppression, patriarchy, homophobia, racism, casualized contracts and the instability that it gives rise to, unfulfilling work, poor living conditions, and so on. Even if we recognize these social causes in theory, we cease to look them fully in the face and seek to find ways to resist them. Instead we adopt the strategy of not trying to change our society but instead putting the burden on individuals to change their attitudes towards the problems they face.

Objection 4: A potentially transformative view applies only to milder, short-term cases of depression

A potentially transformative view seems best suited to milder and shorter-term cases of depression; it can be difficult to see how it applies to severe and permanent cases of depression. In Nouwen's case, his depression lasted for under a year. The fact that it was 'fertile ground' is due in part to the therapy he undertook as part of his recovery process. This therapy meant that he was not only cured, or able to recover: he also experienced a deeper kind of healing that meant that in his post-depression state he was happier than he had been in his pre-depression state. It would be simplistic to say that it was his recovery and the accompanying therapy rather than the depression per se that proved to be fertile ground: it was these things in combination. And yet the example of Nouwen raises the question of what a potentially transformative view has to offer to someone whose depression is both too severe for the kind of psychological exploration Nouwen's therapy involved and also long-term or permanent, so that there is no recovered state from which the person can reflect on the experience of depression with hindsight.

This is a serious objection, since a Christian response to depression (or to any kind of suffering) needs to speak to all instances of suffering and not only mild, moderate or short-term cases. A potentially transformative view of depression is not adequate if it comforts people who suffer mild or moderate amounts of suffering but has nothing to say to those who experience suffering most severely.

Responding to these objections

Response 1: Choice and blame

Is the emphasis on choice we noted in Moore's advice essential to a potentially transformative view, such that we can't have a potentially transformative view without it? Admittedly, we see something like this emphasis on choice even in a more sophisticated thinker such as Nouwen. Thus, in the last of his journal entries written during his depressive episode, when he was well on the way to recovery, Nouwen writes to himself:

> As you conclude this period of spiritual renewal, you are faced once again with a choice. You can choose to remember this time as a failed attempt to be completely reborn, or you can also choose to remember it as the precious time when God began new things in you that need to be brought to completion. Your future depends on how you decide to remember your past.[46]

Here, Nouwen sounds not a million miles from Moore. Choice is at the centre of both accounts. We have already seen in Chapter 1 some of the problems with an overemphasis on choice. Is a potentially transformative view, then, doomed on account of its implicit and intrinsic voluntarism?

I think not, because a central difference between Moore's and Nouwen's accounts lies in the fact that Nouwen is speaking only of his own experience, whereas Moore claims to be speaking to everyone's experiences of suffering. The medium is important to the message: Nouwen is writing autobiography; his account is merely descriptive of his own experience.[47] Moore is writing a self-help book; his account claims to apply to other people's experiences too, and so is prescriptive.

Surely, it might be responded, Nouwen would think that the emphasis on choice is true not only of his own experience but of other people's too. In fact, it is far from obvious that this is the case. A non-Pelagian Christian account of human nature holds that people sometimes, but don't always, have a choice, such as the choice Nouwen regards himself as having at the end of his period of depression. That humans have free will doesn't mean that their free will is unlimited or absolute. There are times and situations in which we do not have the choice that Nouwen had in front of him, or the ability to respond to an apparent choice in a particular way.[48] Transformation may have been possible for Nouwen, but it might not be possible for everyone, at least in the present life.

A potentially transformative view need not – and should not – be voluntaristic: it need not – and should not – say that people always have a choice about whether to respond to depression or another kind of suffering in a positive or fruitful sort of way. Correspondingly, it need not – and should not – put pressure on people to find good things in distressing experiences, or attribute blame to people who do not find their experience of suffering transformative in the way that Nouwen and others seem to have done.

Response 2: Glib and insensitive responses

Relatedly, that a potentially transformative view can encourage glib and insensitive responses to suffering is not an intrinsic feature of a potentially transformative view. It is something that can be guarded against by remembering that not everyone finds their experience of depression transformative: for many people, depression is merely a painful experience they would rather not have or have had. It is also a matter of practical wisdom to know whether, when and how to raise possibilities such as that a particular person's suffering might ultimately give rise to something of positive value in their lives.

Response 3: Social and political apathy

At the heart of a potentially transformative view is the idea that suffering itself is an evil and must be treated as such: it is something we should seek to eradicate and not idealize. In this, it is in contrast to the 'either-or' dark night view of mental distress attributed by some to Mother Teresa's experience, and rejected in the previous chapter. The suffering involved in depression is an evil we should hope people avoid; if they do suffer from it we should hope for their recovery and seek a cure. Provided that we remember that suffering is an evil, we shouldn't get so caught up in the possible benefits of depression that we forget that it would be better if the person did not have depression in the first place. In reality, for those of us who have significant experience of depression – whether of ourselves or of loved ones – idealizing the suffering involved in depression is, I think, unlikely.

Relatedly, we should not forget that our first priority is always to try to minimize or eradicate those social and political evils that are significant causes of depression, and to provide resources for the healing of those who suffer from depression already. In fact, one of the ways in which suffering can be transformative is that it can lead to social and political action, and so away from apathy. We see this in the life of Nouwen, for example in his ministry to people with HIV/AIDS. The transformation that can take place isn't just an interior sort of personal or spiritual growth: it is something that is worked out in the world and in relation to others. This is true not only for the suffering involved in depression but in relation to other kinds of suffering too. Ehrenreich's experience of cancer was a catalyst for her writing a much-needed critique of the harmful positive thinking movement. Rosa Parks' ongoing experience of racist oppression led to her resistance of bus segregation, and her work in advancing workers' rights and racial equality. A potentially transformative view of suffering only encourages apathy if the spirituality that accompanies it is individualistic and dualistic and concerned only with an alleged private interior life.

Response 4: A potentially transformative view applies only to milder, short-term cases of depression

There are some possible exceptions to the idea that a potentially transformative view applies only to less severe and shorter-term cases of depression. For example, David Karp talks about how his realization that his depression is almost certainly permanent has caused him to move beyond a simply problem-solving approach to mental illness to a transformative and spiritual one:

> The recognition that the pain of depression is unlikely to disappear has provoked a redefinition of its meaning, and re-ordering of its place in my life. It has taken me more than two decades to abandon the medical language of cure in favour of a more spiritual vocabulary of transformation.[49]

Nevertheless, the objection seems broadly correct. In the case of Nouwen we saw that transformation was made possible not just by the experience of depression but also by his recovery process and the therapy that took place as part of that. As we have seen, one of the ways in which Nouwen sees suffering as transformative is that it is the basis for being a good healer of others. While the woundedness is conceived of as in some sense ongoing, it nevertheless seems that the person must have accepted and understood their woundedness, and have enough distance from it to reflect on it, even if they are not completely cured of it. Being in the midst of a very severe depression is not likely to be a place from which we can minister to or help others. If depression is both severe and permanent, it is less easy to see how the person's suffering might be transformative.

Here a Christian response might point beyond the present life to future hope. As we saw in Chapter 3, for Christians the resurrection of Christ isn't just something that happened to Jesus: it is the basis of Christian hope for the future transformation of the world and for the lives of people and other creatures within it. In the present life, through the life of Nouwen and others, and perhaps through our own experience, we might see 'in a mirror, dimly' (1 Corinthians 13.12) how even experiences of suffering can be transformative. However, it is only at what gets called the general resurrection, at the creation of a new heaven and a new earth, and not just as individuals but in communion with others, that our own transformation and the transformation of our suffering will be complete.

Conclusion

In this chapter I have argued that suffering such as that involved in depression is potentially though not necessarily transformative in this life. I have maintained that suffering itself is evil, and should not be idealized. Relatedly, I have argued that we should seek to eradicate the sources of suffering. At the same time, the Christian story tells us not only that God brings about good despite evil but that God even brings good out of evil. Good might be brought out of evil in this life, though we are called to look forward to the next life for complete transformation. This provides hope for people who suffer, including those whose suffering is severe and permanent.

I will return to this theme of resurrection and hope in Chapter 8. Before that, I want to consider an alternative (though not necessarily mutually exclusive) emphasis that is sometimes put forward in Christian responses to depression. This is the fairly recent idea that God suffers with sufferers, and is the topic of Chapters 6 and 7.

Notes

1 Henri Nouwen (2009), *The Inner Voice of Love: A Journey through Anguish to Freedom*, London: Darton, Longman and Todd, pp. 97–8.

2 Andrew Solomon (2001), *The Noonday Demon: An Anatomy of Depression*, London: Vintage Books, p. 499.

3 Alister Hardy archive, 000435.

4 See Anastasia Philippa Scrutton (2020), 'Beauty experience in depression recovery', in *The Philosophy of Suffering*, ed. Michael Brady, Jennifer Corns and David Bain, London: Routledge.

5 Some people have argued that suffering is not in itself an evil. For example, John Swinton argues that evil only occurs where suffering is accompanied by 'the absence of hope that there is meaning and order in the world or a God who offers providential care', but that suffering per se is not evil. In order to illustrate this, he gives the example of a young woman who killed herself after experiencing many years of child abuse at the hands of her father and brother. At the end of her life, she questions the existence of a loving God. It is because of this, Swinton argues, that her suffering was not just 'tragic suffering' but actually 'evil' (John Swinton (2007), *Raging with Compassion: Pastoral Responses to the Problem of Evil*, Cambridge: Eerdmans, p. 59).

We should reject this move, and maintain that suffering itself is evil. The suffering of the child was itself evil, and would be evil even if it hadn't led her to question her faith. To say otherwise is not only counterintuitive. It is also to let the socially and politically apathetic features of soul-making theodicy in through the back door: perhaps this or that kind of suffering will actually bring someone closer to God rather than the reverse, so why should we not resist it or consider it actually good? It is also not clear why we would seek to avoid the suffering of non-human animals or other humans who don't have the cognitive capacity to question God's existence or love on the basis of suffering – unless we say that their suffering may make more cognitively able humans question God's love or existence. To do this would be to instrumentalize the suffering of non-human animals and people with cognitive impairments. This is both dangerous and objectionable.

It is true that sometimes instances of suffering have some good consequences. But it is part of the potentially transformative view that I am arguing for here that this is a case of God bringing good out of evil, not suffering being good. Likewise sometimes a smaller amount of evil might be necessary for some good end. That doesn't mean that the evil isn't itself evil. A woman may experience suffering (morning sickness, labour pain) in order to bring a child into the world. The fact that a child being brought into the world is a good thing doesn't mean that we shouldn't seek to find ways to relieve or cure morning sickness and labour pain. It just means that there are lesser evils that people voluntarily go through for a greater good.

6 Michael Ford (1999), *Wounded Prophet: A Portrait of Henri J. M. Nouwen*, New York: Doubleday, p. 72.

7 Jean Vanier, cited in Ford, *Wounded Prophet*, p. 152.

8 Ford, *Wounded Prophet*, xiv, p. 31.

9 Ford, *Wounded Prophet*, p. 54.

10 Ford, *Wounded Prophet*, p. 216.

11 Nouwen, *Inner Voice*, x, xi.

12 Ford, *Wounded Prophet*, xv, p. 73.

13 Henri Nouwen (2008), *The Wounded Healer: Ministry in contemporary society*, London: Darton, Longman and Todd, p. 84.

14 Ford, *Wounded Prophet*, pp. 59, 66, 140–1.

15 Anon, cited Ford, *Wounded Prophet*, p. 141.

16 Nouwen, cited Ford, *Wounded Prophet*, p. 211.

17 Nouwen, *Inner Voice*, p. 17.

18 Nouwen, *Inner Voice*, p. 17.

19 Nouwen, *Inner Voice*, p. 28.

20 Anon, cited in Ford, *Wounded Prophet*, p. 170.

21 Ford, *Wounded Prophet*, p. 166.

22 Gavigan, cited in Ford, *Wounded Prophet*, p. 167.

23 Henri Nouwen (2009), *Home Tonight: Further Reflections on the Parable of the Prodigal Son*, London: Darton, Longman and Todd, pp. 114–15.

24 Nouwen, *Inner Voice*, pp. 97–8.

25 This idea of a happy accident or *felix culpa* is also found in the early and medieval Church. For example, the fourth-century bishop St Ambrose of Milan describes Adam's Fall as a 'fortunate ruin', since on account of his sin, greater good came to humanity than would have come had Adam remained innocent. See Victor Haines (1982), *The Felix Culpa*, Washington: American University Press.

26 See Nouwen, *Wounded Healer*, p. 82.

27 Nouwen, *Wounded Healer*, pp. 81–2.

28 Nouwen, *Wounded Healer*, p. 82.

29 Carl Gustav Jung (1995), *Memories, Dreams, Reflections*, London: Fontana, p. 134; Nouwen, *Wounded Healer*, xii; Nouwen, *Inner Voice*, p. 88. Recently, some research has suggested that in general having suffered might decrease rather than increase people's empathy for people suffering the same thing – see https://hbr.org/2015/10/its-harder-to-empathize-with-people-if-youve-been-in-their-shoes. Some nuance is required in how these results should be applied to individual cases, but they certainly serve as a warning against the idea that suffering is always or automatically transformative.

30 James Hillman (1967), *Insearch: Psychology and Religion*, New York: Scribner and Sons; Jung, *Memories*, p. 156.

31 Hillman, *Insearch*, p. 5.

32 Ford, *Wounded Prophet*, p. 81.

33 Anton Boisen (1960), *Out of the Depths: An Autobiographical Study of Mental Disorder and Religious Experience*, New York: Harper and Brothers, p. 91, n. 92.

34 Boisen, *Depths*, p. 135, n. 92.

35 Nouwen, n.d., as cited in Ford, *Wounded Prophet*, p. 91.

36 See Edward Schillebeeckx (2014), *The Collected Works of Edward Schillebeeckx, Vol. 10: Church: The Human Story of God*, London: Bloomsbury T & T Clark, p. 32: 'human beings, not God,

prepared the cross for Jesus – though God did not allow himself to be checkmated by this'.

37 See William James (1906), *The Varieties of Religious Experience: A Study in Human Nature*, Pennsylvania: Pennsylvania State University Press. James describes the post-melancholy state not as a 'mere reversion to natural health' but as a kind of 'redemption' and as involving 'a deeper kind of consciousness' than the person could enjoy before (p. 156).

38 This raises the question of whether and to what extent people need to have the concept that something good might come out of a negative experience in order to have the experience of this being the case, or whether they might have this experience without a pre-existing concept of or commitment to the idea. Evidence suggests that it is likely that having the concept that something good might come out of a negative experience would increase the chances that people would make sense of their experiences in this way, and this would be a more fruitful framework for transformative experience than one that denied the possibility. See, for example, Samuel B. Thielman and Glenn Goss (2018), 'Ethical considerations for mental health providers responding to disasters and emergencies', in John R. Peteet, Mary Lynn Dell and Wai Lun Alan Fund (eds), *Ethical Considerations at the Intersection of Psychiatry and Religion*, Oxford: Oxford University Press, pp. 221–33; esp. pp. 228–9.

39 See Anastasia Philippa Scrutton (2015), 'Two Christian theologies of depression', *Philosophy, Psychiatry and Psychology* 22.4, pp. 275–89. Reprinted in *Psyche and Geloof*, 2017, 28.1, pp. 3–17. Thanks to two anonymous peer reviewers of this paper for raising these objections.

40 Thomas Moore (2005), *Dark Nights of the Soul: A Guide to Finding your Way through Life's Ordeals*, London: Piatkus, p. xvi. See also, for example, Ann McNerney (n.d.), *The Gift of Cancer: A Call to Awakening*, Baltimore: Resonant Publishing: 'cancer is your ticket to your real life. Cancer is your passport to the life you were truly meant to live' (p. 183); 'Cancer will lead you to God. ... Cancer is your connection to the Divine' (p. vii), cited in Barbara Ehrenreich (2009), *Smile or Die: How Positive Thinking Fooled America and the World*, London: Granta, p. 29.

41 Ray Anderson (2002), *Dancing with Wolves, Feeding the Sheep: Musings of a Maverick Theologian*, Eugene, OR: Wipf and Stock, p. 11, cited Swinton, *Raging with Compassion*, p. 19.

42 Swinton, *Raging with Compassion*, p. 13, my parentheses. Here I have substituted 'theory' for Swinton's 'theodicy' in order to show how the quotation applies to a potentially transformative view as well as to a soul-making theodicy (since I take 'theory' to include both).

43 Ehrenreich, *Smile or Die*, p. 32.

44 Ehrenreich, *Smile or Die*, p. 44.

45 Swinton, *Raging with Compassion*, p. 28.

46 Nouwen, *Inner Voice*, p. 96.

47 Thanks to Theodora Hawksley for pointing out the relevance of the genre here.

48 St Augustine of Hippo cites Philippians 2.13, Romans 9.16 and 1 Corinthians 4.7 in defence of the view that divine grace is required not just to act in a particular way but also to will a particular thing. This, he thinks, is due to the fallenness of humanity – to the fact that human nature is fractured and broken rather than being how it was intended to be at creation and how it will come to be through redemption.

49 David Karp (2001), 'An unwelcome career', in N. Casey (ed.), *Unholy Ghost: Writers on Depression*, New York: Morrow, pp. 138–48, p. 148.

6

Can God suffer?

Introduction

In her 2017 book *Toward a Theology of Psychological Disorder*, psychologist and theologian Marcia Webb argues in favour of passibilism – the idea that God suffers – as the most helpful theological response to mental illness. It is by acknowledging the reality of God's suffering that the Church, and in particular all those within the Church who have psychological disorders, will come to know greater comfort and strength.[1]

Before we consider the detail of these claims and their relevance to depression, it is necessary to take a step back and consider the theological background of the ideas involved. Questions about whether God can suffer, and in what sense God can suffer, are bones of contention in Christian theology. One important split is between impassibilists – people who believe that God cannot suffer in Godself – and passibilists – people who believe that God suffers in Godself. Impassibilism was the majority voice up until the beginning of the twentieth century, and passibilism was even regarded as a heresy by the early Church (called 'Theopassianism'). Around the beginning of the twentieth century, much Christian theology, and especially liberal Protestant theology, did something of a U-turn and increasingly affirmed passibilism instead. As Marcel Sarot puts it towards the end of the twentienth century:

> during this present century the idea that God is immutable and impassible has slowly but surely given way to the idea that God is sensitive, emotional and passionate ... By now the rejection of the ancient doctrine of divine impassibility

has so much become a theological common place, that many theologians do not even feel the need to argue for it.[2]

One reason sometimes given for passibilism is that, in Dietrich Bonhoeffer's frequently cited words, 'only the suffering God can help' in the face of extreme suffering. Writing from prison on account of his work for the anti-Nazi German resistance movement, Bonhoeffer was speaking of the way in which the Pauline idea of strength in weakness, embodied in the life and death of Jesus, may enable Christians to challenge a political regime that values brute power and invulnerability. Many people have found that Bonhoeffer's phrase resonates with problems faced today, which include the stigmatization and alienation of people with mental illness. An emphasis on vulnerability and fragility within the divine life, passibilists such as Webb argue, has the potential not only to comfort those who experience distress but also to challenge stigmatizing attitudes to mental illness within churches and beyond. In contrast, impassibilism can be explained by the fact that:

> over the millennia the Church has sometimes hesitated to admit her members may be vulnerable and suffer because we have not always accepted a God who chose to be vulnerable and to suffer ... We have too often failed to recognize God's strength in weakness; in this, we have misunderstood our God and also ourselves.[3]

Of course, claims about a suffering God are more likely to be comforting or helpful if the person believes them to be plausible. They're less likely to be comforting or helpful if the person feels unable to believe them to be true.[4] Someone might reject passibilism because they see it as hard to reconcile with other things believed about God, or think it misunderstands the nature of God altogether. In addition to this, many impassibilists disagree with the claim that a suffering God is helpful or comforting. They say that it's precisely in *not* suffering, in God's blissful equanimity in the face of suffering, and in the reassurance that gives that all will in the end be well, that comfort lies. So, there seem to be two distinct though related issues we need to deal with in order to examine a passibilist theology of mental disorder. One is about whether it's plausible that God can suffer, given other things Christians think about God, and the other is about whether God being able to suffer is helpful, pastorally and politically. This and the following chapter concern these two issues. In this chapter, I'll look at whether the idea of a suffering God is plausible. Consequently, this chapter will be fairly theology and philosophy heavy. This will prepare the ground for Chapter 7, in which I'll talk about the helpfulness (or otherwise) of passibilism, particularly in the context of mental illness.

I have argued for a form of passibilism elsewhere, but my aim is not to do that in this chapter.[5] Rather, it is to come to some understanding of what motivates people to think that God suffers or doesn't suffer, which I hope may enable readers to reach a decision about where their theological commitments lie for themselves, while also enabling sympathy with people who reach the other conclusion. Because my aim is to foster under-standing of both positions rather than to advance my own, I've opted for an imaginary student radio panel discussion format. This enables both sides of the argument to be heard, and might make for easier reading. A summary is provided at the end for readers who find that metaphysical discussions induce a yawn and who want to skip the main body of the chapter.

The discussion panel consists of an interviewer – a student who is part of a college Theology Society that runs a student radio programme – and two of her (imaginary) professors: Greg, a passibilist, and Catarina, an impassibilist who is strongly influenced in her view of God by the work of the medieval philosopher Thomas Aquinas. Greg's and Catarina's positions represent two significant strands within the Christian tradition on the topic of passibilism today.

Does God suffer? A radio panel discussion

Catarina, Greg and the interviewer enter to Shakira's 2005 song, 'How do you do'.[6]

Interviewer: Hello everyone, and thank you for joining us for our discussion panel today. Today in the studio we have Greg Keelham and Catarina Ribeiro, both professors in the Department of Theology, Philosophy and Religion.

Welcome Greg, and welcome Catarina, and thank you for coming today to tell us about why you think God does or doesn't suffer. Catarina, let's start with you. It may seem strange, especially given the Christian emphasis on the suffering of Jesus and the revelation of God's love in the person of Jesus, that the traditional Christian line is that God does not suffer or (in Shakira's words) 'walk in our shoes'. Why might the vast majority of the Christian tradition up until the twentieth century ever have thought this?

Catarina: Well, because susceptibility to suffering is difficult to reconcile with some of the other things Christians traditionally think about God. God is thought of as all-powerful, and yet suffering overcomes us and is beyond our control. God is thought of as unchanging, and yet suffering requires change. God is thought of as eternal or outside time, rather than everlasting and within it, while suffering requires a being to be in time.

Interviewer: OK. I think some people might be listening in and asking, but what about Jesus? Isn't it the case that Jesus suffered, and Jesus is God, and so obviously God suffered?

Catarina: That's a very good question. The key difference is that for a significant part of the Christian tradition – articulated, for example, at the Councils of Chalcedon and Ephesus in the fifth century – the way in which God suffers is solely and only to do with the suffering of Jesus. It's quite true that Jesus is God, and Jesus suffered on the cross, and so we can say that God suffered. But, according to this sense of 'God suffers', we could also say that 'God died', 'God was born of Mary', 'God spoke Aramaic and had a beard' – and, conversely, that 'that person, Jesus, created the world'.[7] In saying that, we wouldn't mean that God in Godself was actually born or died or spoke Aramaic and so on. Crucially, according to this traditional view, God is impassible – invulnerable to suffering in Godself – just as God is incorporeal (has no body), immutable (incapable of change), and eternal (outside time).

Interviewer: So, Christians could say things like 'God suffered', but without thinking God suffered in Godself. Isn't that a bit ... disingenuous?

Catarina: Well, it would be if they were doing it to be deliberately misleading! But they weren't – they went down that line because they wanted to take seriously the unity of the person of Jesus. They wanted to say that Jesus was both human and divine, but that Jesus wasn't two separate persons – just one person with two natures.

Interviewer: And so they were looking for a way of speaking that made sense of the belief that Jesus is God, and that Jesus had certain experiences that you'd expect a real human being to have?

Catarina: Yes, exactly. And they were doing that while also recognizing that God doesn't have experiences like being born and suffering and dying and so on. They're the sort of things that happen to creatures, but not to God – at least not to God in Godself, or in God's own nature.

Interviewer: OK! So let's consider why we might think suffering isn't the sort of thing that could happen to God, at least in God's own nature. You said a minute ago that God is eternal or outside time, rather than everlasting and within it. Could you explain a bit about what you mean by that, and why you think suffering requires a person to be in time instead?

Catarina: Yes. A distinction is sometimes made between the idea that God is eternal (timeless or outside time) and the idea that God is 'sempiternal' (everlasting, and in time). Beginning with Augustine of Hippo and Boethius, the idea that God is eternal has historically been the dominant position in Christian theology and philosophy. Boethius draws several analogies to explain what eternity might be like. One is of a person at the top of a mountain, who is able to take in at a glance everything beneath her: God is like that person, but for God the 'everything' that is being taken in at a glance is spread across time as well as across space. Another analogy compares God to the centre of a circle. The centre of the circle bears the same relation to all points on the circumference of the circle, just as God bears the same relation to every point in time.[8]

For Boethius, the idea that God is eternal is important. Without it, it's hard to see how God could have foreknowledge and humans have free will. If God knows I am going to eat cake tomorrow, how could I be free to choose not to eat cake tomorrow? By denying that God is in time, Boethius denies that God has foreknowledge – instead, God has present knowledge of my eating cake tomorrow, just the same as God has present knowledge of my talking to you about eternity now. Both tomorrow and right now are immediately present for God, and so the problem of God's foreknowledge undermining my freedom not to eat cake doesn't arise.

Eternality is difficult to reconcile with divine suffering, because eternality means that God is outside time, and so doesn't change. Perhaps we could say that in theory it is possible that God suffers eternally, rather than in time. But the implications of such a view are theologically horrible! Far from being blissful, an eternally suffering God would never cease to suffer. Even if creation were redeemed and human suffering and sin ceased, God's suffering would remain as real as ever.[9] And what's more, if the blessedness of the saved consists in sharing in the divine joy, it couldn't be achieved, since God could never experience perfect happiness. So, I don't think eternality can be reconciled satisfactorily with divine suffering.
Interviewer: Thanks, Catarina. That raises an interesting challenge for someone who thinks God can suffer. Greg, do you agree that passibilists have to reject divine eternality, and if they do, how can they answer Boethius' concern about foreknowledge and free will?
Greg: I agree that if we accept that God suffers, we have to give up divine eternity and be sempiternalists instead – we have to think that God is inside time rather than outside it. But there are other ways of answering Boethius' concerns about free will

and God knowing things in advance, and so being a sempiternalist doesn't worry me.

Interviewer: OK, what other ways of answering Boethius' concerns have you got in mind?

Greg: Well, there are several possibilities that get discussed, but here's just one possibility ... We might think that the future doesn't exist yet, and so in that case it doesn't make sense to say that statements about the future are true or false.[10] If that's right, then statements about the future that concern things that we might or might not do (such as 'Catarina will eat cake tomorrow') aren't either true or false – they're just undecided. And if that's right, then 'foreknowledge' or knowledge of things we will do in the future isn't a possible kind of knowledge, because facts about it don't yet exist. God can't be deficient in not having knowledge of certain facts if there's no knowledge of those facts to be had! There are other possibilities too ... But I think this is enough to show that Boethius worried too much about foreknowledge and free will.

Interviewer: Yes! OK, let's get back to the question of divine suffering. Catarina has given one reason why she thinks God can't suffer – namely, that it just doesn't fit with the other things we think about God. Could you explain why you're so keen on the idea that God does suffer? Some people have recently argued that a God who couldn't suffer couldn't offer consolation, and so would be deficient rather than a perfect being[11] – is that why you believe in a suffering God?

Greg: Hm, well, to be honest I'm not a big fan of that argument, at least as it's usually expressed. One reason is that not everyone thinks a suffering God *is* consoling. Some people, on the contrary, find a God who does not suffer – who is blissful in the face of suffering and points beyond it – far more consoling.[12] So, the argument you mentioned presupposes that we should take religiously helpful characteristics as evidence of God's nature – which is questionable in itself – but doesn't take account of the fact that people have differing intuitions about what is, in fact, religiously helpful. We would, at the very least, have to make an argument for why a suffering God *should* be considered more consoling in spite of *some* people's intuitions to the contrary.

Relatedly, there are different kinds of consolation. The kind of consolation we get from someone who suffers exactly the same thing as us at the same time – say, when members of a family grieve together over a relative's death – is not the same as the kind we get from someone who's been through something similar in the past and has undergone healing, but who can still remember enough of what it's like to enter the suffering person's predicament. And that's different again from the kind of consolation we get from someone who transcends suffering altogether, but who instead points beyond it to a much happier state and gives us confidence that ultimately our own suffering will be overcome. The idea that a God who suffers with us is consoling gets put forward, but it raises difficult questions. What kind of 'suffering-with' does God have? Why is it consoling? Who's it consoling to? And those things aren't specified in much detail by passibilists – claims are made that 'God suffers with us' but what that involves is never really spelled out. So I'm not impressed by those arguments for passibilism.

Catarina: I totally agree!

Greg: Yes! But I think there are some better reasons for thinking that God suffers … One reason is based on the idea that God knows all there is to know, and starts with a thought experiment. Imagine there is a person called Mary who is imprisoned from birth in a black and white room. Mary becomes a brilliant scientist who specializes in colour and colour perception, which she learns about via black and white books, and using a black and white computer. So up until this point, Mary has only ever seen black and white, and no (other) colours. One day, Mary escapes, and sees a red flower – the first time she has ever seen red in her life, despite knowing everything there is to know about red, and about seeing red. The thought experiment asks us: Do you think Mary learns something new when she sees red for the first time? And how would you describe what it is that she learns?[13]

I (and many others) think that one thing that Mary learns is what seeing the colour red is *like*. Learning what the colour red is like can be described as gaining a kind of 'experiential knowledge', whereas the knowledge of colour perception that she had before she saw red was only a kind of 'proposi-tional knowledge' – at that point, Mary only had knowledge of true facts about colour perception. Importantly, experien-tial knowledge does not seem to be reducible to propositional knowledge. If Mary had stayed in the black and white room, then she might have learned even more facts about colour per-ception, perhaps as more knowledge of the human brain and colour perception became available. But that could never have given her experiential knowledge – knowledge of what the experience of seeing red is actually like.

If God really knows everything, then we might think that God should have experiential as well as propositional knowledge.[14] God should not only know facts about colour perception, but also know what it's like to see red. In addition to colour per-ception, we might think that an omniscient God would know what it's like to have feelings or experience emotions, and this kind of knowledge can only be got by actually having feelings or experiencing emotions. Some of these emotions are going to involve suffering – for example, I would want to say that God knows *what it's like* to feel sadness and so on. It seems strange to think of a God who knows all the true facts about the world but doesn't know what it's like to feel sad – something that's an integral part of human and other animal existence. It would mean that God is all-knowing in some respects (for example, in relation to propositional knowledge), but really quite ignorant in other respects (for instance, in relation to what it's like to feel sad).

Interviewer: Catarina, are you persuaded by that?

Catarina: Well, not really. I don't think it always follows that we need to have experienced something to know what it's like to experience it. Think of the film *Blade Runner*. In it, there are robots – who don't know they're robots and who have emo-tions just as you and I do – who have false memory implants. They think they've experienced things when they haven't. You could imagine a robot who came into being five minutes ago, but who thinks she experienced a certain kind of suffering 30 years ago. I think in that case you'd want to say that she knows what that suffering was like, in the same way you or I do when we have a memory of suffering. But she hasn't actually experienced that suffering, she only believes she has. So knowing what suffering is like, and having experienced suffering, could conceivably come apart. Someone doesn't necessarily have to have experienced suffering to know what suffering's like.

But a much bigger problem with Greg's argument lies in its implications: what happens when we apply it to other aspects of human experience? I mean, as Greg has expressed the argument, in order to be all-knowing, God would have to know what it's like to feel everything humans experience. And it seems he thinks that knowing what it's like to feel whatever it is involves actually feeling whatever it is. But what happens when we apply this to other aspects of human experience? Must God know what it's like to feel, and have experienced feeling, envious – or sadistic – or horny?[15] (*Embarrassed laughter.*)

Greg: That is a big problem! The best solution I've come across to help with this relates to the idea of empathy. Empathy – at least as Edith Stein and others define it – is second-person knowledge of a first-person emotional state. So if I empathize with your grief, say, it doesn't mean that I feel the grief exactly as you feel it. In that case it'd cease to be empathy, and simply be grief! Rather, I feel for and with you as you feel grief.[16] So maybe God might be able to experience those problematic feelings – sadism and envy and so on – in a second-person or empathetic kind of way, rather than in Godself.

Catarina: Well, it seems pretty dodgy to me to say that God empathizes with feelings of sadism and horniness and the rest of it. But suppose we accept that there are some kinds of empathy that would make that OK. You're left with another puzzle: why shouldn't we say that God also *suffers* in this empathetic, second-person kind of way? What makes suffering rather than sadism or horniness something that we should ascribe to God in Godself, rather than just experiencing it in a second-person sort of way?

Greg: I think it's this ... At the heart of the Christian faith is the promise that all will be well – but it's difficult to see how we can trust that all will be well unless God knows just how 'bad' the badness really is. In particular, we know that human suffering does not end as soon as external forces – say torture, rape, war – cease to inflict harm on people. Rather, severe evils cause ongoing psychological damage. Someone who is tortured may experience depression or post-traumatic stress disorder. That all will in the end be well requires not *only* that no new suffering will be inflicted by external forces; it requires that the hurt caused by past sufferings will be healed. So, the Psalms say that God will 'heal the broken-hearted and will bind up their wounds', and in Revelation we're told that God will 'wipe every tear from our eyes'.

To me, this raises the question: how is a God who has no experiential knowledge or understanding of, no personal acquaintance with, extreme suffering able to claim that he is going to heal the broken-hearted, the traumatized, the people whose spirits are broken by the pain they've been caused? Such a being would be unable fully to know the 'badness' of the damage caused to the person – and so unable to assess whether the healing they offer will be adequate to heal those whose suffering is deep-rooted, whose suffering has affected their personality deeply and over time. Note that this is not about goods in the afterlife that 'make up for' or compensate for the badness. It's about whether certain kinds of wounds – those that have been most deeply inflicted – could be healed through an encounter with God. Ultimately, I suggest, if the God who promised these things were incapable of suffering, and so of knowing the nature of the harm caused, God's claim to heal wounds and make all things well would lack credence or ring hollow. And so, to my mind, thinking that God cannot suffer calls into serious question Christian eschatological hope – hope about what will happen at the end of time.

Interviewer: I've got a couple of questions coming in from listeners. First, Greg, you said earlier that you reject the argument to do with consolation, but this one sounds quite like it. Does that mean you do agree with the argument about consolation after all?

Greg: Thanks for getting me to clarify. I think they are different arguments, but in the same ballpark in that they are both related to quite practical or pastoral concerns, rather than primarily metaphysical ones. The consolation argument says that if God is impassible then God is not able to console, and if God isn't able to console then God can't be a perfect being, and if God isn't a perfect being then God wouldn't be God after all – and so we have to say God is passible. I reject that because I think that the idea that if God is impassible then God is not able to console is questionable – some people find an impassible God more consoling. I also think there might be other problems with the bit that says that if God isn't able to console then God isn't a perfect being. I don't think we can so easily derive things about God's nature from what is (thought to be) religiously helpful. We could easily end up constructing a God based on wish fulfilment that way.

The argument I'm putting forward instead is to do with what we might call 'epistemic warrant' – what we (and God) can claim to know and why. I can claim to know what it's like to be a white male in academia, but if I said, 'I know what it's like to be a black woman in academia', Catarina could rightly say, 'No, you don't, you've never been one.' So, I have epistemic warrant to say that I know what it's like to be a white male, but not epistemic warrant to say what it's like to be a black woman – if I claimed to, I'd rightly be criticized for overstepping the mark epistemically. I'm saying that an impassible God wouldn't have epistemic warrant to claim that she will make all things well and heal every wound unless deep and lasting woundedness is something God has experienced herself. Unless God has experienced deep and lasting woundedness, the promise seems like an empty one, rather than one that's based on experience and that we can trust.

Interviewer: OK, so here's another question from a listener. Why can't you just say that God knows the 'badness' of trauma but propositionally rather than experientially? Surely that ought to give God sufficient knowledge of the 'badness' of the trauma to assess whether the healing God is able to give will be sufficient?

Greg: That's a really good question. To me, that seems like a problematic way of knowing the badness of something. Knowing the 'badness' of the trauma caused, but propositionally rather than in an experiential sense, suggests a non-qualitative kind of assessment of the badness – perhaps a quantitative assessment instead – so the badness might be measured as a 4 out of 5, rather than it being 'like this'. It would not be the qualitative, experiential knowledge of the badness of the suffering, which is what would be needed in order for the being (here, God) to assess whether healing of deep-rooted psychological damage is possible.

Interviewer: Mm, thanks. And what do you think, Catarina?

Catarina: Well, as a Thomas Aquinas fan, I don't think God has experiential knowledge *or* propositional knowledge, as such. I don't think an impassible God is like Mary the scientist before she saw red, but with emotions rather than colours. Rather, I think God has knowledge in virtue of the fact that God creates us, and knows us more intimately than we can be known by any part of the created order. Teresa of Avila and others saw God as findable in the innermost part of our souls, not as another person who's outside us. 'Before I formed you in the womb I knew you', the prophet Jeremiah says.[17] God knows us even better than we know ourselves; 'we live and move and have our being' in God.[18] God isn't another being, separate from ourselves – though it's hard to get away from that idea because as soon as we start to talk about 'God' we seem to make God into another object, because of the limitations of our language. When we speak of God coming to know things about us through this or that route – propositional knowledge and experiential knowledge and whatnot – we speak as though God is another being in the world who is separate from ourselves, rather than that God is in me and has more intimate knowledge of me than I have of myself. We start to say things like 'God helps those who help themselves' as though there are two separate beings, me and God, acting as separate agents. Because of the limitations of our language, we misunderstand what we mean by 'God', who isn't this kind of separate agent at all![19]

Greg: Hm ... I suppose the idea of God knowing us intimately, and thus knowing our trauma, on account of having created us, is possible. But it seems mysterious – so vague as a kind of knowledge that it's hard to engage with. I understand that God is not just another human or another part of the created order – but I don't want that to give us a licence to say anything we like, including things that don't seem possible. Philosophers of religion often say that God can't do logically impossible things, like create married bachelors or square circles. In a similar way, I don't see how 'knowing us intimately' could really be that intimate, if it doesn't involve knowing (in some kind of experiential sense of 'knowing') what it is we're going through, when we go through particularly bad times. I think it's *part* of knowing us intimately that someone – including God – would know what it's like to be us, in the sense of knowing experientially what our suffering is like.

Catarina: Well, according to my view, God still has a lot of understanding of that kind of knowledge, which is gained in the usual human, experiential way too. As a Christian I believe that Jesus suffered during his earthly life – and in particular that Jesus suffered the trauma of torture and execution at the very end of his life. He even experienced the despair of feeling that God had forsaken him: 'My God, my God, why have you forsaken me?'[20] God can be said to suffer, by virtue of the incarnation, in the person of Jesus, in Jesus' human nature. Given, then, that God *does* have experiential knowledge through the person of Jesus, we can say that God does have experiential knowledge of the kind of suffering that inflicts lasting psychological damage – the kind of suffering that causes trauma. I mean, does that meet your concerns?

Greg: I think the problem with making the crucifixion the only kind of suffering that God knows experientially is that it's only one kind of suffering. Different kinds of suffering vary widely in what they feel like. Jesus knew the pain and humiliation of being tortured, and the fear of execution. For me, Jesus' life and death reveal what God is like in Godself: God's relationship with creation is characterized by suffering love. But God's suffering love doesn't stop with the earthly life of Jesus – and, if it did, that would be really inadequate. Jesus did not know the pain and damage caused by ongoing domestic abuse, or by rape and what it's like to try to live after it, or by grief at the death of one's own child, or by being separated from one's family and placed in a detention centre, or by being put in solitary confinement, or by living every day for a long period with severe depression. And so the suffering of the incarnate Christ, while real and while severe, does not seem to me sufficient for God to know the nature of different kinds of deeply rooted psychological trauma, and so not sufficient to give us confidence in God's promise to heal the broken-hearted.

Catarina: But you're forgetting that Jesus does not stop being human after his earthly life – Jesus continues to have the human capacity for empathy with people who suffer today.[21] Humanity is not just a temporary 'costume' Jesus wears until the ascension! In addition, Jesus' resurrection gives us the guarantee we need that all will in the end be well – that God has the power and the knowledge to overcome sin, suffering and death.

I'm reluctant to give up the idea of divine eternality and timelessness ... not just for itself, but also because situating God in time and as a victim of suffering seems far too much like making God like just another creature, too much like the Greek and Roman gods, who loved, suffered, got jealous, envious, sadistic, horny, and so on.[22] To my thinking, that kind of God – a God who is another subject in the world – is not a firm foundation for Christian hope.

Greg: It's interesting what our differences come down to, isn't it? Really different intuitions about the kind of God we can put our faith in, and the importance of experience within that.

Catarina: Yes! For me it's really important to maintain the distinction between the Creator and the created, and not just think of God as another albeit bigger person or part of the created order.

Interviewer: All right. This leads on nicely to another feature of the debate I want to talk about: the issue about divine omnipotence or all-powerfulness and whether that means one should be an impassibilist or a passibilist. Catarina, how does the idea of divine omnipotence affect your thinking on impassibility?

Catarina: For me, divine omnipotence is at the heart of God's impassibilism. God is insusceptible to suffering – insusceptible to being hurt or harmed by bad things that happen in the world, bad things that people do. Events in the world are part of creation's matrix of cause and effect. As Creator, God is outside this matrix – God holds the world in being. God is not controlled or limited by the world in the way that creatures are.

Interviewer: And Greg, how about for you?

Greg: I see omnipotence as suggesting divine possibility, not the reverse. One reason for this is that impassibility seems like a lack of power – an inability to experience suffering, an inability to know experientially things other beings know. Like a lot of passibilists, I want to say that God does not experience suffering in the same way that creatures experience it. Creatures are involuntarily susceptible to suffering, to being hurt and harmed by the bad things others do. God, according to most passibilists, is not involuntarily susceptible to suffering: God freely chooses suffering, out of love for creation. And because the suffering is chosen, God remains master of it and is not overwhelmed by it in the way creatures are.[23]

Interviewer: Catarina, would the idea that God chooses suffering and is not overwhelmed by it answer your concerns about suffering diminishing God's power?

Catarina: No, in fact it seems to raise further problems to me. It's part of creaturely suffering that we usually do not choose it, and that we do not have control over it. As Simone Weil says, 'it is the essence of affliction that it is suffered unwillingly'.[24] According to passibilists who think that God chooses suffering, God only mimics suffering rather than suffering authentically. I would much rather say that God does not suffer at all.

Interviewer: And Greg, what do you think? Is a God who suffers voluntarily merely mimicking creaturely suffering?

Greg: No – because I reject the idea that in order for suffering to be authentic it has to be involuntary. Women might choose to suffer to bring new life into the world. Martyrs choose to suffer in order to stand true to and witness to their beliefs. Political activists choose to suffer to bring about a better world. Stories of saints include people choosing poverty in order to minister to others. We would not want to say in these cases that suffering is not authentic.

To my mind, when suffering is taken on voluntarily, the important question is what the sufferer's motive is. Usually when someone chooses to suffer, it's a means to some greater good. If someone chooses to suffer – I don't know, to make themselves look good or get sympathy or something – there would be something inauthentic about their suffering. But if someone chooses suffering for a greater good that's of real value, then the suffering seems totally authentic to me. So in the case of the woman who goes through morning sickness and childbirth, or the martyr who stands up for their beliefs and so is tortured and executed, I think we would want to say that these have good motives – and so although their suffering is chosen, it's still authentic. And likewise, God's suffering, which is freely chosen out of love for creation.[25]

Interviewer: So God's suffering is real, is authentic?

Greg: Yes, totally. God's suffering is just as real as yours or mine. It's just a bit more like the suffering of a woman who chooses to have a baby or a martyr who chooses death to stay true to and witness to their faith – it's chosen by God for some greater good, not inflicted on God involuntarily.

Interviewer: And Catarina, what do you think of that?

Catarina: I agree with Greg's point that suffering might not need to be involuntary to be real or authentic, provided that the choice is well motivated. But the cases given all suggest a forced choice. A woman might choose pregnancy and childbirth because without it she can't produce a new life. A martyr might choose torture and death because otherwise she will have to renounce her faith, and send out a message to others that her religion is not worth dying for. A saint might choose poverty, because without it she can't fully minister to others. The passibilist would presumably say that God chooses suffering, because unless God suffers God cannot fully love. But I reject the view that God has a forced choice involving suffering or else not being able to love. I think it's perfectly possible for God to love and not to suffer. At the heart of love is that we want the beloved's good – we want them to be well, happy, good, be fully themselves, flourish, or however you want to put it. But willing the beloved's good is totally compatible with not having the emotional responses, including suffering, that are typically involved in love for humans.

In addition to this, passibilists usually claim that not only does God freely choose suffering; God's suffering is always within God's control and God is not overwhelmed by it. That seems to affect the quality of God's suffering. In the case of creaturely suffering – even in cases where suffering is freely chosen, as in the case of the woman and the martyr – the suffering can still be overwhelming somewhere down the line. The woman who is six months pregnant or about to go into labour can't suddenly change her mind and decide not to go through with it after all. The martyr can't say to the impending lions 'actually, I've had second thoughts'. The suffering may have been chosen for a greater good in the first place. But the experience of being totally in control throughout the course of suffering is not characteristic of human suffering, or at least of severe human suffering. To my mind, the suffering of God in Godself would be so different from human suffering that it wouldn't be consoling or comforting in the way passibilists tend to assume.[26]

Interviewer: That's really interesting. Thank you. I'd like to talk much more about this topic, but I'm aware that we're coming to the end of the programme – and we've got a few questions listeners have been sending in that I want to discuss before we end. First, one for Catarina – what do you think of the objection that the God you believe in is the God of Greek philosophers, and not the God of the Bible?

Catarina: That was quite a popular line of argument at one point, and you can see why – divine attributes like immutability or changelessness and so on are far closer to Plato than they are to the God described in the Hebrew Bible, who changes his mind, has emotions, and so on. But in the Bible God is also spoken of as having hands and feet – we usually make sense of those by saying that they are metaphors rather than attributing a body to God. I think we should do the same when God is described as having emotions.

Interviewer: Greg, what would you say to that?

Greg: Oh, I'm fine with the logic of that! And I'd add that the 'Greek rather than biblical' criticism is dubious on various grounds – for example, it overlooks the huge influence Greek thought had on various biblical writers.

Interviewer: Great, thank you. Here's another question. Catarina, don't you think that impassibilism idealizes invulnerability, while vulnerability is at the heart of the Christian gospel? This question comes from someone who says they are worried about the pastoral implications of impassibilism – people who suffer might be alienated because suffering and vulnerability are not part of God's life.

Catarina: That's a really important question. I can see why you might think that. I think that's not the case, because of the place of Christ's suffering and vulnerability in Christian theology and worship. In fact, I think impassibilism may be the more helpful pastorally. Passibilists say that suffering is part of the divine life, and that can romanticize or idealize suffering – it can make it into a good in itself. Christian impassibilists instead look to the suffering of Christ, and this of course is understood in the light of Christ's resurrection. Therefore we look to the transfiguration of suffering that has happened already in Christ and will happen to the whole creation at the general resurrection. We do not idealize suffering but have a place for it within a bigger narrative about victory over suffering.[27]

Interviewer: OK. We have two more minutes before the end of the programme, and one more question from a listener – so please keep your answers brief. Let's start with Greg this time: do you think there's a way beyond the impasse between passibilists and impassibilists?

Greg: I think there's a way beyond it in relation to passibilism where that's defined as whether God has emotions – emotions is such an umbrella term, we might want to say that God has some kinds of emotions and not others ...

Catarina: Yes! I agree with that! Aquinas, for example, made a distinction between passions and affections – he thought that it's possible that God has affections, but not passions, which are involuntary and bodily ... That's important since affections are still subjectively warm and lively states.[28] It's not like an impassibilist God is apathetic, in the modern sense of that term!

Greg: Yes! But I think it's very hard to see how there could be a reconciliation between the idea that God *suffers* and the idea that God *can't suffer* ...

Interviewer: Yes, I see! OK, thank you. We really need to end the show now. I'd like to thank you both for joining us.

Greg: I mean, the passibilist and impassibilist strands within Christianity rely on quite different views of love for a start ...

Catarina: Yes, for my tradition love is seen as willing the good of the beloved – love is not an emotion ...

Greg: Whereas my tradition would insist that suffering is a part of love, when the person who is loved suffers, or when they are not flourishing as they should ...

Interviewer: I can see there are lots of different aspects concerning the debate that God suffers, but we need to wrap up there ...

Catarina: And my tradition would say that that's only true of human love – because emotions such as the emotions involved in suffering are appropriate to humans but not to God ...

Cut to programme theme music. Greg and Catarina can still be heard debating in the background.

Summary and discussion

Through this radio programme sketch, we get a sense of what motivates passibilism for some and impassibilism for others. For Catarina, passibilism would mean giving up other important traditional divine attributes, such as divine eternity and omnipotence. Catarina is concerned not to elide the distinction between creator and creature and thus (as she sees it) to make God like the pagan gods or just another being in the world (albeit a more perfect one). The God Catarina believes in is not cold, indifferent or apathetic (as some passibilists believe the impassibilist God to be). Catarina points to the person of Jesus, who knew significant suffering in his earthly life, and who continues to have the human capacity for empathy. Catarina also thinks that God in Godself can be regarded as loving us and as having intimate knowledge of us, even though God (in God-self) cannot experience emotional states, and doesn't suffer for or with us. Indeed, she sees impassibilism as more consoling for the sufferer – because it points beyond suffering to ultimate victory over it through Christ's resurrection and in the hope of our own resurrection. Catarina defines love as a will for the good of the beloved – and God's love for us is shown not only in God's creating and sustaining of us, but also in the incarnation, suffering and death of God in the person of Jesus.

On the other hand, Greg thinks that God can't really love us and can't really know us unless God has emotions and knows what our suffering is like. For Greg, it's not the case that God in Godself can just know us intimately but non-passibly (as Catarina would have it). This is because Greg thinks that to know someone intimately requires knowing what their lived experience is like, and loving someone requires suffering with them when they suffer. God loving and knowing intimately but without emotion and the possibility of suffering are as impossible as God creating married bachelors or square circles, or God deciding to cease to exist or doing something bad – they are things that are simply not within the realm of possibility, even for God. Furthermore, for Greg it's important given the hope and faith Christians place in God, and in the idea that in the end God will make all things well, that God knows what God's getting into when God makes promises that all will be well. Greg thinks that it's worth giving up divine eternity in order to have a God we can relate to and who loves us in a way that includes suffering with and for us. And Greg thinks that omnipotence is compatible with thinking that God suffers, so long as God's suffering is freely chosen out of God's love. For passibilists like Greg, Jesus' suffering reveals God's suffering love, but God's *suffering* love doesn't stop there.

Catarina and Greg disagree about passibilism even though they find themselves agreeing about lots of things. They disagree with each other in their overall conclusions primarily because they have different instincts about what's most important, and what's worth sacrificing for that. A passible God ends up looking quite different from an impassible God, not only in terms of emotions but in other things too, such as how God relates to and is affected by creation and time. At the beginning of this chapter we saw that Webb, following other passibilist theologians, sees divine suffering as the core focus for a positive and helpful theology of mental illness. This, of course, presupposes that divine suffering or passibility is a plausible option.

The aim of this chapter is not to convince you to agree or disagree with passibilism or impassibilism, but to help you to see why people end up disagreeing about the topic, and to reach a conclusion about what you think, why you think it, and what thinking it involves, for yourself. This prepares the ground for the following chapter, which looks at why or how a suffering God might be thought to be helpful. It also explores whether and how the helpful aspects of a suffering God can be met by other means for impassibilist Christians.

Notes

1 Marcia Webb (2017), *Toward a Theology of Psychological Disorder*, Eugene, OR: Cascade, p. 149

2 Marcel Sarot (1992), *God, Passibility, and Corporeality*, Campen, The Netherlands: Kok Pharos Publishing, p. 113.

3 Webb, *Theology*, p. 148.

4 The person could be a fictionalist about passibilism: they could commit to passibilism but only as a comforting and helpful fiction. I think in this case their commitment to passibilism might be accompanied by some degree of comfort, but this is likely to be more superficial and less lasting than the comfort derived from genuine belief in passibilism. An analogy might be to the emotional responses we get when watching a fictitious film. Emotions such as sadness, joy and fear are felt, but they are not felt as deeply as emotions relating to real-life events, and they are not as long-lasting. Thanks especially to Sam Lebens and Simon Hewitt for discussions on this topic.

5 Anastasia Philippa Scrutton (2011), *Thinking through Feeling: God, Emotion and Passibility*, New York and London: Continuum.

6 Available at www.youtube.com/watch?v=b8xOKjb-C2Q (all websites in Chapter 6 notes accessed 13.12.19).

7 This is by virtue of the 'communication of idioms' (or *communi-*

catio idiomatum) which in order to emphasize the unity of Jesus' divine and human natures means that experiences and attributes relating to one of Jesus' natures (i.e. human or divine) can be referred to Jesus' other nature too.

8 See Natalja Deng (2018), 'Eternity in Christian thought', *Stanford Encyclopedia of Philosophy*, available at https://plato.stanford.edu/entries/eternity/.

9 Notably, eternality probably also means that God can't experience joy either, since joy requires some duration. Rather, for the eternalist-impassibilist, God experiences what would be experienced as joy in humans: because God fulfils all potentiality (on a Thomistic view), there is no need or lack in God. This is what divine blissfulness would consist in. However, the absence of affective joy in divine blissfulness seems less theologically problematic than the idea of God experiencing suffering eternally. Thanks to Sam Lebens and Simon Hewitt for conversations about this.

10 Whether you think this argument works will depend on your understanding of the nature of time. See Ned Markosian (2014), 'Time', *Stanford Encyclopedia of Philosophy*, available at https://plato.stanford.edu/entries/time/.

11 E.g. Sarot, *God*, p. 80: 'in the case of severe suffering one is sometimes better able to console someone when one feels sympathy, compassion or fellow-suffering. If God is not able to have these feelings, in these cases He will not be able to give perfect consolation. This is an important reason for holding God to be passible.'

12 E.g. Karl Rahner (1986), cited in Jürgen Moltmann (1991), *History and the Triune God*, London: SCM Press, p. 123.

13 See Martine Nida-Rümelin (2009), 'Qualia: The knowledge argument', *Stanford Encyclopedia of Philosophy* (Summer 2015 edn), available at https://plato.stanford.edu/archives/sum2015/entries/qualia-knowledge/.

14 See Linda Zagzebski (2008), 'Omnisubjectivity', in Jon Kvanvig (ed.), *Oxford Studies in Philosophy of Religion*, Oxford: Oxford University Press, available at www.baylor.edu/content/services/document.php/39971.pdf.

15 See Richard Creel (1986), *Divine Impassibility: An Essay in Philosophical Theology*, Cambridge: Cambridge University Press, p. 129.

16 See Zagzebski, 'Omnisubjectivity'.

17 Jeremiah 1.5.

18 Acts 17.28.

19 The idea that God is not separate from ourselves could be misinterpreted as pantheism. However, within Catholic theology and especially mystical spirituality the thought is rather that there is a deep union between God and the self so that God is to be found by looking in the self. This is not the same as saying that God is reducible to or

identical with the self. See, for example, Teresa of Avila's *The Interior Castle* or Francis Thompson's *O World Invisible*.

20 Mark 15.34; Matthew 27.46.

21 Thanks to David Efird and Simon Hewitt for conversations about this.

22 See Herbert McCabe (1987), *God Matters*, London: Geoffrey Chapman, pp. 39–51.

23 For this view see, for example, Jürgen Moltmann, cited in Richard Bauckham (1990), 'In defence of *The Crucified God*', in Nigel M. de S. Cameron (ed.), *The Power and Weakness of God*, Edinburgh: Rutherford House Books, p. 106; Paul Fiddes (1988), *The Creative Suffering of God*, Oxford: Clarendon Press, p. 62; Webb, *Theology*, pp. 148–9.

24 Simone Weil (1974), *Gateway to God*, London: Fontana, pp. 87–8. See also Origen, who defines suffering as an experience 'outside the control of the will' (*Contra Celsum* 2.23).

25 See Anastasia Philippa Scrutton (2009), 'Living like common people: Emotion, will and divine passibility', *Religious Studies: An International Journal for the Philosophy of Religion* 45.4, pp. 373–93.

26 Thanks to Ann Catherine Swailes OP for this point.

27 Thanks to Ann Catherine Swailes OP for this point.

28 See Scrutton, *Thinking through Feeling*.

7

Would a suffering God help?

Introduction

In this chapter, I will take as my starting point the idea that a passible God – by which I mean a God who suffers in Godself rather than solely in the person of Jesus during his earthly life – is helpful. Taking hints from passibilists such as Marcia Webb, I will look at two ways in which a passible God is thought to be helpful in the context of mental illness. First, in being in Alfred North Whitehead's powerful phrase a 'fellow sufferer who understands',[1] a passible God provides consolation to sufferers. Second, by affirming a place for suffering within the divine life, churches are discouraged from holding, and are motivated to challenge, negative and stigmatizing views of people who suffer.

I will argue that while it might be the case that a passibilist God is helpful in these respects, it is not the case that *only* a passible God can help. Rather, it is the depiction of non-sanitized suffering of religiously significant figures (which could be God, but could also include non-divine figures such as saints) that provides consolation and the means to challenge negative views of mental illness. In this respect, I disagree with the way in which Bonhoeffer's phrase 'only the suffering God can help' has been appropriated in passibilist discourse.[2]

My aim in arguing this is not to undermine the idea of a passible God and the consolation and social-political resources it provides for those who do find it helpful and plausible. Rather, I seek to give due recognition to the fact that not all Christians find the idea of a passible God helpful, and many may not even find it plausible – perhaps for some of the reasons Catarina articulated in the previous chapter. This seems important, given the emphasis on passibilism as the Christian response to suffering in much theology over the last century.[3] While passibilists seek to transform the experience of suffering by situating it in the divine life, in fact passibilism could leave Christians who do not feel consoled by a passible God – or who regard the idea of a passible God as based on a misunderstanding – feeling left out in the cold.

Some of this chapter involves looking at the way in which significant but non-divine religious figures such as saints have been received and interpreted. I will argue that saints and other venerated figures have sometimes been interpreted in such a way as to console people who suffer in particular ways, and to challenge stigma against them. On the other hand, saints and venerated figures have sometimes been represented in such a way as to further alienate people, for example by emphasizing only sanitized forms of suffering that are exclusionary. Notably, the issue here is not about the figures themselves but about reception: about how they have been interpreted and represented. And the tension between these two kinds of representation – the destigmatizing and the sanitizing – is found not only within Christian traditions that emphasize the communion of saints but also across Christian traditions in the representation of Jesus' suffering on the cross.

Whether Christian communities affirm a passible God, or whether they emphasize some other non-divine form of fellow-suffering, I will argue, is not the crucial factor in determining whether they provide consolation or have the capacity for combatting stigma. Rather, what is crucial is how the suffering of significant religious figures – whether divine, human, or both human and divine – is portrayed. In addition to this, stigma against mental illness is not the only stigma that needs challenging in relation to people experiencing mental illness. Other forms of stigma – for example relating to sex and sexuality – affect many people suffering from depression and other forms of mental illness, and these need addressing by the Church and wider society. If we tackle only stigma relating to mental illness, we do not take into account the way in which this form of stigma intersects with other aspects of people's experience and identities, some of which are also stigmatized within churches. It is not enough for someone not to experience stigma in relation to their depression to help with their depression – they must also be welcomed and affirmed in relation to being female, or gay, or trans, or black, or poor, or all of these things.

Is divine passibility consoling?

Philosophers and theologians express radically different intuitions about whether divine passibility is a consolation to sufferers, or rather the reverse. For example, theologian Karl Rahner writes that:

> it does not help me to escape from my mess and mix-up if God is in the same predicament ... God ... is in a true and authentic and consoling sense that God who does not suffer ... What use would that [i.e. passibilism] be to me as a consolation in the truest sense of the word?[4]

Jürgen Moltmann, otherwise an admirer of Rahner, describes himself as 'deeply shocked' by Rahner's position on this, since, he argues, 'Only a God in whose perfect being there is room for pain can comfort us.'[5] This is because of the necessity of fellow-suffering (or empathy or compassion) in a consoler:

> An impassible God is capable of neither love nor feeling. Empathy is impossible for such a God. So such a God is not in a position to console people either. One can only console when one shares another's feelings. And one can only share another's feelings if one has empathy. And having empathy means being passible and not impassible. I cannot imagine an impassible God as a God who consoles in a personal sense. He seems to me to be as cold and hard and unfeeling as cement.[6]

Rahner and Moltmann highlight an important conundrum. Are we more consoled by God's being outside suffering and able to point beyond our current predicament to future bliss? Or would this mean that God is incapable of offering consolation because God is entirely lacking in empathy or fellow feeling?

The substance of these differing intuitions is echoed by many others.[7] For those who find a passible God consoling, an impassible God would be irrelevant and distant in the face of suffering. For impassibilists, what is more consoling is a God who is a guide or help in overcoming suffering, or who can see beyond suffering to the ultimate good. Whether a passible God is consoling or the reverse seems to be a major motivating factor for passibilism or impassibilism, regardless of whether it's seen as an argument,[8] or simply a psychologically powerful motivating force.[9]

In their favour, the passibilists are drawing on the wounded healer tradition, according to which in Petrarch's words: 'No one's solace penetrates a saddened mind more than that of a fellow sufferer, and therefore the most effect[ive] words to strengthen the spirits of the bystanders are those which emerge from actual torments.'[10] Given this, we might wonder, what are impassibilists to do if they seek consolation? Or perhaps, why do traditions and communities that lean towards the idea that God is impassible still seem to be psychologically and pastorally satisfying, in spite of the absence of a divine fellow sufferer consoler?

Fellow suffering consolation in impassibilist theology: communities, Scripture and the saints

One answer to the question of fellow suffering consolation for impassibilists is going to be that impassibilist Christians have access to fellow suffering consolation through the life and death of Jesus. This was a very real and very terrible form of suffering, and a source of consolation to many sufferers. And yet it seems limited as a source of consolation, since Jesus did not experience every type of suffering. As Frances Young notes:

> It is often stated that the person who can help a sufferer is someone who has experienced a similar kind of suffering and come through it. The impact of the story that God suffered and died has depended on its implication that God is like such a person, a conviction which has undoubtedly had a profound psychological effect upon suffering believers who have felt that God could understand their predicament.
>
> Yet there are many forms of suffering which Jesus of Nazareth (i.e. in terms of this account, God-in-Christ) did not experience.[11]

And, as Greg notes in the previous chapter:

> Jesus did not know the pain and damage caused by ongoing domestic abuse, or by rape and what it's like to try to live after it, or by grief at the death of one's own child, or by being separated from one's family and placed in a detention centre, or by being put in solitary confinement, or by living every day for a long period with severe depression.

Nevertheless, impassibilists can still appeal to Jesus as a fellow sufferer who understands, not least because, as Catarina pointed out, Christ did not cease to be human after his earthly life. Jesus, then, continues to have the capacity for empathy with people today.

For impassibilists, the kind of consolation that comes through fellow suffering can come not only through Jesus but also from other, non-divine, sources. This might include the consolation of fellow suffering humans within the same communities, churches, or friendship groups as us. Of course, having communities that include fellow sufferers who console is in no way specific to particular Christian groups, or even to Christianity as a whole, or even to religions more generally, and so might be overlooked in theological discussion. But it seems an important theological point that we are formed and sustained not only in our relations with God but also in our relations with other people, whether inside or outside the Church. Some passibilist discourse can seem to suggest that our relationship with God must be sufficient for every aspect of our life or our every need. But this is surely to overlook the fact that we are bodily, social creatures – indeed, animals – who need others and for and with whom others were created in order to flourish fully as human beings. The desire for a fellow sufferer who understands is often held alongside a desire for a figure who is not caught up in the same 'mess and mix-up' (as Rahner puts it), but who heals, consoles and points beyond suffering. It does not seem surprising if the desire for fellow sufferers is met in some communities principally by other humans, rather than by divine or saintly figures.

In addition to other people in our communities, fellow suffering consolation might be found in Scripture, and in the way in which Scripture is used both privately and communally in worship. This may be particularly true of the psalms, which describe in first-person terms some of the experiences and feelings characteristic of depression.[12] Psalms are often joyful, and at first sight it might seem as though these, rather than ones that experience mental distress, will be better suited to consoling people with depression. This might be true for some, and yet people with depression sometimes report that solely joyful forms of worship can be alienating.[13] More helpful, they say, is worship in which one is welcomed into the community, even if one is unable to experience joy or happiness. And not only the response of the community but also the form of worship will be important here. Some of the psalms, such as the Psalms of Individual Lament, include first-person expression of distress and frustration:

You have put me in the depths of the Pit,
in the regions dark and deep.
Your wrath lies heavy upon me,
and you overwhelm me with all your waves.
You have caused my companions to shun me;
you have made me a thing of horror to them.

I am shut in so that I cannot escape;
my eye grows dim through sorrow.

(Psalm 88.6–9)

As we saw in the introduction, a common experience in depression is alienation from the interpersonal world, or feeling cut off from others. If we are in a communal setting in which others are expressing joy that we cannot feel, then we are likely to feel more alienated and cut off still. In contrast, if we are reincorporated into the interpersonal world or community by being allowed to experience sadness, sorrow and despair, we may feel some sense of comfort, of the lessening of the gap between ourselves and others.[14] We know this from other areas of life – for example, people often report that when they feel sad they are consoled by sad (rather than happy) music.

In addition to this, that there is nothing sinful about having these negative emotions may be implied by the fact that the psalmists' laments are part of Scripture and a core part of the Christian tradition. And the structure of each Psalm of Individual Lament moves from despair to hope, thus allowing people to take part in a narrative journey, which may be suggestive to people with depression that their current state is not the only state they can hope for.

In addition to human communities and Scripture, fellow suffering consolation might also come from non-divine but still religiously significant figures, such as the saints. Perhaps it is no accident that some impassibilist traditions (such as Roman Catholicism) are also the traditions that emphasize the role of saints. Saints are particularly good candidates for fellow suffering consolation, because different saints have known different kinds of suffering. In addition to this, they offer consolation both by knowing what it's like to have experienced a particular kind of suffering and by pointing beyond it to future healing and joy. This can give sufferers hope for the future, and perhaps also hope that their suffering has some transformative value. Here, by way of example, I describe the case of Matt Talbot, whose life seems to offer fellow suffering consolation to people struggling with addiction.

Fellow sufferers who understand: the example of Matt Talbot

On a devotional website, one writer discusses the fact that when she first experienced mental illness she felt ashamed and distant from God because of it, but that examples of the saints who experienced mental distress showed her that there is nothing sinful about having mental illness. One of the main examples she gives is of Matt Talbot, a significant figure for people seeking to recover from substance and alcohol abuse and addiction.[15]

Matt Talbot was born into a large and poor family in Dublin in 1856, the men of which were all heavy drinkers. He left school aged 12 to work in a wine store, and was an alcoholic by 13. He then worked in a whisky store, and ran up debts to buy drink, eventually scrounging, pawning clothes and money and stealing to buy alcohol. One day, when he was 28, after lingering unsuccessfully outside a pub in the hope that someone would buy him a drink, he returned to his mother and announced he was going to 'take the pledge' (i.e. give up alcohol). According to popular accounts, his mother was preparing the midday meal; when she saw him she remarked, surprised, 'Matt, you're home early and you're sober!' When he announced his intention to remain sober she said, 'God give you strength to keep it.'[16]

Matt took the pledge initially for three months, then six, and then for life. The first seven years of sobriety were especially hard, but Matt found strength in prayer and attending mass. He repaid his debts, and searched for people from whom he had stolen in order to repay them. When he was 34 he became a Lay Franciscan and became known for his generosity to others and his frugal lifestyle. Following his sudden death when he was 69, it was discovered that he wore chains under his clothes, a mortificatory practice. As a result, enquiries were made by the Vatican into his alleged holiness, leading to his veneration in 1975 – a step before canonization (or being recognized as a saint, for which evidence of a miracle is required).

While his mortificatory practices were the catalyst for the

Church's interest in his life, it is his struggle with and recovery from alcoholism that most inspires devotion to him. There are addiction recovery and community centres named after Matt Talbot worldwide,[17] and Catholics who themselves or whose friends or family face addiction will sometimes appeal to the example of Talbot for strength in recovery, and pray to him for help. Talbot is seen as a fellow sufferer, because he experienced being an alcoholic and the difficulties faced by people on the long road to recovery. In words attributed to him: 'Never go too hard on the man who can't give up drink. It is as hard to give up drink as it is to raise the dead to life again.'[18] He is seen as a consoler, because he experienced severe alcoholism, and yet was able to overcome his addiction, thus offering hope to those struggling with addiction. And so a prayer suggested for people with addictions and their friends and family says:

> Lord, in your servant Matt Talbot you have given us a wonderful example of triumph over addiction ... May Matt Talbot's triumph over addiction bring hope to our community and strength to our hearts through Christ our Lord.[19]

One devotional website includes the following reflection:

> In looking at the life of Matt Talbot, we may easily focus on the later years when he had stopped drinking for some time and was leading a penitential life. Only alcoholic men and women who have stopped drinking can fully appreciate how difficult the earliest years of sobriety were for Matt. He had to take one day at a time. So do the rest of us.[20]

As these quotations show, the example of and devotion to Talbot is reminiscent of the therapeutic method employed by Alcoholics Anonymous. People who are fellow sufferers and yet who have overcome addiction are regarded as the real experts and thus are able to provide a more powerful form of therapy than someone who has not been an alcoholic would be able to do.[21]

So far in this chapter, I have argued that passibilists who think that 'only the suffering God can help' when it comes to consolation are mistaken.[22] While a passible God may be both plausible and consoling to some, passibilism may be implausible and non-consoling to others, for whom God's blissful equanimity in the face of suffering is a much greater source of consolation. For these people, there are still fellow sufferers who understand and who offer consolation. Christ himself is chief among these, and his suffering points beyond suffering to victory over it and the transfiguration of it. Saints and saintly figures such as Matt Talbot are fellow sufferers who understand, and this is indicated by the content of devotions such as prayers to them and reflections on them. Scripture and other people within our communities may also offer fellow suffering type consolation. With respect to Scripture and in other ways, communal worship can be alienating to people with depression, by demanding that people feel joy when they cannot. On the other hand, Scripture and communal worship can be an instrument for healing by helping to reincorporate people with depression back into the community and the interpersonal world. This is especially the case when it allows them to express and share feelings of distress.

In the next section I will explore a further way in which a passible God might be thought to be helpful to people with mental illness: that by situating suffering within the divine life Christians are less likely to adopt stigmatizing views of mental illness, and are more likely to challenge them in wider society.

Divine suffering as destigmatizing

What has passibilism or impassibilism got to do with destigmatizing mental illness? According to Webb:

> an emotionally restrained Savior – and an entirely impassible God – may be the preferred correlates to negative lay theologies [Webb's term for sin and demon accounts of mental illness] which portray Christian life as absent of all mental distress. Such a depiction of God is more conducive to the ideal of human invulnerability found in these theologies.[23]

Webb bases this conjecture on studies that show that people's depictions of God correlate with their self-understanding – so, for example, people who regard God as generous are more likely to describe themselves as generous.[24] In the background of all this is the Feuerbachian idea that views of God are projections of human desires and aspirations. A person or community's view of God, on this view, tells us about what that person or community regards as valuable or admirable or to be aspired to in human beings. Thus, a community with an impassibilist theology is likely to hold in high esteem humans who are self-sufficient, not weak, invulnerable to suffering, and perhaps lacking in emotion – or at least those emotions that detract from self-sufficiency and autonomy. Furthermore, admiring those characteristics in humans is likely to lead to critical, judgemental and stigmatizing attitudes to depression and other forms of mental illness, where people's vulnerability, dependence on others and emotionality are highly evident. If that's right, then it seems not only that people with judgemental theologies of mental disorder will prefer impassibilist theology, but that people with impassibilist theology will tend to have negative theologies of mental disorder. And if that's right, then impassibilism is practically problematic, because it is reflective of, and reinforces and perpetuates, stigmatizing attitudes to mental illness.

Feuerbachians are probably on to something when they say that people's views of God are or at least can be projections of a person's or a community's own ideals, aspirations and natures. At the same time, we should be cautious about inferring correlations between people's theology and their ideals of human perfection and own behaviour too quickly. We need to pay attention to the reasons they have the beliefs about God that they do (Catarina does not seem to be an impassibilist because she values self-sufficiency or autonomy in humans), and to the possible disparity between people's ideals of human perfection and their actual behaviour (people do not always embody the principles they value or assert that they have). While a priori speculation may give us a working hypothesis, we need to look at real-life examples before reaching our conclusions. For instance, the Roman Catholic Church teaches impassibilism,[25] and yet while regarding God as invulnerable to suffering Catholic theology will frequently speak of the potential value, purpose and worth of human suffering, and the inalienable dignity of people who suffer.[26] In addition, while there may be exceptions at the level of local communities, the Catholic Church does not tend to be stigmatizing or judgemental in its attitude to people with mental illness. Interviews with and surveys of people with experience of both mood disorders and Christianity seem to suggest that Catholic churches have less negative (e.g. sin or demon related) views of mental illness than some other churches, and a rich theology of suffering in relation to depression.[27] It seems, then, that we should be suspicious of the idea that impassibilist theology is going to be more stigmatizing in relation to mental illness.

One of Webb's motivations is, I think, to combat and overcome the stigma of people with mental illness, and she sees passibilism as best suited to achieving this aim. Combatting and overcoming the stigma of people with mental illness is crucial within churches, which have the potential to provide significant forms of help and support for people with mental illness when they respond positively. Indeed, provided that they offer support, churches and other religious communities may form buffers against mental illness, and be conducive to better and swifter recovery from it.[28] But in addition to the hope that churches themselves do not respond in alienating ways to people with mental illness who are part of their communities, churches have the potential to be catalysts for social and political change in the wider world, outside the Church, which includes combatting and overcoming stigma there as well. And so if passibilism were indeed best suited to combatting stigma against mental illness, this would make it a more attractive position than impassibilism in at least one extremely important respect.[29]

I have already suggested that we have several reasons to be suspicious of the idea that impassibilist theology is more stigmatizing than passibilist theology. I want to look briefly at a further reason. Webb seems to presuppose that impassibilist theology will be accompanied by belief in 'an emotionally restrained Savior'.[30] While this would be nice and neat, in reality it is often impassibilist Christian theology that emphasizes the real suffering of Jesus (consider, for example, the Catholic devotional practice of the Stations of the Cross). An impassibilist such as Catarina is likely to feel that the vulnerability and suffering of God in the person of Jesus, throughout the incarnation and particularly during his torture and death, is significant in overcoming stigma. She might point to the fact that Jesus is thought to have been free from sin, and yet suffered psychologically and physically. This fact seems to be a significant corrective to theologies that regard depression as a sign that the person is sinful, and other forms of victim blaming. In addition to the person of Christ, it might be pointed out, there are saints and other figures who experienced a vast range of different kinds of human suffering. This includes some forms of human suffering most frequently stigmatized. Reception to these figures – for example, devotion to Matt Talbot by recovering alcoholics – indicates the potential these figures have not only for providing comfort and hope to sufferers but also for overcoming stigma.

It would be nice to end this chapter on a saintly note, but there's a fly in this ointment. Christian traditions that emphasize the communion of saints often highlight the suffering of Jesus, Mary and the saints as a consolation to sufferers, and as a reminder to communities to fully include those who suffer in their communities. But too often the emphasis on the suffering of Jesus, Mary and the saints becomes powerless to destigmatize. This is because their suffering has often been sanitized: 'respectable' kinds of suffering have been foregrounded while other kinds have been downplayed. Here are a few examples of saints, and of the ways in which aspects of their lives have been emphasized, interpreted and depicted, to illustrate this point.

Saints who have been sanitized

In discussing why it is that medieval English mystic Margery Kempe was never canonized, historian Katherine Lewis draws attention to the fact that people canonized during that period (the High Middle Ages) tended to be men, usually of high status, or else female virgin martyrs – again, often of high status.[31] The married and sexual, highly unconventional and sometimes turbulent middle-class and probably illiterate Margery was unlikely to establish a significant cult or number of devotees, or win the favour of the Church.

St Maria Goretti, an 11-year-old girl from Italy, was murdered in 1902 while resisting a man who was trying to rape her; he choked her and then stabbed her repeatedly when she refused to have sex with him. The attack was the culmination of ongoing attempted rapes by the man, which had previously included persistently seeking sex from her, and threatening her with a weapon when she refused. An important factor in the canonization of and devotion to Maria Goretti is that the rapist failed, and so she is considered a virgin martyr. A further important factor is that Goretti forgave the murderer before she died.

The Catholic Church teaches that Mary the mother of Jesus is a perpetual virgin – not only was she a virgin when she conceived Jesus, but she remained a virgin throughout her life. While not the official teaching of the Catholic Church, it is sometimes also taught that Mary did not experience childbirth pain. This is because Mary is thought in Catholic theology to be conceived without the stain of original sin – and childbirth pain is thought to be a punishment for the Fall. And so the pain of childbirth is transferred to the emotional pain Mary feels when she watches Jesus' suffering at the crucifixion.

The Ugandan martyrs were a group of young men who converted to Christianity in the late nineteenth century and were executed by the king, Mwanga. The reason why they were executed is unknown, and so we can only talk about the ways in which their execution has been represented in later accounts. Many of these, written by Christians who see the Ugandan men as martyrs, attribute the execution to the young men's refusal to have sex with the king.[32] The idea that the martyrs were first and foremost Christian resistors of homosexuality has been emphasized in anti-gay propaganda,[33] and was used to garner support for the 2014 Ugandan Anti-Homosexuality Act, according to which consensual homosexual activity would be punishable by life imprisonment.[34] If one were to take the later Christian accounts that point to refusal to have sex as the reason for execution at face value[35] – we can't be sure that this isn't a later accretion to the story – it would be possible to depict the Ugandan martyrs as resistors of state-instituted rape. Instead, they are repeatedly depicted as resistors of the 'shameful' practice of homosexuality.[36]

As these examples indicate, there are certain sticking points for the Catholic Church, in the Church's treatment of suffering, and in the Church's depiction of the fellow suffering of the saints. These sticking points often centre around sexuality, particularly (any) female sexuality, and homosexuality among men. Saints can be fellow sufferers, but female fellow sufferers are much more likely to become saints if they are virgins, even if this means resisting rape to the point of death. So, for example, Maria Goretti and others who resisted rather than living through rape and its aftermath are the patron saints of rape victims.[37] This is unlikely to send out a hopeful message about post-rape healing in the way that Matt Talbot is a hopeful example about recovery from addiction. In addition to this, it can foster guilt or remorse that the person who was raped did not try to resist, or did not succeed in doing so.

Mary the mother of Jesus remains a virgin throughout her life, and her suffering is thought to be unlike the suffering of other women who are mothers, since she is thought to be exempt from the pain of messy and undignified forms of pain such as childbirth. It's been argued (rightly, I think) that perpetual virginity would be associated with female freedom from dependence on men, rather than being anti-sex, in most historical periods, given that the options available to women were very different. But the way in which it is depicted within the Church today often downplays the autonomy implied by Mary's virginity, and instead suggests her purity in contrast to sexual women.

Unlike Maria Goretti, the Ugandan martyrs are not regarded as patrons of rape victims, despite the fact that according to various accounts they too died resisting forced sex. Indeed, to my knowledge there are no male patron saints of rape victims. That the Ugandan martyrs are not regarded as such may be because the rape of men is often overlooked or trivialized, and the issue of homosexuality has dominated the way in which their stories are told.

The suffering of the saints includes people like Matt Talbot, whose struggle with and recovery from alcoholism not only offers comfort but has the potential to destigmatize struggle with addiction and other forms of mental illness in the Church. But suffering is frequently sanitized by the Church, and this means that some forms of suffering – most notably that bound up with sex and sexuality, and especially female and homosexual sex and sexuality – are likely to continue to be stigmatized. By sanctifying only sanitized suffering, the stigma remains. Notably this is not simply a case of the Magisterium imposing problematic views of sex and sexuality on to parish clergy and lay members of the Church, since canonization – the process by which people come to be recognized as saints – reflects and takes as its starting point popular devotion. The problematic emphases within the representation of the communion of saints is, rather, a much wider issue to do with the culture of the Church as a whole. And this does not occur in a vacuum – while churches can be particularly problematic in this respect, it reflects patriarchal and (relatedly) homophobic elements in wider culture.

What has any of this got to do with the destigmatization of depression? This is indirectly relevant to people with depression since depression is reported as being higher among women[38] and gay people than among the rest of the population.[39] There is also a strong correlation between depression and other forms of mental illness, and having been the victim of sexual violence.[40] That female sexuality, homosexuality, and being a victim of sexual violence are still stigmatized, including through the cult of saints – otherwise a potentially destigmatizing force – is likely to continue to alienate people and contribute further to depressive feelings of guilt and remorse. To issues regarding sex and sexuality we could add issues of ethnicity and race:

people from minority ethnic backgrounds are more likely to be diagnosed with mental health problems, and also to experience a poor outcome from treatment.[41] It is noteworthy in relation to this that where churches include black saints, they will still sometimes depict Mary and Jesus as white.[42] And again, we might mention poverty – which is also correlated with mental health problems[43] – given the aristocratic background of many of the most popular saints.[44]

The issue around emphasizing some saints rather than others may relate more directly to depression as well, though the question of stigmatizing certain kinds of suffering is less clear-cut – because the examples are less widespread – than in the case of sex and sexuality. The most famous patron saint of mental illness is St Dymphna, who was not herself someone who experienced mental illness first-hand. Rather, she was the victim of her father's incestuous desire for her, which resulted from grief at the death of his wife and mental illness, and eventually caused him to kill her (she is another virgin martyr). This raises the possibility that having St Dymphna as the patron saint of mental illness might in fact contribute to stigma around mental illness, because her story portrays a mentally ill person being violent. However, legends about St Dymphna suggest that she miraculously healed people with what we would now call mental illness, and this was the reason for her patronage. Perhaps, then, St Dymphna is an example of a saint who is not caught up in the 'mess and mix-up' with us, but who instead offers healing and help. Yet, we might think that figures such as Blessed Clara Isabella Fornari, who experienced significant periods of mental distress during which she was unable to remember the ecstasy of her visions, and who contemplated suicide, might be emphasized in relation to mental illness rather more. These figures might offer resources, as patrons of people with mental illness, to destigmatize and to offer hope and consolation to those who themselves suffer from it.

How is all this relevant to Christian traditions who do not emphasize the communion of saints? The issue of stigmatizing representations and emphases is of relevance to all Christians, whether Protestant or Catholic, and whether passibilist or impassibilist, because it relates significantly to the representation of Jesus' suffering at the crucifixion. For passibilists, Jesus' suffering reveals the suffering of God in Godself. For impassibilists, Jesus' suffering reveals God's love, expressed in human form. In both cases, Jesus' suffering is of central importance in relation to human suffering. It is common for churches to represent the physical pain of Jesus, but what is less common is representation of the humiliation that would have been a part of Jesus' execution, or the respects in which people who were crucified, including Jesus, might be considered victims of sexual forms of violence. Crucifixion not only involved severe physical pain. Far from the loinclothed (and armpit-shaved) figure of most depictions of Jesus' death, crucifixion involved nakedness, incontinence, and humiliation and degradation through, for example, involuntary and public stripping. David Tombs has recently argued that involuntary and public stripping is a form of sexual violence, suggesting that the fact we do not recognize it as such probably reflects a cultural tendency to view male and female nakedness differently: a camera's heterosexual male gaze means that whether we are men or women, gay or straight, we are more likely to identify naked women but not men as sexual objects. This is to the detriment of both women and men: of women because they are overly sexualized, and of men because sexual violence often goes unrecognized.

Women who experience sexual violence often feel shame and are frequently met with stigmatizing attitudes such as victim blaming ('Were you drunk?' 'Why did you go out wearing that?' 'Why were you out that late at all?'). Men who experience sexual violence are often ridiculed or not taken seriously. Whether stripping would have been considered a form of sexual humiliation requires attention to the historical context of Jesus' crucifixion, which is beyond the scope of this book. But recognizing and accepting the possibility that Jesus was a victim of sexual violence could help to combat stigmatizing attitudes. Again, this is not about historicity, but reception. That being a victim of sexual violence is itself stigmatized – that it is still taken as an indication of lack of purity or sanctity – is shown by some responses to Tombs' research on this topic. Some people have responded that to claim that Jesus was a victim of sexual violence is 'insulting and demeaning to all Christians', and is also to 'feminize Christ', presumably because women and not men are perceived as 'naturally' the victims of sexual violence.[45] Here, as in the cases of some of the saints we have discussed, stigmatizing and alienating attitudes are in full force. These are most obviously relevant to women, to gay people and to people who have experienced sexual violence. But stigmatizing and alienating attitudes towards these groups intersects with stigmatizing and alienating attitudes towards people with mental illness, and many people who suffer from depression will also be women, and/or gay, and/ or have experienced sexual violence, and so will experience several forms of stigma on this basis. Churches can too easily become contexts in which people feel alienated, because they are mentally ill and for other reasons, and all these things – not just stigma against mental illness – are detrimental to their mental health.

Conclusion

In this chapter, I have argued against the claim that passibilist theology is more consolatory and more able to combat stigma than impassibilist theology. This is for many reasons, including that a fellow sufferer is not the only form of consolation – someone who is beyond the 'mess and mix-up' who can heal and save is an important form of consolation too. But in particular, I have suggested that in traditions in which God is thought to be impassible (and consolatory precisely on account of being impassible), the saints are well suited to provide consolation, including fellow suffering consolation. This is not least because different saints are familiar with the different kinds of suffering humans can experience, and yet point beyond current suffering to the hope of future healing, in this life or the next. At the same time, I have indicated that too often depictions of the saints fall short in this respect, because the ways in which their lives are told embody rather than challenge exclusionary attitudes. And this is not only the case with the saints and in Christian communities that emphasize the saints. It is the case for all Christian tradition, because of the tendency to sanitize Jesus' suffering at the crucifixion.

These exclusionary attitudes are relevant to people with depression not only because of possible stigma surrounding mental illness. There is particular stigma around female sexuality, and homosexuality, and this will affect many people with mental illness, many of whom will be women and/or gay. Intersectionality is key here: the way in which a woman with depression is treated by others is not just the way in which a woman and someone who has depression are treated stuck together, but a significantly and qualitatively different way of being treated.[46] And other aspects of identity, such as being gay or from an ethnic minority, or poor, will again significantly and qualitatively affect the way in which one is treated. In order to overcome alienation of people with mental illness within communities, then, churches – and also wider society – need to tackle not only stigma against people with mental illness but also stigma surrounding sex and sexuality, ethnicity, poverty, physical disability, and so on.

Consolation and stigma busting are, of course, not the only ways in which Christian traditions and communities can respond to depression and other kinds of mental illness. Depression needs to be treated with recovery in mind, whether through medicines, talk therapies, healing rituals, changes in the person's circumstances, or some combination of these things. The partners and families of people with mental illness need the moral and practical support of communities, without which they can become isolated, unable to support the person with depression; they may also become mentally ill themselves. Some of the root causes of depression and other forms of mental illness, and especially those often named 'social' – poverty, insecure job contracts, unfulfilling work, insecure housing – need to be addressed. The Christian tradition has particular and distinctive resources for understanding and responding to these things. In the next and final chapter, I will consider some of these further.

Notes

1 Alfred North Whitehead (1978) (1929), *Process and Reality: An Essay in Cosmology*, corrected and edited by David Ray Griffin and Donald W. Sherburne, New York: Free Press, p. 351.

2 E.g. Richard Bauckham (1984), 'Only the suffering God can help: Divine passibility in modern theology', *Themelios* 9.3, pp. 6–12, available at https://theologicalstudies.org.uk/article_god_bauckham.html (all websites in Chapter 7 notes accessed 13.12.19). Bonhoeffer was probably talking (solely) about the suffering of God in the person of Jesus on the cross. Bonhoeffer saw an emphasis on vulnerability and strength in weakness as a way of countering the Nazi ideology, which prized brute power and invulnerability. However, Bonhoeffer's phrase has often been appropriated by passibilists who want not only to affirm divine suffering in the life of Jesus but to make much bigger claims about the suffering of God in Godself.

3 E.g. Jürgen Moltmann (1991), *History and the Triune God*, London: SCM Press, pp. 219–27. Moltmann's view is that in Jesus' cry of dereliction ('My God, my God, why have you forsaken me?'), Jesus himself experiences God-forsakenness and takes up humanity's protest of suffering against God.

4 Karl Rahner (1986), *In Dialogue: Conversations and Interviews 1965–1982*, ed. Paul Inhof and Herbert Biallowons, trans. and ed. Harvey D. Egan, New York: Crossroad, cited in Moltmann, *History*, p. 123.

5 Moltmann, *History*, p. 29.

6 Moltmann, *History*, 123.

7 See for example Richard Creel (1986), *Divine Impassibility: An Essay in Philosophical Theology*, Cambridge: Cambridge University Press, pp. 156–7; Marcel Sarot (1992), *God, Passibility, and Corporeality*, Campen, The Netherlands: Kok Pharos Publishing, p. 78; Paul Fiddes (1988), *The Creative Suffering of God*, Oxford: Clarendon Press, p. 31; Kenneth Wollcombe, 1967, 'The pain of God', *Scottish Journal of Theology* 20, pp. 129–48, p. 143.

8 Sarot, *God*, p. 78.

9 Fiddes, *Creative Suffering*, p. 31.

10 Petrarch, 2: 380–1.

11 Frances Young (1979), 'Incarnation and atonement', in *Incarnation and Myth: The Debate Continued*, ed. Michael Goulder, Canterbury: SCM Press, p. 102.

12 See for example Kathryn Greene-McCreight (2015), *Darkness is My Only Companion: A Christian Response to Mental Illness*, Ada, MI: Brazos Press, and Robert Griggs (2014), *A Pelican of the Wilderness: Depression, Psalms, Ministry, and Music*, Eugene, OR: Cascade.

13 For example, one person reports feeling alienated on account of being confronted with lots of 'joyful' Christians (https://depressionmarathon.blogspot.com/2011/01/why-so-sad.html#axzz5SPo8gY4A). See also Hilfiker, *Mental Illness*.

14 See Anastasia Philippa Scrutton (2018), 'Depression and aesthetic experience', *Discipline Filosofiche* 2, pp. 105–22 (in a Special Issue on Affectivity and Psychopathological Experience).

15 See www.catholicstand.com/suffering-saints-mental-illness/.

16 See www.catholicireland.net/saintoftheday/matt-talbot-the-wor kers-saint/.

17 e.g. Seattle (www.mtcenter.org/treatment-programs); Nebraska (www.mtko.org/); New Jersey (http://mtrcinc.com/); Sydney www.vin nies.org.au/page/Find_Help/NSW/Housing/Matthew_Talbot_Hostel/).

18 See https://uk.reuters.com/article/uk-pope-ireland-drinker/pope-to-pay-tribute-to-irelands-holy-drinker-who-may-become-saint-idUK KCN1L91TU.

19 See http://venerablematttalbotresourcecenter.blogspot.com/2008/09/matt-talbot-prayer-card.html.

20 See www.franciscanmedia.org/venerable-matt-talbot/.

21 Thanks to Wendy Dossett for raising this point.

22 Note that this differs from Bonhoeffer's likely emphasis: 'Only a *suffering* God can help'.

23 Marcia Webb (2017), *Toward a Theology of Psychological Disorder*, Eugene, OR: Cascade, p. 147.

24 See Webb, *Theology*, p. 145.

25 First Vatican Council, *Dei Filius*, 1870: 'The holy, catholic, apostolic and Roman church believes and acknowledges that there is one true and living God, creator and lord of heaven and earth, almighty, eternal, immeasurable, incomprehensible, infinite in will, understanding and every perfection. Since he is one, singular, completely simple and unchangeable spiritual substance, he must be declared to be in reality and in essence, distinct from the world, supremely happy in himself and from himself, and inexpressibly loftier than anything besides himself which either exists or can be imagined.'

26 See e.g. *Salvifici Doloris*, available at http://w2.vatican.va/content/john-paul-ii/en/apost_letters/1984/documents/hf_jp-ii_apl_11021984_salvifici-doloris.html.

27 Thanks to Anthea Colledge for conversations about this, in relation to her (currently unpublished) research for her PhD. See also research by Edna Hunneysett, which finds that Catholics and Anglicans in the UK are more supportive of people with mental illness than people in Evangelical and Pentecostal congregations (Edna Hunneysett, 2006, *Christian Congregations and Mental Illness: A Survey of Contemporary Attitudes in their Historical Context*, North Yorkshire: Fryup).

28 Harold Koenig, Dana King and Verna Carson (2012), *Handbook of Religion and Health*, Oxford: Oxford University Press.

29 This presupposes that we might choose our theology on the basis of its ethical virtues (for example, choose a passibilist theology because it is destigmatizing). This relates to a wide philosophical literature on pragmatic reasons for belief (see e.g. William James (1896), *The Will to Believe and Other Essays in Popular Philosophy*, New York NY: Longmans, Green, and Co.). My own position on this is that we can't usually derive anything about the truthfulness of a belief from the belief's (ethical or other kind of) helpfulness. However, where the arguments for or against the truthfulness of something seem to be equal, pragmatic considerations about the belief's helpfulness might be a tipping point in deciding what to believe. (See Anastasia Philippa Scrutton (2015), 'Why not believe in an evil God? Pragmatic encroachment and some implications for philosophy of religion', *Religious Studies: An International Journal for Philosophy of Religion* 52.3, pp. 345–60.) I think in these cases the quality of our belief might be different from when we think there is overwhelming evidence for something. In particular, there might be an element of agnosticism about it ('I don't know x for sure, but I choose to believe it because ...'). A related question is whether and to what extent we can indeed choose what we believe (my view on this is: 'sometimes and to some extent').

30 Webb, *Theology*, p. 147, cited above.

31 Katherine J. Lewis (2004), 'Margery Kempe and saint making in later medieval England', in John H. Arnold and Katherine J. Lewis (eds), *A Companion to the Book of Margery Kempe*, Cambridge: D.S. Brewer, pp. 195–215.

32 For example, a British Catholic priest recounts the testimony of a Baganda man, Kiwanuku: 'At that time, the king practised the works of Sodom. Moslems and pagans were prepared to do those things with the king, but the Catholics absolutely refused. For that reason the king began to detest us, and deliberated with the pagans and Moslems about putting us to death' (Thoonen, cited in John Blevins (2011), 'When sodomy leads to martyrdom: Sex, religion, and politics in historical and contemporary contexts in Uganda and East Africa', *Theology & Sexuality* 17.1, pp. 51–74, pp. 53–4).

33 E.g. Pentecostal preacher Martin Ssempa characterizes Mwanga as 'a deviant homosexual who used his demigod status to appease his voracious appetite for sodomy by engaging in these unmentionable acts with his pages at court' (Ssempa, cited in Rahul Rao (2015), 'Re-membering Mwanga: Same-sex intimacy, memory and belonging in postcolonial Uganda', *Journal of Eastern African Studies* 9:1, pp. 1–19.

34 See Blevins, 'Sodomy'. Blevins draws attention to the role of the story of the Ugandan martyrs in the 2009 Anti-Homosexuality Bill which gave rise to the 2014 Act; he was writing before the Act was

passed. The Bill (though not the Act) included the possibility that some homosexual acts (ones involving people with HIV or people with disabilities) would be punished not by life imprisonment but by death.

35 See Rao, 'Re-membering', for a discussion of some different ways in which the martyrologies can be interpreted. My concern here is the way in which saints' lives are interpreted and represented, and not with the historical facts of their lives.

36 See Blevins, 'Re-membering', for examples. It might be objected that this tells us nothing about the Catholic Church and simply reflects the view of homosexuality within African Christianity. In its favour, it should be noted that Pope Paul VI did not mention homosexuality during the canonization of the martyrs in 1964. However, it is mistaken to characterize African Christianity as overwhelmingly homophobic, and the anti-gay account of the events seems to come not initially from African Christians but from European ones (see Kevin Ward (2002), 'Same sex relations in Africa and the debate on homosexuality in East African Anglicanism', *Anglican Theological Review* 84.1, pp. 81–111; Rao, 'Re-membering').

37 There are other patron saints of rape victims but these are also people who resisted rape – e.g. St Agatha, St Dymphna, St Solange of Bourges, Blessed Antonia Mesina.

38 Reasons given for the significantly higher depression rates among women when compared with men include not only social factors but biological ones, and the possibility that women report (rather than suffer from) depression more than men. It is possible that all these factors play a role. Arguments that biological factors alone play a role tend to presuppose the remarkable idea that Western societies have successfully vanquished patriarchy. See Paul R. Albert (2015), 'Why is depression more prevalent in women?', *Journal of Psychiatry and Neuroscience* 40.4, pp. 219–21, where the idea that social factors give rise to high levels of depression among women is met with the objection that changes in social attitudes to promote equality have 'been occurring in the West and ... yielded no clear change in the female:male depression ratio'.

39 See www.mentalhealth.org.uk/statistics/mental-health-statistics-lgbt-people.

40 www.mentalhealthamerica.net/conditions/sexual-assault-and-mental-health.

41 www.mentalhealth.org.uk/a-to-z/b/black-asian-and-minority-ethnic-bame-communities.

42 A Baroque church I visited in Ouro Preto, Brazil was built by slaves from Africa who had been brought over to work in the gold mines. The slaves were allowed their own church building and could include black saints in it – provided that Jesus and Mary were always presented as white. The oppressive message the slave owners sought to

drive home through this legislation is clear: black people can be among the faithful, and yet, it says, white people are the masters – and this is written into the divine order. Today, anything as explicit as this is unlikely to be the case, and some churches in majority black countries – for example, the Ethiopian Orthodox Church – have a long tradition of black iconography. In recent decades in Africa the Catholic Church has made efforts to 'inculturate' Christian art. However, the 2016 'Jesus de Greatest' statue in Nigeria, the largest Jesus statue in Africa, which was built with Catholic money, represents Jesus as white. In Pentecostal circles, religious images are also usually white. Thanks to Adriaan van Klinken for conversations about this.

43 www.mentalhealth.org.uk/statistics/mental-health-statistics-poverty.

44 See Lewis, 'Margery Kempe'.

45 See Katie Edwards and David Tombs (2018), '#HimToo – Why Jesus should be recognized as a victim of sexual violence', available at https://shiloh-project.group.shef.ac.uk/himtoo-why-jesus-should-be-recognised-as-a-victim-of-sexual-violence/.

46 See Kimberlé Williams Crenshaw, 'What is intersectionality?', available at www.youtube.com/watch?v=ViDtnfQ9FHc.

8

Towards a Christian response
to depression

To all of us, in sickness or in health, in sanity or in madness, in the vigor of youth or in the decrepitude of senility, God speaks these words which he spoke once to St. Augustine: *Currite, ego feram, et ego perducam, et ibi ego feram ...* Run on, I will carry you, I will bring you to the end of your journey and there I also will carry you.[1]

Introduction

In this book, I've reviewed some existing Christian responses to depression and separated some of the more helpful responses from those that are harmful. It is sometimes assumed that Christian theology should have something distinctive to say about mental illnesses, because it is thought that *mental* illnesses have a particularly strong relationship to the spiritual, whereas *physical* illnesses do not. In fact, if my analysis over the last seven chapters is broadly correct, it is in trying to 'spiritualize' mental illness that Christian responses to depression often go wrong. For example, trying to find a distinctively Christian aetiology of or explanation for depression – whether this is that depression is a result of a sinful lifestyle, or of demonic affliction, or is caused by God as a sign of holiness – often leads to problematic theology and damaging pastoral advice, as well as obscuring the rather more helpful biopsychosocial model and leading people away from possible sources of help. Is there, then, anything distinctive that Christian theology can offer in response to the reality of depression?

I think there is – and in this chapter, by way of a conclusion, I will draw out four emphases for a Christian response to depression that have been touched on in the course of the previous chapters. At the end of the book, I will suggest some pastoral and some clinical implications of this book.

Towards a Christian response to depression: four core emphases

Christ's solidarity with those who suffer

In his book on the historical Jesus, New Testament scholar José Pagola explains that:

> Every culture experiences sickness in a different way. It is not the same thing to be sick in the western society of our time, as in Lower Galilee in the decade of the 30s of the first century. Sickness is not only a biological condition. It is also an experience that one interprets, lives and suffers within the cultural framework of one's own society.[2]

Pagola's focus is on the decade of the 30s in the first century, the time at which Jesus was practising his ministry. Pagola goes on to talk about the way in which people with illnesses such as leprosy experienced not only debilitating skin conditions but also shame, humiliation and alienation from their community. This was accompanied by a sense of judgement: why doesn't God bless these people like everyone else? Surely they must have done something to displease God. Jesus responded to this culturally formed experience of illness by showing his solidarity with lepers and others who were excluded:

> The historical fact is beyond doubt: Jesus was devoted to them above everyone else. He came near to those who were seen as Godforsaken, touched the lepers whom no one else would touch, gained the trust of those who could not enter the temple, and brought them into the people of God as he understood it.[3]

The God of Jesus, then, is the God of those who suffer abandonment and exclusion. God is on the side of those who suffer, not on the side of those who are against them.

The focus of the book you are reading now is on the way in which one illness – depression – is experienced today. Pagola is right when he says that sickness is an experience that one interprets, lives and suffers within one's particular cultural framework. In this book, I have tried to show how different interpretations of the illness we call depression affect the meaning people give it and shape their experience of it. People not only experience having depression, they experience having depression *as a result of sin, as a result of demonic affliction, as a biological condition*, and so on.

Yet there are some notable similarities between the experience of depression today and that of leprosy in the first century discussed in the Gospels. In both cases, the illness is not just about the distressing and debilitating condition itself. It often includes loneliness and alienation from the community, and judgement and the suggestion of sin. How these things are manifested is indeed different across the two cultures. For example, unlike first-century lepers, people with depression today are not explicitly excluded from religious services, but may be implicitly so – perhaps because an overemphasis on joy, and moralization of its absence, makes being in church unbearable. Yet, despite cultural differences, the way in which alienation and judgement attend these illnesses is remarkably similar.

Whether God suffers is a matter of debate.[4] What we do know is that in his life Jesus shows us God's solidarity with those who suffer. This is depicted well in the painting on the front cover of this book: Jewish artist Marc Chagall's *White Crucifixion*. This was painted in 1938 in response to the horrendous events of *Kristallnacht*, the night of the broken glass, in Nazi Germany. In the painting we see violent acts against Jewish people: murder and the destruction of synagogues and homes. Jesus is shown on the cross, with a tallith or prayer shawl rather than a loincloth, a menorah at his feet and a light from the scroll of the Torah moving up towards him. In these ways, Chagall emphasizes that Jesus was Jewish.

Historically, Jesus' crucifixion has sometimes been used as a way of justifying the persecution and genocide of Jewish people. Jews have been accused of being 'Christ-killers' and Jesus' own Jewishness has been downplayed. *White Crucifixion* is remarkable because it reminds us of Jesus' Jewishness and solidarity with the Jewish people in their suffering.[5] Given the historical background – the context of oppression and persecution of the Jewish people – it also points to Jesus' solidarity more generally with those who suffer and are oppressed. Jesus is in solidarity not only with persecuted Jewish people but with all who are persecuted, oppressed or alienated.

The Gospels show Jesus' solidarity with those who suffer over and over again. Jesus' ministry is to the poorest of the poor. Jesus heals those who are ill, including those who have the most stigmatized illness of their time, and who therefore suffer not only illness but also alienation and loneliness. Jesus is friends with women in a society in which women are valued primarily for their procreative function and whose lives are shaped by patriarchal oppression.[6] Jesus is even friends with those women who are regarded as abhorrent and condemned on account of their sexual conduct.[7] Jesus is in solidarity with those who suffer, not with those who oppress them. Jesus' solidarity with those who suffer should be foremost in our minds when we think theologically about depression.

Sin and demons revisited

White Crucifixion also reminds us of the social and political dimension of much suffering. Human brutality is the cause both of Jesus' crucifixion and of the Nazi persecution of the Jewish people. There is a less obvious relationship between human brutality and depression, but nevertheless the relationship is still there. We know, for example, that depression and other kinds of mental illness such as post-traumatic stress disorder are strongly correlated with the displacement and torture many asylum seekers today have undergone.[8] We know that mental illness is also correlated with other forms of suffering including poverty, loneliness and social isolation, being implicitly or explicitly a victim of discrimination, and having insecure and/ or poor housing or being homeless.[9] These things – poverty, social isolation, discrimination, insecurity and homelessness – are not necessary features of the way the world is, but the result of political and social choices that are made, often to protect the interests of the wealthy and most powerful.

Thus, while the voluntarists we discussed in Chapter 1 associate depression with *individual* sin, in fact it seems that depression has far more to do with *social* sin: with the systemic injustices that make people poor, force them to live in unstable conditions, and make them vulnerable to violence and discrimination. People who suffer from depression are less likely to be the primary perpetrators of these kinds of sin than they are to be the victims of it.[10] In Chapter 1 I argued against the idea that depression is the result of sin. Here I am suggesting that we should resuscitate it. However, when I talk here about sin in the context of depression, it is with this 'social' kind of sin foremost in mind.

Likewise, there is an important and perhaps essential place for language of the demonic within the Christian tradition.[11] However, if we are to be true to the gospel, this needs to be understood in the light of Jesus' ministry of liberation as a whole. This requires understanding it in a political and social rather than merely individualistic way. That this is the case can be seen when we ask the question, 'Why does Jesus' compassionate ministry of healing and exorcism raise the hackles of the authorities so much?' Healers and exorcists were common in the first century, and yet were not generally met with hostility.[12]

Jesus' healing and exorcism ministry was so incendiary because it wasn't a sideline to his teaching; rather, it was part and parcel of the way in which he announced and manifested the kingdom of God, and so threatened the Roman empire and the power of those who had an interest in maintaining the status quo. In his healing and exorcism ministry, Jesus showed God's love for the poor and marginalized; he reintegrated them into their communities and challenged established social boundaries; he overcame illness and demonic possession and so the ways in which oppression was manifested; he unapologetically dealt with the effects of social sin and the political demonic. The rich and powerful were correct to fear Jesus in this respect. The idea that Jesus' ministry threatened the status quo was not some tragic misunderstanding on the part of the Jewish and Roman leaders: it was the logical conclusion of his disruptive compassion for the poor and oppressed and of his proclamation that they are loved by God. The warfare Christians are called to be a part of is not, then – contrary to advocates of the 'spiritual warfare' worldview – 'in our minds',[13] though of course it involves our minds (our mental lives are not isolated from our social structures). Rather, it is against the demons of poverty, oppression, war, torture, injustice and inhumane politics today, and the ways these afflict people in many forms, including in the form of depression and other kinds of mental illness. Theologian James Cone puts this well when he says:

> the exorcisms disclose that God in Jesus has brought liberation to the poor and the wretched of the land, and that liberation is none other than the overthrow of everything that is against the fulfilment of their humanity.[14]

The account of the relationship between mental illness on the one hand and Christian faith and spirituality on the other that I have offered in this book is largely deflationary: I have argued that we should not regard mental illnesses as having a special relationship with faith and spirituality any more than, say, physical illnesses or other kinds of suffering. This is related to the fact that I am buying into the language of depression as a kind of illness. An attentive reader might raise the point that in associating mental illness with social sin and the demonic I am relating mental illness and the spiritual life in a particular way – I am saying that there is a special relationship between experiences like depression and the spiritual life after all. Surely I am driving a wedge between depression and some other kinds of mental illness (on the one hand) and physical kinds of illness (on the other)?

In fact, I think that physical illnesses do have a close relationship with social sin and the political demonic – to poverty, oppression, injustice and so on – though this often goes unnoticed. For example, today HIV is experienced very differently in wealthy countries, where antiretroviral medications are widely available, from how it is experienced in poorer countries, where they are not. Where antiretroviral medication is taken, people with HIV are often able to live full and normal lives, can cease to be infectious to others, and might not develop AIDS. In poorer countries, where antiretroviral medication is not widely available, the condition usually progresses to full-blown AIDS, and is still life-threatening. In addition to the availability of medication, living conditions – for example, whether cleanliness is easy or difficult to maintain; whether one's diet is good or bad – affect whether one will succumb to an infection that will prove fatal if one's immune system is weakened by the HIV/AIDS virus. HIV is not exceptional as a physical illness in this respect: I could equally well have talked about asthma and exposure to air pollution, or cancers and exposure to carcinogens, or lung diseases suffered by coal miners and people exposed to asbestos. I could talk about not only what illnesses affect what kinds of people in the first place, but whether medications or other treatments are available and to whom, and which illnesses receive funding for research to prevent or cure them.

As these examples suggest, in highlighting the way in which depression relates to social sin and the political demonic, I'm not saying that this is something special about depression or mental illness more generally. Rather, the role of social sin and the political demonic is something that can and should be talked about in relation to a range of different kinds of suffering, including physical as well as mental illnesses. Illnesses, mental and physical, may be unfortunate things that just happen to some people and not others in one sense – but these unfortunate things that just happen do not occur in a political or social vacuum. What the political and social valancing is, and why some people are more likely than others to become depressed, or suffer from asthma, or get a lung disease, is one of the things with which language about sin and the demonic is properly concerned.

Resurrection and hope

In his letter to the Romans, St Paul speaks of the way in which creation has been 'subjected to futility' so that we have not experienced the fullness of life for which God created us. This includes our susceptibility to illness, including mental illness. Suffering is not something God wants for us; it is something that has gone wrong with the world. God does not want us to be unhappy or ill. It is certainly not something God inflicts on people, for example as a sign of holiness.

In the resurrection of Jesus, we see God's plan for the redemption of the whole of creation to live the life for which we were created – without sin but also without suffering. The ancient hymn the Exultet, sung on the night before Easter Day, celebrates this:

This is the night,
of which it is written:
the night shall be as bright as day,
dazzling is the night for me, and full of gladness.

The sanctifying power of this night
dispels wickedness, washes faults away,
restores innocence to the fallen, and joy to mourners,
drives out hatred, fosters concord, and brings down the
    mighty.

In Chapter 5 we saw Henri Nouwen refer to Anton Boisen as a man whose woundedness – his experience of severe mental illness – was 'a source of beauty in which even the weaknesses seem to give light'. In the context of the Christian theology in which both Nouwen and Boisen were embedded, Nouwen's words call to mind the image of the risen Jesus whose wounds remained visible and tangible but which, instead of causing suffering and death, give rise to his disciples' faith and strength to preach the gospel (see Luke 24.39–43; John 20.19–28). Nouwen too, and those who knew him, saw his own depression as having given rise to what we might call 'beauty' – his joy in human relationality; his ability to love and trust; his ministry to people with HIV and AIDS. This occurs partially in the lives of Nouwen and Boisen and many others – including perhaps many people who will read this book. It is one of the central beliefs of Christianity that the resurrection – the overcoming of suffering and sin and death, and the transformation of woundedness, shown first in the resurrection of Jesus – will happen fully and to all of creation.

Animality and the senses

In his book *Things My Dog has Taught Me about Being a Better Human*, Rabbi Jonathan Wittenberg describes the way in which his dog Mitzpah (meaning 'Blessing') takes part in a Jewish ritual that takes place in their family home. As Wittenberg recounts, Mitzpah

> knows when it's Passover, the festival towards which, in accordance with the biblical injunction to eat no leavened foods, we rigorously remove all bread, biscuits, cereals, pasta and flour-based products from the house. He especially enjoys the ritual of 'searching for the leaven', the ancient custom of checking that the house is truly free of all proscribed products. The practice is to search the home by the light of a candle at dusk on the night before Passover for any remaining undiscovered crusts and crumbs. To ensure that the activity is taken seriously, a small bit of bread is consumed in each room prior to the search. In our family, the women generally do the hiding and the men the looking; Mitzpah, who counts among the latter, offers his team a considerable advantage since he frequently sniffs out the hidden pieces well before his humans find them.[15]

Non-human animals tend to be associated strongly with the senses: with sniffing out and eating food, with being stroked and feeling the sun on their backs; with hearing interesting noises, or sensing small creatures in the undergrowth to chase, or large creatures from whom to flee. To be an animal is to be bodily and sensory.

While Christianity has sometimes been linked to a denial of human animality, it is interesting that Christianity, Judaism and other religious traditions particularly involve the senses. We see this in practices such as the one Wittenberg's dog takes part in, and others besides: hiding and finding food and sharing a meal, lighting a candle in the dark and feeling its warmth, smelling incense as we enter a church, singing hymns or plainchant or worship songs, dancing in response to music, extending touch to others in prayer or during the Peace. In addition to this, religious traditions bring us together as communities. In churches people are not autonomous individuals with a negligible relationship to the physical world, but part of the body of Christ.

This is significant for mental illness, in terms of both healing and prevention. We know that alienation, isolation and loneliness are particularly implicated in mental illness. Churches can be healing because they can provide real communities and places to belong. We know that engaging or re-engaging the senses can be therapeutic. For example, art and music therapy can be especially good for people who have experienced trauma and for whom talk therapies re-trigger distress, and for people who do not have the linguistic capacities to describe their feelings and experiences. Provided that they are not accompanied by a pressure to achieve a particular standard, performing and listening to music or creating and looking at visual art can provide a way of allowing people to explore their thoughts and feelings non-confrontationally. They can absorb us and take our minds off the way we are feeling or prevent us from ruminating. They can connect us to others, and remind us of the presence of beauty in the world without demanding that we respond joyfully to it.

People with depression sometimes report feeling sad, lonely, distant or anxious in the face of beauty, reflecting a more general sense of being cut off from the interpersonal world.[16] This is especially the case if people feel pressured to feel joy at beauty – for example, if attention is drawn to their inability to feel joy at beauty. Parker Palmer, who experienced depression, describes this well:

> I had folks coming to me, of course, who wanted to be help-ful, and sadly, many of them weren't. These were the people who would say, 'Gosh, Parker, why are you sitting in here being depressed? It's a beautiful day outside. Go, you know, feel the sunshine and smell the flowers.' And that, of course, leaves a depressed person even more depressed, because while you know intellectually that it's sunny out and that the flowers are lovely and fragrant, you can't really feel any of that in your body, which is dead in a sensory way.[17]

At their best, religious practices can awaken our senses from their deadened state and remind us that we are thoroughly bodily, and not incorporeal souls temporarily incarcerated in a bodily prison. At their best, religious practices can gently remind us of the beauty of creation, without demanding a par-ticular emotional response from us or confronting us with our 'failure' when we do not feel happy. They can draw us into communities, and counter and combat the alienation that is a common experience in our societies today.

This emphasis on the sensory is not just an aesthetic add-on to the Christian tradition. As we saw in Chapter 3, it's part of the Christian tradition to see who we are (and who we will be) not in terms of individualism and disembodiment but rather as thoroughly corporeal and sensory, and as involving not only the human world but the whole of creation.

Therapeutic implications

Finally, what are the therapeutic (pastoral and clinical) impli-cations of this book? Many of the pastoral implications of this book are negative: I've counselled against telling someone their depression is a sign of sin, or of demonic possession, or else not biological or (on the contrary) solely biological, or a dark night of the soul rather than a mental illness. I have also counselled against telling people that depression will probably turn out to be a gift, or that they ought to find a bright side to their suffering.

Among the more positive pastoral implications of this book is the idea that, taking Christ's solidarity with those who suffer as our example, the best first response might involve simply being with those in distress, rather than offering any kind of advice or explanation. Whether and in what context to talk theologically – for example, about Christ's solidarity with those who suffer, or social sin and the political demonic, or the hope of transformation and resurrection – is a matter of 'know how' rather than 'knowledge that'. It may be helpful in some cases, but which cases those are is a matter of practical wisdom that can hardly be stipulated in a book.

Theology is not only about what we say but also about what we do. Healing often takes place through the senses. Different Christian traditions have different aesthetics, and some are more explicitly sensory than others. But all have significant resources for engaging and awakening the senses. We have seen some of the things that can go wrong here – for example, when a community insists that emotions like joy and wonder are the only acceptable ones in the context of worship, and meets their absence with judgement or, more well-meaningly, tries to prompt people to feel joy or see beauty when they cannot. As Palmer's words quoted above show, putting pressure on people to feel happiness or joy when they are unable to may only burden them further and make them feel more alienated. Hilfiker makes a similar point when he says:

> I need my community not to require that my spirituality bring me any particular joy – for if joy is some measure of spirituality, I'm a long way from home … I need my community to enter into the darkness of my distance from God. I need their willingness to bring *their* relationship with God into my

darkness and hold it there without imposing it on me. Can they be there even if I don't respond very much?[18]

Encouraging people to engage with the world in an act of communal worship can be therapeutic, provided that they don't feel they have to respond joyfully or have somehow failed if they cannot. Acts of worship that are not emotionally prescriptive can engage the senses, foster a sense of belonging, distract the person from rumination and, by being non-pressuring, might even provide a more conducive context for joyful emotions to emerge.

It is significant here that people with depression often turn to the psalms, which use rich sensory images and involve joy but also sadness, hopelessness, fear and despair.[19] Psalms give voice to significant mental distress; people may find relief in the acceptability of saying or singing sorrowful words in a liturgical context. Psalms are, of course, only one example – there are doubtless many others.

How about implications for clinicians? One issue is whether and to what extent clinicians should ask about or engage with people's religious beliefs. Clinicians are often reticent about doing so, for numerous reasons. Clinicians may worry that the conversation will move into difficult territory or get out of control; they may feel that religion is private and a 'taboo' subject; they often feel that they are under-qualified or lack theological expertise.[20] One of my aims in this book has been to address some of these concerns by familiarizing readers with different beliefs about depression in the Christian tradition and with theological and philosophical criteria for evaluating them. However, the question remains: 'What should I do if a patient seems to have damaging religious beliefs about their depression? What should I do, for example, if a patient has a deeply held belief that depression is the result of their sin, or has been told this by someone in their church?'

There is unlikely to be a 'one size fits all' answer to this. Perhaps it might be worth bearing in mind that the options are not binary: a range of different responses is available, between the extremes of arguing with the person on the one hand or ignoring their belief on the other. One therapist told me that she sometimes gently points to the fact that there are different Christian interpretations of depression available, without directly challenging their current belief. Often someone on the receiving end of a sin account, say, will have been told that a sin account is *the* Christian interpretation of depression: it can be liberating to hear that there are other Christian views out there. Whether and when this is the right approach is, again, a matter of practical wisdom.

Discussion of therapeutic (clinical and pastoral) implications usually focuses on interventions that psychiatrists, counsellors, religious ministers, carers and others can implement at an individual level. And yet we know that these interventions deal with only the tip of the iceberg when it comes to responding to and preventing mental health problems. Psychiatrists sometimes lament that all they can do is offer a 'sticking plaster' when faced with patients who have experienced trauma and abuse and continue to live with instability and in poverty.[21] Yet this 'sticking plaster' can be life-saving, and cuts to mental health provision jeopardize vulnerable people's lives.

At the same time, if we wish to respond to depression not only reactively and at an individual level, we all need to think collectively about our societies and the political systems that underpin them. In the Introduction we saw that depression is often characterized by a sense of being cut off from others, or of alienation from the interpersonal world. The interpersonal is also political. Societies can invite people to participate in the interpersonal world, or they can force separation and alienation. If we wish to combat the root causes of depression, we need to think socially and politically about how our culture can enable people to live as communities and with sensitivity to the needs we have as human animals, rather than foster anxiety, loneliness and alienation.

Notes

1 Maurice O'Connor Drury (2019), *The Danger of Words*, in *The Selected Writings of Maurice O'Connor Drury on Wittgenstein, Philosophy, Religion and Psychiatry*, ed. John Hayes, London: Bloomsbury, p. 329.

2 José A. Pagola (2009) (Eng. trans.), *Jesus: An Historical Approximation*, Miami, FL: Convivium Press, p. 158.

3 Pagola, *Jesus*, p. 160.

4 See Chapters 6 and 7.

5 Richard Harries (2004), *The Passion in Art*, Farnham: Ashgate Publishing, p. 109–11.

6 Much of Jesus' teaching should be better understood against the backdrop of the inequality between men and women at the time. For example, Jesus' prohibition against divorce in Matthew's Gospel is about inequality: men were able to divorce women but women were not able to divorce men. If a man divorced a woman she could be left without any means of support.

7 John 8.1–11; Luke 7.36–50.

8 A 2009 study carried out by the Scottish Refugee Council with 349 refugees found that 57% of women were likely to have post-traumatic stress disorder, 20% reported suicidal thoughts in the last 7 days, and 22% of women said that they had tried to take their own life. (See Scottish Refugee Council & London School of Hygiene and Tropical Medicine (2009), *Asylum-Seeking Women: Violence and health: Results from a Pilot Study in Scotland and Belgium*, London: London School of Hygiene & Tropical Medicine and Scottish Refugee Council.)

9 See e.g. 'Fundamental facts about mental health' (2015), available at www.mentalhealth.org.uk/publications/fundamental-facts-about-mental-health-2015 (all websites in Chapter 8 notes accessed 13.12.19).

10 See e.g. Psalm 73.12–14.

11 Language of the demonic can be argued to be infungible (or not substitutable for other language) because it provides a way to speak about the power and agency of evil systems in a way that other language about evil does not. This is the case, regardless of whether language of the demonic should be regarded as referring to real demonic entities or as metaphorical.

12 See Ched Myers (2008), *Binding the Strong Man: A Political Reading of Mark's Story of Jesus*, Maryknoll, NY: Orbis Books, p. 141

13 Chip Ingram (n.d.), 'Spiritual Warfare 101: What is the invisible war?', *Living on the Edge with Chip Ingram*, available at https://livingontheedge.org/broadcast/spiritual-warfare-101-what-is-the-invisible-war-part-1/daily-radio#.XDNbhGngrIU.

14 James Cone (1975), *God of the Oppressed*, London: SPCK, p. 77.

15 Jonathan Wittenberg (2017), *Things My Dog has Taught Me about Being a Better Human*, London: Hodder and Stoughton, pp. 51–2.

16 See Anastasia Philippa Scrutton (2018), 'Depression and aesthetic experience', *Discipline Filosofiche* 2, pp. 105–22 (in a Special Issue on Affectivity and Psychopathological Experience).

17 Parker Palmer (2009), 'Transcript for Parker Palmer, Andrew Solomon, and Anita Barrows: The Soul in Depression', *On Being with Krista Tippett*, available at https://onbeing.org/programs/the-soul-in-depression-mar2018/.

18 David Hilfiker (2002) (May and June), 'When mental illness blocks the spirit', available at www.davidhilfiker.com/index.php?option=com_content&view=article&id=33:when-mental-illness-blocks-the-spirit&catid=14:spirituality-essays&Itemid=24.

19 See Kathryn Greene-McCreight (2015), *Darkness is My Only Companion: A Christian Response to Mental Illness*, Ada, MI: Brazos Press; Robert Griggs (2014), *A Pelican of the Wilderness: Depression, Psalms, Ministry, and Music*, Eugene, OR: Cascade.

20 G. Durà-Vilà, M. Hagger, S. Dein and G. Leavey (2011), 'Ethnicity, religion and clinical practice: a qualitative study of beliefs and attitudes of psychiatrists in the United Kingdom', *Mental Health, Religion and Culture* 14.1, 53–64.

21 Relatedly, I have heard people with broad sympathy for the anti-psychiatry movement blame clinicians and mental health professionals for taking attention away from the social causes of depression by treating them instead with medicines. Reacting against the biomedical or bio-bio-bio model I criticized in Chapter 3, they put forward the socio-socio-socio model of mental illness instead: depression has only social causes and there is no place for medical or psychological treatments. To do this not only overlooks other important aspects of our being such as our bodiliness and animality: it is also to blame the wrong people, and so in fact to draw attention further away from social and political evils we should be addressing. See Tasia Scrutton and Simon Hewitt (2018), 'All in the mind?', *Labour Briefing*, available at https://labourbriefing.squarespace.com/search?q=all+in+the+mind.

Glossary

Biomedical: The biomedical model can be dubbed the 'bio-bio-bio' model. In theory it's been replaced by the biopsychosocial model, but in practice its legacy continues. The biomedical model sees depression and other kinds of mental illness solely in biological terms, in both aetiology and treatment. Unlike the biopsychosocial model, it does not take into account the psychological and social causes of depression, or look to these as sources of treatment.

DSM: The *Diagnostic and Statistical Manual of Mental Disorders*, currently in its fifth edition. This is the book used by psychiatrists in the USA to help them decide whether and what kind of diagnosis is appropriate to someone showing signs of mental distress. Diagnosis is typically based on sets of symptoms, alongside considerations to do with duration and context. In the UK and Europe, psychiatrists might use the ICD (*The International Classification of Diseases*) alongside or instead of the DSM.

Dualism: Dualism is the idea that there are two kinds of thing. In the context of this book, the two kinds of thing according to dualists are mental things (e.g. our minds, God, our souls) and physical things (e.g. our bodies, the world we can see, non-human animals). Although not essential to dualism, dualists often see mental things as more important than or superior to physical things. Dualism is often seen as an alternative to physicalism, though there are many options besides everything being physical, or everything being physical and mental. A major problem for dualists is to explain how the mental and physical, which are thought to be separate things, interact. See E. J. Lowe (2000), *An Introduction to the Philosophy of Mind*, Cambridge: Cambridge University Press.

God in Godself: In Christian theology, the phrase 'God in Godself' is used to be distinct from 'God in the person of Jesus'. Christians believe that Jesus is one person with two natures: divine and human. In order to emphasize that these two natures are united in one person (against various early Church heresies that denied this), Christians are allowed to say of God things that are true of Jesus ('God was born of the Virgin Mary'), and vice versa ('the creator of the world walked the earth'). However, sometimes Christians want to say things about God that are different from things they want to say about God in the person of Jesus. They might want to say that God is incorporeal (body-less), or eternal (outside time), or immutable (changeless) by nature, even though Jesus had a body, existed in time, and changed. In order to stress that they are not talking about God in the person of Jesus, they talk about 'God in Godself'.

Gnostic: This is an umbrella term for a range of religious groups who were or are strongly dualistic. A common characteristic of Gnosticism is the belief that matter or the physical world is evil while the world of the spirit is good. Gnostics also typically believe or believed in two gods: an unknowable god of the spirit world, who is good, and an inferior god, who created the material world and is often identified with the God of the Old Testament or Hebrew Bible. Gnosticism was a significant presence in first- and second-century Christianity. Because Gnostics believed that matter was evil, Gnostic Christians struggled with the idea that God really became human in the person of Jesus, and that Jesus died on the cross (rather than merely appearing to). The New Testament writings – especially the Gospel of John – reveal internal debates relating to Gnosticism and incarnational Christianity (see, for example, John 1.14; 11.35; 20.27). See Elaine Pagels (1979), *The Gnostic Gospels*, New York: Vintage Books, available at https://static1.squarespace.com/static/52cdf95ae4b0c18dd2d0316a/t/53e-074cee4b0ea4fa48a5704/1407218894673/Pagels%2C+Elaine+-+The+Gnostic+Gospels.pdf (accessed 13.12.19); and Raymond E. Brown, 1978, *The Community of the Beloved Disciple*, New Jersey: Paulist Press.

Impassibilism: This either means the idea that God cannot have emotions, or that God cannot suffer. In this book, the emphasis is on the latter. Christianity has traditionally held that God in Godself is impassible – but that God can be said to suffer in the person of Jesus. Reasons for impassibilism include distinguishing God from the morally imperfect Greek and other pagan gods, and compatibility with other divine attributes. Divine immutability (changelessness), eternality (being outside time), incorporeality (body-lessness) and bliss are among the divine attributes thought to preclude divine suffering.

Mental distress: I use this general term to describe an instance of suffering that is strongly psychological in character, whether or not it is properly describable as depression or another mental illness. For example, Mother Teresa is best described as experiencing 'mental distress' because (to our knowledge) she never saw a doctor about her mental state, and we do not know whether she would have been diagnosed as having depression (or another kind of mental illness) if she had seen a doctor.

Passibilism: This either means the idea that God has emotions, or else that God suffers. In this book, the emphasis is on the idea that God suffers – and, in particular, that God suffers with us. The turn towards passibilism in Christian theology occurred from the late nineteenth century onwards. Some reasons for passibilism include the idea that God's suffering is required for divine omniscience (all-knowingness), divine love (since humans suffer when those they love suffer), and consolation (for some, an impassible God seems cold and apathetic in the face of suffering). See Anastasia Philippa Scrutton (2011), *Thinking through Feeling: God, Emotion and Passibility*, New York and London: Continuum.

Pelagianism: The belief that humans are capable of choosing good or evil without divine grace. Pelagianism takes its name from the British monk Pelagius in the fourth and fifth century who emphasized the role of free will when he encountered Christians in Rome leading what he regarded as sinful lifestyles. However, Pelagius seems to have denied many of the things attributed to him by Pelagians. Pelagianism has come to be associated with the idea that humans can earn salvation by their own merits, and that the value of Christ's life lies in being an example. St Augustine of Hippo responded to Pelagianism by emphasizing the need for grace, and by developing the idea of original sin: that, because of the sin of Adam, we are no longer free to choose the good without divine grace. See Carol Harrison (2000), *Augustine: Christian Truth and Fractured Humanity*, Oxford: Oxford University Press.

Physicalism: The idea that everything real is physical. Physicalism is reductive because it holds that things we normally categorize in mental, spiritual or experiential terms are ultimately in fact physical things. For example, our thoughts are ultimately reducible to the physical things that are happening in our brains. A problem for physicalism is to explain how to characterize phenomena that do not seem to be captured by, say, neurons in the brain – for example, the feeling of what it's like to desire coffee. See Thomas Nagel (1974), 'What's it like to be a bat?', *The Philosophical Review* 83.4, pp. 435–50, available at https://warwick.ac.uk/fac/cross_fac/iatl/study/ugmodules/humananimalstudies/lectures/32/nagel_bat.pdf (accessed 13.12.19).

Reductive: Suppose I claim that heat *is nothing more than* kinetic molecular energy. In claiming this, I'm making a reductive argument. You might be fine with my claim, or you might think there's something missing about that characterization of heat: you might think it describes the chemical aspect quite well, but misses other characteristics of heat, such as that heat feels warm. To take another example: suppose I claim that my desire for coffee is nothing more than particular neurons firing in my brain. Again, I'm making a reductive argument. In particular, I am reducing what sounds like a mental state to a purely physical one. Whether you think being reductive is a good or bad thing in this context will depend on whether you think the neuron explanation captures the whole of what my desire for coffee consists in, or whether there are important – and real – aspects left over. See also: **physicalism**.

Sanitize: If you cut your hand, perhaps you might clean the wound before you bandage it, to make sure there are not germs that will cause an infection. In cleaning the wound, you're 'sanitizing' it: you're making it free from dirt and germs. An analogous use of sanitizing occurs in the context of ideas rather than germs: we might sanitize Grimm's *Fairy Tales* or our narrative of Spartacus' uprising in order to make them less gruesome, upsetting, offensive or challenging. Sanitizing, then, means making something more palatable by removing difficult or challenging aspects. Unlike cleaning a wound, sanitizing in this ideological sense is often problematic because it can remove what is most powerful and important in an image or narrative.

Stigma: A stigma is a mark that sets one apart from others. Reasons for being stigmatized can include being mentally ill, being disabled, and being gay in a heteronormative context. Stigma is closely related to alienation: a stigmatized person is likely to find it harder to make close friendships, since others are wary of the person's differences. Stigma is also closely related to discrimination – for example, someone who is stigmatized might find that they lose out on a job to someone else because people don't want to take a chance on someone different or find it more difficult to interact with them. Stigma is therefore a cause of poverty, insecure employment and housing, and so on.

Voluntarism: Voluntarism refers to an emphasis on choice and free will (it derives from the Latin word for 'will', and we get our word 'voluntary' from it). So, for example, in philosophy, 'doxastic voluntarism' is the idea that we can choose what beliefs we have. In this book I'm interested in all kinds of voluntarism – voluntarism about beliefs, emotions, actions and so on – as these relate to depression. Interpretations of depression are highly voluntaristic if they presuppose we can choose particular beliefs, emotions and actions that make us depressed. Because we can choose our beliefs, emotions and actions, it is claimed that we effectively choose to be depressed – and we thus are responsible for it. See also: **Pelagianism.**

Further Reading

James Cone (1975), *God of the Oppressed*, London: SPCK.

Celia E. Deane-Drummond and David Clough (eds) (2009), *Creaturely Theology: On God, Humans, and Other Animals*, London: SCM Press.

Maurice O'Connor Drury (2019), *The Danger of Words*, in *The Selected Writings of Maurice O'Connor Drury on Wittgenstein, Philosophy, Religion and Psychiatry*, ed. John Hayes, London: Bloomsbury.

Barbara Ehrenreich (2009), *Smile or Die: How positive thinking fooled America and the world*, London: Granta.

Thomas Fuchs (2013), 'Depression, intercorporeality, and interaffectivity', *Journal of Consciousness Studies* 20, No. 7–8, pp. 219–38, p. 228, available at www.klinikum.uni-heidelberg.de/fileadmin/zpm/psychatrie/fuchs/Literatur/Depression_Intercorporeality_and_Interaffectivity.pdf (all websites in Further Reading accessed 13.12.19).

Kathryn Greene-McCreight (2015), *Darkness is My Only Companion: A Christian Response to Mental Illness*, Ada, MI: Brazos Press.

Kathleen J. Greider (2007), *Much Madness is Divinest Sense: Wisdom in Memoirs of Soul-Suffering*, Ohio: Pilgrim Press.

David Hilfiker (2002) (May and June), 'When mental illness blocks the spirit', available at www.davidhilfiker.com/index.php?option=com_content&view=article&id=33:when-mental-illness-blocks-the-spirit&catid=14:spirituality-essays&Itemid=24.

William James (1896), *The Will to Believe and Other Essays in Popular Philosophy*, New York NY: Longmans, Green, and Co., available at www.mnsu.edu/philosophy/THEWILLTOBELIEVEbyJames.pdf.

William James (1906), *The Varieties of Religious Experience: A Study in Human Nature*, Pennsylvania: The Pennsylvania State University Press, available at https://csrs.nd.edu/assets/59930/williams_1902.pdf.

Kay Redfield Jamison (2006), 'The many stigmas of mental illness', *Lancet*, 533–4.

Kenneth Leech (1981), *The Social God*, London: SPCK.

Herbert McCabe (1987), *God Matters*, London: Geoffrey Chapman.

Jürgen Moltmann (1991), *History and the Triune God*, London: SCM Press.

Henri Nouwen (2009), *The Inner Voice of Love: A Journey through Anguish to Freedom*, London: Darton, Longman and Todd.

Henri Nouwen (2008), *The Wounded Healer: Ministry in Contemporary Society*, London: Darton, Longman and Todd.

Henri Nouwen (2009), *Home Tonight: Further Reflections on the Parable of the Prodigal Son*, London: Darton, Longman and Todd.

José A. Pagola (2009) (Eng. trans.), *Jesus: An Historical Approximation*, Convivium Press.

Matthew Ratcliffe (2015), *Experiences of Depression: A Study in Phenomenology*, Oxford: Oxford University Press (International Perspectives in Philosophy and Psychiatry Series).

Tasia Scrutton and Simon Hewitt (2018), 'All in the mind?', *Labour Briefing*, available at https://labourbriefing.squarespace.com/search?q=all+in+the+mind.

Andrew Solomon (2001), *The Noonday Demon: An Anatomy of Depression*, London: Vintage Books.

John Swinton (2007), *Raging with Compassion: Pastoral Responses to the Problem of Evil*, Cambridge: Eerdmans.

John Swinton (2000), *Resurrecting the Person: Friendship and the Care of People with Mental Health Problems*, Nashville, TN: Abingdon Press.

Kevin Timpe (2013), *Free Will in Philosophical Theology*, New York: Bloomsbury.

Marcia Webb (2017), *Toward a Theology of Psychological Disorder*, Eugene, OR: Cascade Books.

Ludwig Wittgenstein (1970), *Lectures and Conversations on Aesthetics, Psychology, and Religious Belief*, Berkeley and Los Angeles: University of California Press, compiled from Notes taken by Yorick Smithies, Rush Rhees and James Taylor, ed. Cyril Barrett, available at http://psych.nyu.edu/pelli/papers/wittgenstein.pdf.

Tom Wright (2007), *Surprised by Hope*, London: SPCK. An e-book version is available at www.difa3iat.com/wp-content/uploads/2014/07/N.-T.-Wright-Surprised-by-Hope_-Rethinking-Heaven-the-Resurrection-and-the-Mission-of-the-Church-2008.pdf.

Linda Zagzebski (2008), 'Omnisubjectivity', in Jon Kvanvig (ed.), *Oxford Studies in Philosophy of Religion*, Oxford: Oxford University Press, available at www.baylor.edu/content/services/document.php/39971.pdf.

Index of Names and Subjects

demons 20, 56–83
 belief in as cause of mental
  illness 87
 language about 222 n11
 and personal sin 63, 75
 possession/oppression by
  60–1, 70–1, 73
depression
 Christian interpretations of
  1–6, 208–21
 diagnoses 7, 224
 phenomenology of 7–9,
  39–43, 46–8
 as potentially transformative
  22, 129, 133–5, 142–54
 salutary or pathological
  124–6
 terminology 7–11
 see also biological model;
  biopsychosocial model;
  recovery
Descartes, René 12–13
devil, the 68–9
devils 85 n23
diagnosis 7, 12–14, 46,
 72–3, 224
Dissociative Identity Disorder
 72–3
doxastic voluntarism 41
Drury, Con 36–7, 208
dualism 12–14, 105, 224
Durà-Vilà, Gloria 124–6
Dymphna (saint) 199

Ehrenreich, Barbara 148, 152
emotions
 choice of 37–8
 see also feelings

empathy 168, 187
 of Jesus 173
epilepsy 67
evil, suffering is 135
exorcism 20, 57–8, 60,
 62–3, 81
 by Jesus 64–7, 70, 75
 practical approach to 81–2
experience, shaped by
 interpretation 4–5

faith 41–2
 absence of 61–2
 in Aquinas' thought 55 n35
Fall, the 140
feelings
 of God's love 43
 of guilt 19, 45–6, 49, 78
 of happiness 42–3, 218,
  218–19
 of isolation 7–8
 of worthlessness 45–9, 78,
  138
Feuerbach, Ludwig 193
Font i Rodon, Jordi 123–4
Fornari, Clara Isabella 199
Francis of Assisi 108
free will 30–32, 37, 39–42,
 165, 228
Fuchs, Thomas 46, 47

Gerasene demoniac 65, 71
Giles (saint) 108
Gnosticism 91, 225
God
 eternal 163–5
 experience of 43
 foreknowledge 165